THE
COMPLEXITIES
OF AN URBAN
CLASSROOM

New York · Chicago · San Francisco · Atlanta · Dallas · Montreal · Toronto · London

LOUIS M. SMITH

WILLIAM GEOFFREY

Graduate Institute of Education, Washington University, St. Louis, Missouri

HOLT, RINEHART AND WINSTON, INC.

THE COMPLEXITIES OF AN URBAN CLASSROOM

AN ANALYSIS TOWARD A GENERAL THEORY OF TEACHING

Louis M. Smith and William Geoffrey
The Complexities of an Urban Classroom

Cover photograph by Monkmeyer Press Photo

PREFACE

We think *The Complexities of an Urban Classroom* is probably the most intensive analysis that has been made of a single classroom. It is most likely the first time a college professor has spent all day every day within a slum classroom as an observer. It is probably the most intensive cooperative effort between an elementary school teacher and an educational psychologist to bring their varying points of view to bear on the day-to-day issues of teaching. Finally, the self-conscious attempt to describe carefully the mundane day-to-day events and then to interpret these within an internally consistent language makes the book a unique attempt to theorize about the problems of teaching. In consequence, it possesses a general as well as a particularistic point of view.

We believe our book will have several audiences, for it has several unusual features and can be read from several vantage points. Because the problems of urban education are timely, the layman, who usually has no clear perception of life in a classroom of a slum school, should profit from the extended detail reported in the fieldnote excerpts. Our intent has been to build clear and realistic images for readers whose elementary school backgrounds are foreign to the lower-class culture and yet whose positions in contemporary society require them to make intelligent decisions in this area. If we have made clear the magnitude of the urban education problem and some of its specific dimensions, we will be heartened. We have strong faith in the power of an aroused and informed citizenry to improve its present-day circumstances and institutions and in the power of public education to produce citizens who will approach the problems of the next generation with intelligence and courage.

For the undergraduate education major studying educational psychology and principles of teaching, we hope to have written a book which bridges some of the gaps between the two areas of study. Once again, the descriptive accounts in our book should provoke clear images of the realities of the classroom and provide illustrative material against which the education student can test his growing set of concepts and principles of psychology and teaching. We have made a self-conscious effort to explore the classroom from the point of view of the teacher. While we included many accounts of what the children did, said, and thought, we continually returned to the impact this had on the teacher in his intentions, plans, and alternatives. We hope this contributes to the change of perspective from college student to teacher. Perhaps though, the most important impact for the undergraduate education student should be the awareness that behind the sensational reports he reads in novels and newspapers, an equilibrium exists; the reality of the school has a rhythm and a pattern to it. One can observe it, learn it, and in time help shape it toward one's own personal ideals. There is a silent language that, as one comes to know and feel it, allays the anxiety lying in an unknown and potentially uncontrollable and hostile environment.

Perhaps most of all, though, we hope to speak to the graduate student interested in the psychology of teaching and the instructional process. He will have his own images of classroom reality and will long since have developed a clear conception of the equilibrium of the school and, moreover, his own relationship to it. In our experience, however, most graduate students have not been involved intensively in the exciting experience of working toward an axiomatic theory of teaching. The language systems to which they have been exposed are frequently prescriptive, for example, "The good teacher should. . .," rather than descriptive and analytic. We think we have made a significant beginning in this effort, as we have tried to implement the orientation of such social scientists as George Homans (1950) and Hans Zetterberg (1965). Our many diagrams and figures are, in reality, miniature theories about teaching. We hope they are persuasive enough to challenge teachers to test them against their own experience and powerful enough to illuminate further that experience. To the graduate student who is about to engage in more formal verificational research, our many models contain concepts in the form of hypotheses which need testing. As he joins the quest, we hope that *The Complexities of an Urban Classroom* will provide a fruitful starting point and that his results will cumulate in a more potent and provocative conception of the psychology of teaching.

Writing for several audiences poses serious dilemmas. Although these choices occur throughout a manuscript, they arise most critically at introductory and concluding points; for example, to whom do the authors direct the opening and closing messages? On occasion we resolved such dilemmas by writing to ourselves; the last chapter possibly illustrates this best. If our audience should be as varied as we might hope, the kind of summary we could write also might vary dramatically. For instance, rather than speaking directly to the lay citizen who wants to improve urban public education, to the neophyte teacher who is about to face her first class, to the experienced teacher who is reflecting upon her years in the classroom, or to the research-oriented graduate student who wants to design a verificational study, we elected an egocentric and possibly artistic alternative. We asked ourselves, "What has the book added up to? What is its message?" To us, the message centers on complexity. The beginning of school in the fall is deceptively simple and can be described simply; yet we think the first few weeks have important implications for the implementation of the activity structure (the instructional program) and for the development of the authority structure (achieving classroom control). Similarly, the teacher's casual comments and humor have implications for pupil roles and belief systems. Simple resumés or elaborate concluding prescriptions seem to fall far short of reality. Each teacher's personality, each school's way of doing things, and each classroom's aggregate of pupils must be entered into the equations. The real world will not tolerate anything less. In our view, each reader must do his own summarizing and reflecting along the way.

For us, as authors, the last chapter gave us a chance to speculate on next steps, further pieces of the complex educational puzzle which need exploration, clarification, and analysis. To use an apt expression, which is rapidly becoming a cliché, "the medium is the message." We have struggled through a particular educational episode, a teacher's coping with a group of pupils over a semester. We have tried to develop new concepts and ideas. We have indicated some specific problems which we think are important and interesting. Hopefully, each reader will have an agenda of his own. Although we may be rationalizing, this is our interpretation. We feel it is reasonable and that it has integrity.

Our gratitude to the officials of "Big City" who must remain anonymous is unbounded. Their willingness to let us be around for a semester is deeply appreciated. We hope that their faith in our ability to see clearly and interpret carefully has been justified. As in all research of this kind, responsibilities exist regarding the confidentiality and anonymity of the people involved. The names of the school, the teachers, and the children are all fictitious. We have assumed that all large cities have a Washington School and that it probably lies in an older part of the community, as does our school.

The U.S. Office of Education through its small-grant program in the Bureau of Research aided us financially at a critical moment with its support of project S-048, *Toward a model of teacher decision making in an urban classroom*. The Central Midwestern Regional Education Laboratory (CEMREL) appointed Smith as Senior Research Associate which faciliated completion of the work.

Washington University and its Graduate Institute of Education have provided an environment where one can get his work done. Our secretarial staff, headed by Pat Carpenter and Jan Williford and assisted by Dorothy Clark, Vera Costain, and Jane Saenger, knows no equal. The process from field notes, to final report, to book is long and arduous. The support of the administration and our colleagues has been limitless. Although the GIE is obviously not unique in this regard, such a setting seems rare. We are fortunate to have had the benefits of working here.

As we tried to turn a large, rough research report into a book, Dale Harris of Pennsylvania State University and Bruce Biddle of the University of Missouri patiently read our manuscript and kept pointing out soft spots which we tried to remedy. If we had listened better, many of the remaining problems might have been clarified also. We are most appreciative of their efforts.

The two people to whom we owe the greatest intellectual debt are W. W. Charters, Jr., and Laurence Iannaccone, our long-time mentors, colleagues, and friends. Our obligation is an unusual one, for they have seen little of the final manuscript, and, consequently, are not to be held responsible for it, but they were part of its early aspects as stimulators and models to whom we turned in our initial groping. Charters, the superlative analyst, convinced us that theory was a worthy objective and tried to show us how the process worked. Iannaccone, the perceptive clinical field worker, gave us the conviction that participant observation was not only legitimate but great fun.

Finally, our wives and children have borne well the emotional burdens that involvement in a project such as this entails.

L. M. S.
W. G.

St. Louis, Missouri
January 1968

C O N T E N T S

x   Contents

C H A P T E R O N E

THE NATURE OF CLASSROOM MICROETHNOGRAPHY

PROBLEM

Several years ago we[1] began what we thought was a relatively simple project dealing with the central problem of how a middle-class teacher copes with a group of lower-class youngsters. Our intent paralleled the views of anthropologist Edward Hall, who makes a vivid case in his book, *The Silent Language* (1959), for the importance of the analysis of what we call the "real world". His essay begins with problems of teaching American citizens to work as government and business representatives in foreign countries. Many difficulties lie in their lack of understanding of the foreign culture and the cues foreigners give to others by their behavior. Hall's major point states that this transaction of a culture to an individual and the in-

---

[1] Louis Smith conceived the project—partly as a result of comments by William Geoffrey, who was then a student in a graduate class. The possibilities of an extended relationship were explored and found feasible, personally, professionally, and administratively.

dividual to a culture amounts to a "silent language": much of it is unspoken, unconscious, and often quite subtle. Our primary intent was to describe the silent language of a culture, a classroom in a slum school, so that those who have not lived in it will appreciate its subtleties and complexities. Secondly, we wanted to develop a scientific language about the phenomenon for more productive research about its functioning. Finally, we hoped to state hypotheses that are worthy of intensive verificational investigation.

To illustrate this intent of careful description and model-building, we suggest several brief examples. First, one boy, a troublesome child in past years, had moved into a special relationship with the teacher. He had a quick wit and a quick tongue. He and the teacher frequently engaged in a teasing, joking type of banter. The boy seemed to "get away with" comments and remarks that no one else dared. Nevertheless, he was accepted by the other children. The teacher utilized this relationship to reach important educational goals with the group. However, theory suggests that such joking interaction often shifts pupil sentiments and pupil social rank. Behaving differently toward this child seemed a violation of the norm of fairness, yet apparently this, too, was accepted by the children. From the wealth of field notes we have described the nuances of this child's behavior with the teacher. Then we developed a more careful conceptual statement of this aspect of teacher-pupil interaction.

As a second illustration, the teacher accented the 3R's and tended to give less emphasis to science, art, and music. The norms of the staff indicated that he was supported in this choice. "With these kids, you have to spend more time on the basics," volunteered another teacher. Homans' (1950) theory suggests that the social environment of the group, in this instance the faculty social system, partly determines time allotments of various classroom group activities (3R's versus other curriculum areas). The teacher's decision concerning emphasis reverberated within the faculty social system and indirectly affected other aspects of the classroom system. Observational data of the teacher's relation to the rest of the staff and description of classroom events permitted this phenomenon to be subjected to further conceptualization.

This research, the model-building of the complexities of an urban classroom, has significance for education in several areas. First, the social problem of urban education is a major issue in contemporary American society. Secondly, the need to understand the full impact of urban teaching through the eyes of the regular practicing teacher in his day-to-day work in the "real world" of his classroom seems essential for guiding any future experimentation as well as practical innovation. Thirdly, to prevent such an analysis of urban teaching from merely giving support to another "in vogue" topic in education, it is necessary to take seriously the admonition that educational issues can profit from careful utilization and development of social and behavioral theory.

METHODOLOGY OF CLASSROOM
MICROETHNOGRAPHY

Any endeavor is partially known by its label. This research, in its broadest scope, used the technique of direct observation of an ongoing, naturalistic situation. To say that we collected "anecdotal records" of the events of the classroom casts the project in a mildly disreputable and trivial light. Such a label makes our work seem much less important than our own feelings reflected at the time. Consequently, when one of our colleagues suggested that we were engaged in the "microethnography of the class-room,"[2] we knew immediately that this was what we were doing, that it was high-sounding and important. Beyond the emotional quality of the label, it does suggest two other points of importance. First, we were, as we have indicated, trying to describe carefully the small social system. Secondly, we pursued our problem quite consciously as a social anthropologist might have done.

Perhaps the most novel aspect of the methodology from either a psychological or a social anthropological point of view concerns what we call the "inside-outside" phenomenon. Mr. Geoffrey, the classroom teacher, was a full-fledged participant in the research. He kept daily field notes of his perception of the classroom and its functioning. As the University observer, Louis Smith was equally a full-fledged participant in the research. He kept detailed field notes of his observations of the classroom. While it is not our purpose at this point to analytically develop the distinction between the participant- and the nonparticipant-observer, it should be noted that the classroom was viewed from these two perspectives: the teacher who had an inside look at what was going on and why it was going on and the University investigator who had an outsider's view of what was happening and why it was happening. To the best of our knowledge this procedure has not been utilized in educational research.[3]

The actual layout of the classroom is presented in Figure 1.1. Mr. Geoffrey's desk was on the left side of the classroom toward the front. Mr. Smith's desk was located at a table on the side toward the rear of the room. Mr. Geoffrey, as the teacher, was in the classroom all day, every day, throughout the semester. His records consisted of a daily set of notes in a teacher's plan book, which is kept, hypothetically, by every teacher in the school system, and stenographic summary notes on daily events of the classroom. Generally, these were written in the evening from brief notes he had taken during the day. Mr. Smith, the University investigator,

[2]We are indebted to Fred Strodtbeck of the University of Chicago for this concept.
[3]In a sense, W. F. Whyte's relationship to "Doc" in *Street Corner Society* provides an analogue. "Doc," however, was primarily an informant, Mr. Geoffrey, the research associate, was a coinvestigator trained in professional education and social science theory and research.

was in the classroom almost all day, every day. Actually his University commitments had been lightened and while he was not there literally all day, every day, he was there approximately 80 percent of the time the class was functioning from the beginning of the semester until the last week of the semester. This gave him the opportunity to observe the day-to-day trials and tribulations of the classroom. As will be described in more detail shortly, he kept a running account, copious field notes, of the classroom events.

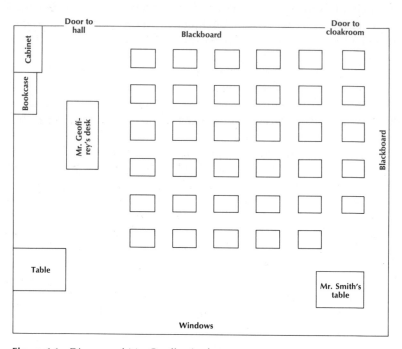

Figure 1.1 Diagram of Mr. Geoffrey's classroom.

Briefly, we would describe the behavior of the nonparticipant-observer, the nature of the field notes that were taken, the behavior of the participant-observer, and finally, the analysis of the data. Because the methodology has not had widespread currency within educational psychology we also kept careful notes on how we behaved throughout the project. Our intent was eventually to write a much more analytical account of this field work in education.

A Behavioral Account of the Method

Basic Guiding Constructs Even when one does not tally on a predetermined observation schedule, attention should be paid to the guiding constructs and social theory that make one selectively perceptive in an observational project such as this. The purpose of the principal investigator was twofold. He wanted to look at the "real world" and describe it carefully and in considerable detail. Then he wanted to back away and conceptualize this "real world" in broader, more abstract terms that would be applicable to any classroom. This latter process is what is meant by developing a model of the classroom. The investigator was interested in learning more about how a middle-class teacher copes with a group of lower-class children. It was his conviction that no one had a very clear idea about how this is done.

There was an element of naïve conviction that if he carefully observed the class and listened attentively to the teacher, then he could make sense out of the experience. In other words, order could be found there. He did not have a previously worked-out statement of how to teach children such as these and there was no commitment to any general point of view in professional education. This resulted in what might be called a nonevaluative orientation. He was not there to criticize but to try to understand and see the relationships among the many facets.

Substantively, the personality theory of McClelland, the social theory of Homans, and the learning theory of Skinner had been his concern as he thought through problems of educational psychology.[4] Most certainly these ideas guided the selection of events that he noted. He had been teaching a graduate class in education entitled "The Classroom as a Social System." This class mainly serves master's degree students in education. A major part of the purpose of the course is to bring relevant social theory to bear upon educational problems. He tries to draw the students, who are generally elementary and secondary school teachers, into lengthy discussion of the nature and problems that they encounter in their day-to-day classroom teaching. The wealth of issues, ideas, problems, and points of view raised by this discussion has considerable bearing on the nature of the methodology. The problem of bias or preconception is a critical one. Malinowski subtly captures the point we are trying to make:

> Good training in theory, and acquaintance with its latest results, is not identical with being burdened with "preconceived ideas." If a man sets out on an expedition, determined to prove certain hypotheses, if he is incapable of changing his views constantly and casting them off ungrudgingly under the pressure of evidence, needless to say his work will be worthless. But the more problems he brings with him into the field, the more he is in the habit of molding his theories according to facts, and of seeing facts in their bearing upon theory, the better he is equipped for the work. Preconceived ideas are pernicious in any scientific work, but foreshadowed problems are the main endowment of a scientific thinker, and these problems are first revealed to the observer by his theoretical studies. [Malinowski, 1922, pp. 8–9]

[4] See L. M. Smith and B. B. Hudgins, *Educational Psychology*. New York. Alfred A. Knopf, Inc., 1964.

We were aware of educational and psychological theory and were concerned with many troublesome, unsolved problems. In effect, our nets were spread to catch some elusive quarry. At the same time, partly because we were so unsure of how one "ought to behave" in teaching these children, we tried to be alert to novelties, incongruities, and new ideas. Serendipity was one of our goals.

With the Children   The observer was introduced to the children as Mr. Smith, a teacher at City University who was interested in problems of how children learn, what they find easy or difficult, what they are interested in, and so forth. The children seemed to accept this without any special concern. They had difficulty differentiating him from previous people, for example apprentice teachers who had been in the classroom. This was clarified by explaining that "Mr. Smith teaches teachers" and was there to find out how lessons go and how children learn. Rather than being bothered or upset, the children generally were amazed that he could write so fast, for often twenty pages of longhand notes were taken each day, and that he could sit so long and be so quiet in the classroom.

In line with prior agreements with Mr. Geoffrey, he did not intervene in classroom activities at any time. He remained outside the discussion and interplay, and did not offer suggestions, criticisms, ideas, or answers to questions. Mr. Geoffrey explained to the children that at any time, except during recitation, they could go back and visit and talk with Mr. Smith if they so desired. The children soon understood that he did not report anything he saw to Geoffrey, whether Geoffrey was in or out of the classroom. The field notes contain several beautiful illustrations. One occurred when a girl was playfully chasing a boy about the classroom while Mr. Geoffrey was away. One of the others said, "You better be careful, Mr. Smith will tell on you." The girl who was in pursuit commented, "Oh, he never tells what we do when Mr. Geoffrey isn't here." As a matter of fact, we did talk a great deal about what the children were doing and what kinds of things were happening, but Geoffrey never used anything we said to take action toward a child. In this sense, no one ever suffered from having been observed. The basic strategy that the observer used was first to never impose himself upon the children; second, to always be interested in them and in what they were doing or what they were saying. Often at recess or during lunch hour when we were out on the playground together, Mr. Smith would wander about while individuals and groups of children came up to raise questions or have informal conversation and chitchat.

On a number of occasions children would come to the observer's table to ask for help on a lesson. Generally this was handled in a very nondirective fashion. He tried to clarify the problem, to point out the possibilities while leaving the decision to the pupil as to exactly what he would put down for his answer. He tried to avoid being caught at a later time when a pupil might say "but Mr. Smith said to do it this way." This never happened in the semester of the project. In similar fashion, an attempt was made to stay out of arguments and not be a part of the authority structure. For instance, on one occasion a pupil seemingly tried to entice him into a conflict by saying, "Mr. Smith, make Alan stop doing that." Fortunately, he was able to quip back "Alan knows better than I do what he should or shouldn't be doing, and doesn't need me to tell him." This went over very well, and the children seemed to sense that he had legitimately evaded the conflict.

With the Teachers   A critical problem centered around the principal investigator's relationship with the teachers in the building. While Mr. Geoffrey had cleared the project with the principal during the prior semester, and had mentioned to the teachers the possibility of his coming, and even though Mr. Smith had made arrangements and secured permission from the administrative hierarchy, the principal and the superintendent, the burden of acceptance came during the fall. He was introduced at the first faculty meeting as an educational psychologist from City University who was interested in the problems of teaching and learning with children from "this kind of a neighborhood," an urban slum area. Initially little more than this was done. During the first days of school, he met informally most of the teachers who were near Mr. Geoffrey's room.

Invariably when a teacher cornered Smith alone the teacher would ask "what are you really doing?" as if he couldn't imagine someone sitting and watching all day, every day, in one classroom. The teachers made comments such as "Isn't it boring?", "What do you write down?", and so forth. With a couple of the more "rough-and-ready" teachers these questions were countered with "In a way it's kind of like Margaret Mead, the anthropologist, who went to the south seas to observe the natives." They would laugh and finish the statement "And we are the natives." The observer would grin back and comment, "I have never lived or taught in such a neighborhood. Teachers have told me it's different. I want to see as carefully as I can this part of the 'real world.'"

Mr. Smith did not go into any classroom except Mr. Geoffrey's. He did not pry into teachers' business or their conversations. Before school, during recess, and at lunchtime, he took part in the hallway social life, essentially by staying about, watching the children, and listening to the conversations. Gradually, as the semester wore on and the teachers came to feel that he was a reasonably pleasant but naïve college instructor who was relatively harmless—at least he didn't gossip—he was able to take a more complete role in the faculty group. Also, the ongoing events of the social system kept dragging him into the system, and moving him from a nonparticipant role into a participant role. Some of these incidents have been described in more detail in the main body of the monograph.

With the Teacher, Mr. Geoffrey   The variety of interdependencies between Geoffrey and Smith requires a conceptualization almost as intensive as the monograph itself. Briefly, the relationship had these background characteristics: (1) Mr. Geoffrey had been a student of Smith's the preceding year, (2) he was an exceptionally able student, (3) he possessed an interest in and flair for analytical, intraceptive behavior, (4) he wrote easily and clearly, (5) he was an accepted member of his school staff. Actually, as the data show, he is a prominent member of the faculty.

Within the classroom, minimal interaction occurred between the two of us. Geoffrey had his teaching responsibilities and Smith had his observational responsibilities. Occasionally Geoffrey would elaborate a point in class to help Smith see an issue clearly, and often messengers would be told to bring their notes to him as well.

We talked at great length before school at Italo's little restaurant, during recess, and at lunch, although the latter occasions frequently involved other teachers. In order for Smith to meet and know the other teachers, Geoffrey set up a "coffee bar" which the second floor teachers frequented before school and at recess. Occasionally Geoffrey would engage in more extended conversations with faculty members to draw them out for the observer's benefit. Unconsciously, Geoffrey echoed Doc's wisdom in helping William Foote Whyte:

> That's right. You tell me what you want to see, and we'll arrange it. When you want some information, I'll ask for it, and you listen. When you want to find out their philosophy of life, I'll start an argument and get it for you. If there's something else you want to get, I'll stage an act for you. Not a scrap, you know, but just tell me what you want, and I'll get it for you. [Whyte, 1955, p. 292]

One of our innovations, which we fell into, consisted in having morning coffee together before school at Italo's. This gave us an opportunity to communicate matters of the day before and to build a growing relationship. On some occasions this meeting was very necessary. The observer had access to most of the information available to the teacher but none of the responsibility for implementing his program. When successes occur, an observer has less reason to feel happy, and alternatively when failures or difficulties arise a mere observer doesn't need to defend himself with any of a variety of mechanisms. Consequently, it is possible for an observer to see the protective mantle as the teacher uses it. On Monday, September 30, the day classes were exchanged,[5] Geoffrey had commented to him that Miss Binder shouldn't have objections about receiving a sibling pair, for

---

[5]This incident appears in full in Chapter Five. A room was closed and most teachers sent many of their students on to a teacher a grade above them while receiving students from a teacher a grade below. Teaching loads were more equitably distributed after these exchanges. Geoffrey had sent brother and sister, Edward and Allison, to Miss Binder.

Miss Carr had three pairs and he himself had two brothers, Harry and Billy, and three sisters, Patty, Rose, and Evelyn. Both Edwin and Allison were difficult children with whom to work. In the observer's notes:

> I opened my mouth about this "rationalization" and caught Geoffrey between the eyes. This was a mistake. Points up the difficult role of friend, instructor, colleague, and participant-observer. Re-emphasizes the importance of morning coffee, exchanging family experiences, passing on inside information regarding the Education Department at City University, in maintaining rapport and some kind of harmony. The sharp eye is necessary as an observer, but the quick tongue creates havoc. A discrimination needs to be made, however. On occasion, when Mr. Geoffrey's own ego is not involved, the ability to make a shrewd inference from minimal cues clarifies my business in being down here. Also continues to validate my ability to see important items.   (9/30)

The observer has an important tightrope to walk.

In summary, it was only when Smith talked to others who have engaged in nonparticipant research, those who have had to find their informants and build their relationships "on the spot", did he truly come to appreciate this one unique role, among many others, played by Mr. Geoffrey.[6] This suggests, in addition, the need for methodological investigations centering on various approaches to obtaining and utilizing informants.

Contrasts in the True Participant-Observer's Behavior

The greatest strength of the classroom teacher as participant-observer is that he usually knows why he proceeds as he does. He knows why he suddenly shifts gears when there is no overt evidence from nonparticipant observation.[7] For example, he may start talking about warm- versus cold-blooded animals and then turn to something else before going into the subject. Why? With no statements of plans and expectations from the participant, or the person being observed, the nonparticipant-observer has difficulty understanding certain courses that the teacher takes. Of course, there also can be difficulty because the teacher may not fully understand why he proceeds as he does and may either be unable to report accurately or may be tempted "to look good" in what he does report. The teacher found it mortifying to admit, for example, that warm- versus cold-blooded animals was a subject introduced and then discarded quickly because of a sudden feeling of inadequacy to make the point intended. But such was the case.

We imagine that there is much more to this than is obvious on the surface. In teaching in the traditional manner the teacher is usually look-

---

[6]We are indebted here to conversations with a number of our colleagues, especially Anne Trask and Laurence Iannaccone.

[7]The importance of this and the succeeding paragraphs for our decision making model only appeared gradually as the project developed.

ing for certain answers, and unless a nonparticipant is thoroughly familiar with the patterns of instruction, problems previously encountered that cause the teacher to use a certain approach are unknown to that nonparticipant. The mere selection of content is a case in point. Why does the teacher start with grammar and proceed later to composition work? (By that we mean the formal instruction of grammar—today we will study nouns.) The participant supposedly could present a logical argument supporting his procedures and practices. The nonparticipant may have no knowledge of these.

Even if the teacher explains his thinking to the nonparticipant-observer, there is no guarantee that the teacher himself fully perceives the reasons for his actions, nor is there a guarantee that he will report in full honesty even if he does know. Thus the participant has the advantage of knowing most of what is going on. Whether or not he can report this honestly is another matter. The nonparticipant alone cannot know the rationale behind practices and procedures.

The participant-observer has other advantages. He can manipulate. In interacting with students he can lead conversations on to get more information. He can move two students so that they sit next to one another, or he can separate them. The nonparticipant must take things as they come.[8]

The participant-observer also has the advantage of being able to hear more than the nonparticipant. Many conversations at the desk or out in the hall are physically beyond the reach of the nonparticipant. Of course, there is a weakness here in that the participant is likewise limited. He misses much of what goes on at the back of the room. Of the two positions, however, the nonparticipant seems to miss much more. This advantage includes access to all notes and other communications that pass across the teacher's desk. It includes conversations with other teachers, the principal, and parents.

One final critical advantage is that the participant-observer is to a certain degree a member of a social system, and from his interactions with other adults in the school he receives a great deal of information not available to the nonparticipant.

There are disadvantages. The greatest is that the almost constant interaction demanded by the participant role and other duties involved prohibit real reporting. The nonparticipant-observer has it all over the participant here. He can sit in the back of the room and fill page after page with notes, while the participant can only jot down a comment here and there, or make rushed notes that cannot survive long amid his constant attention to his classroom duties.

[8]In retrospect this too seems an exceedingly important point. The move toward "quasi-experimentalism" in ongoing classrooms is quite possible and should be exploited in later research.

Another disadvantage is the nature of involvement. It is difficult to view situations with detachment if one has strong positive or negative feelings about the students. It is not impossible, but it is difficult. It is also difficult to report honestly when one is so deeply involved.

A third disadvantage is the improper use of manipulation. Manipulation, while having certain advantages, could present a false picture of the situation, depending upon the data desired. It would not be normal. If a pupil says he is going to the country, perhaps the teacher would not ask normally what he means by "country." Perhaps a question such as this is not very serious. But the opportunity to manipulate might be regarded as a disadvantage, if used at the wrong time.

These are the main advantages and disadvantages of the participant-observer role in relation to the nonparticipant-observer. One perhaps needs further comment—the stated advantage of the participant being a member of the school's social system. What happens when the participant works closely with the nonparticipant and therefore might be identified as an informant?

First, we would imagine there would be a difference between the informant who volunteers to lead the way for the observer into the school system, and the informant who is merely assigned the job. There might be a wide range in how much informing would occur in the case of arbitrary assignment by a third person. Here we will only consider the situation as it actually existed.

The first problem facing the informant concerns the continual explanations to his colleagues. Why is the observer here? What does he want? How does he feel? How long is he going to stay, anyway? The teacher as informant must allay fears, overcome suspicions, smooth paths. In short, depending upon what the observer wants, the informant may have to try to help him into the system.

The second problem is related to the first. What happens to the informant's role in the system? What information that the teacher normally would have was denied Geoffrey because of his close relationship to the observer? How much should he report of what he was told? The other teachers sensed this part of the relationship. Geoffrey felt that he was told most of the things that he normally would have been told. There was a difference in that once at least he was told something in strict confidence, not to be told to the nonparticipant-observer. Thus some sensed the relationship. Many times Geoffrey was told things with the admonition, "Don't tell anyone." This usually meant not only not to tell *anyone* but also not to tell Smith. (The requests were always honored.)

There was harrassment for Geoffrey about the nonparticipant-observer and some extra caution in handling, or being given, certain information.

In addition, some members of the system were inhibited slightly in interacting with Geoffrey such as Mr. Gennep. Geoffrey, too, felt somewhat inhibited in wandering and interacting freely because of a sense of responsibility for the nonparticipant-observer. Fortunately, however, in these areas as well as in the two problems mentioned above, both teacher and observer were able to minimize any difficulties.

Finally, one might ask about the impact of nonparticipant-observers as they come into the system. How do the members perceive them? They do present some kind of threat or elicit some suspicion as far as a faculty is concerned. Teachers are generally not happy about being observed, or about having outsiders around. Or so they claim. A lot may depend upon how well the presence of the observer can be explained at the very beginning and on how he makes his presence felt. The relationship to a teacher already in the system, the preparation of the others for his entrance, and his passive acceptance by the students seem to have clouded any evidence of impact upon the system beyond that which already has been reported. In summary, there are probably many wrong ways to enter a system as an observer that would not enable one to present observation after observation. Fortunately, this was not the case in our project.

On Keeping the Field Notes

After the initial perception of classroom events fades, and new events crowd out earlier ones, the data that become "rock bottom" are the daily field notes and records.

Basically three kinds of records were obtained by the nonparticipant-observer: (1) The longhand record of classroom events contained direct reports of the behavior of the teacher, the children, and others who happened into the classroom, as well as insights, inferences, and interpretative comments that occurred to him as he watched. Usually, the latter, the inferences, were bracketed to set them off from the more concrete behavior, the classroom action itself. (2) The second set of records were entitled "Field Notes: Summary Observations and Interpretations." Generally these were taped on a portable tape recorder in his car as he drove to and from the school. The content of these notes usually reflected events in the building as a whole: they were broader interpretations and reflections on the events of the day, week, or semester. (3) The third set of records were the "documents." These included an array of materials passing through the classroom: occasional work samples, sociometric and other tests, notes from parents, and so forth.

Several points need brief amplification. The notes had to be kept every day. While this is easy to say, it is very difficult to do because the accumulated fatigue and "staleness" mount rapidly and significantly. He found often that he didn't have the energy to talk into the Stenorette on the way home. When that happened he made a special point of recording the following morning.

Another very significant point concerned the temptation to talk about an episode before he had recorded it in the notes. Talking to his wife or a colleague seemed to take the edge off of reporting the incident in the notes. In effect, we think that the reactions and interpretations of the new party were mixed into the summary observations. We do not have quantitative data on this result, but our impression is that the leveling, sharpening, and distorting phenomena noted in research on recall of impressions and research on variations in successive transmissions of rumors are pertinent here. He tried to make a practice of keeping his mouth shut until the item was safely reported in the field notes themselves or dictated into the summary notes.

Another practice the observer followed, which accents the difference between model-building and verificational research, was to record at the time what we call insights and interpretations. For instance, in September, a language lesson was underway and the questions in the text required the pupils to construct sentences containing direct objects. Mr. Geoffrey approached this carefully and systematically as he built on the children's prior experiences. The observer was noting his examples, the children's responses, and so forth. While doing this, it occurred to Smith that the format of constructing one's own sentences was very different from the more usual procedure of identifying the direct object in each of a given list of ten sentences. The possibilities for prompting humor and originality with a statement "If you like, try to think up humorous or unusual sentences" seemed possible. Methodologically, the point we wish to make is that the observer took the time to write down this idea and several brief comments on the implications for the current fad about creativity, the consequences of humor in classroom interaction, a need to look at the structure of questions in textbooks, and the special characteristics of language arts in contrast to arithmetic or social studies. These comments were bracketed and initialed, the code for personal thoughts in contrast to observations.

When we returned months later to the notes, this interpretive comment formed a point of departure for ideas that must be checked throughout the notes for frequency and for relationships with other events. Methodologically, it is important to remember that while writing these supplementary comments many events occurred that could not be recorded. If one were trying at the moment to quantify the frequency of teacher interaction with a pupil for a test of an hypothesis on the amount and kind of teacher-pupil interaction, this interpretive note would not be possible. For our purposes, we were "discovering" rather than "verifying."

On Analyzing the Field Notes

General Problems and Procedures   The twin goals—describing the real world of a slum classroom and building a more general theory of teaching—guided the collection of the data. Similarly these goals guided the behavior of the analysts in working with the accumulated file drawers of notes. Scholars such as Becker (1958) have indicated an ideal type in the process of data analysis. He suggests steps which fall roughly in this order:

1. Selection and definition of problems, concepts, and indices.
2. Checking the frequency and distribution of phenomena.
3. Construction of social system models.
4. Final analysis and the presentation of results.

In a sense, we did this, but for clarity we will indicate precisely our procedures.

While we did know we wanted a monograph that would describe and conceptualize the events of the classroom, we did not know whether to write a chronology section and then a theoretical section or to attempt some blend. Consequently, we started reading through the field notes. In the course of doing this several things happened: first, we reaffirmed our interest in speaking to the issues involved in beginning a new school year. Second, we wanted to present considerable detail about the first few days to indicate the "quality" of our observation and to acquaint the reader with the children and the situation. Third, we immediately began running into the "interpretative insights" interspersed throughout the document. At that point we elected to write short statements, one to five pages, about the insights. These statements involved both descriptions and attempts to conceptualize. Later, after they had been put aside in favor of other problems and issues, new episodes and incidents would occur which were relevant. More cutting and pasting, qualification, rewriting, and consolidating of ideas would then occur.

Fourth, we began listing the concepts we used and the definitions we gave them. Our intent was to get these "on the table" and eventually organize and interlock them in a general axiomatic theory of teaching. We soon found ourselves with problem areas such as the nature of the culturally deprived child in the classroom and social roles in the classroom. Several of these we pursued quickly through notes, cut and pasted our carbons into the total story, and then drew out our more complete description and abstraction. As the ideas came and went we tried to date them to know whether they arose initially in situ or whether they "flashed" as we read and organized.

As we went about this, methodological questions, such as the two realities problem,[9] arose and we stopped to think and write tentative statements about them. Also we invented procedures such as using the inside-outside idea as a means of focusing on decision-making. In like manner we were haunted by the desire to say something about "the ideal," or changes we would make. When we started to phrase these as generalities they sounded glossy and inappropriate. The idea arose to focus on how we would

[9]This point is clarified in the appendix.

change things in terms of each child and in terms of the specific parts of our description and model. We brainstormed this initially and returned again and again to the notes.

In this manner, like Topsy, the social system model grew. Our colleagues thought it very inefficient and time-consuming, as it was, yet we never had the total picture until we had the total monograph. Only then could we enter Becker's fourth phase of final analysis in any true sense. In a less than true sense we did because of another phenomenon. The senior author began to lecture on parts of the data and tried to put together coherent papers. Each of these went through criticisms by Geoffrey for erroneous interpretations and missed nuances. The notebooks arbitrated any continuing disagreements. Similarly, colleagues at City University helped clarify ideas in the thesis and ambiguities in the presentation.

The closest analogy we have found for the "analyst's" behavior is that of putting a jigsaw puzzle together. The pieces are strewn about. One has faith that order exists. Simple fits occur with struggling. Later the sections of green merge with the sections of reds and browns and blues. In time, the whole is there.

A Microethnographic Procedure for Studying Decision-making Processes

As we have indicated, some literature exists on the problems and procedures in analyzing field notes. In the course of the analysis of our data, in the way we came to conceptualize the problem, and in the "inside-outside" type of methodology, we invented a format that seems productive and that might have broader generality. Briefly, it is easiest to report our simple steps and then to expand upon them.

1. Read through and stop at each "insightful" comment or interpretation.
2. Abstract verbatim the incident precipitating the insightful comment and the date of occurrence.
3. If possible, elaborate the significance and implications of the incident.
4. Feed the incident (No. 2) without the insight (No. 1) or the elaboration (No. 3) to Mr. Geoffrey. Ask for reasons concerning his behavior or his perception of others' behavior.
5. Later, if desirable, feed the incident plus insight and elaboration for further commentary.
6. Later, reread jointly each others' comments and talk additional interpretations into a verbatim record.
7. Include an occasional incident that seems innocuous to keep the other honest.

The procedure proves very helpful in making the process analysis related to our interests. One of the basic assumptions lay in the on-going record of insights and interpretations kept by the outside observer. These events were akin to evidence on the "foreshadowed problems" of Malinowski. The record kept them from being lost. The notes also kept separate the concrete event in descriptive terms and the possible implications for abstract problems. The elaboration frequently amounted to a short conceptual essay in which the incident was decomposed into common elements and into a language system used throughout the report. This allowed for the gradual development of a systematic conceptualization of the classroom as a social system. Feeding the episode and the date to Mr. Geoffrey allowed him: (1) to go back to his notes and his general information, (2) to recapture the episode, and (3) to reproduce an approximation of the images and thought occurring at the time. In this way two sets of perceptions and two interpretations could be integrated about an issue. As discrepancies arose step No. 5 was initiated. In the course of critiquing early drafts of the report step No. 6 occurred.

As we have commented, our interest in decision-making processes forced us in this direction. Our independent "inside-outside" record of events permitted the back-and-forth interplay.

One of the major advantages centered on the minor degree of alteration of the natural events. Mr. Geoffrey was a naturally introspective teacher. His keeping a record probably enhanced this. The outside observer by not breaking in with questions probably altered the situation much less than if he had called up, for critical analysis, the events as they arose. At the same time the records were complete enough to minimize distortion in recall.

THE THEORETICAL MODEL

While Homans' *Human Group* (1950) provided a model for substantive concepts and to a degree for the formal characteristics of a theory, it was Zetterberg's (1965) conception of social science theory that more explicitly became our target. For us, he made clear distinctions among primitive and derived concepts, propositions, and theory. A theory is an interrelated set of propositions. A proposition is a relationship between two or more concepts. A concept, or term, is the primary language unit. The initial set of concepts is undefined[10] or primitive; the broader set of concepts used in the propositions are derived from combinations of the undefined or primitive concepts. Further, he states that propositions may be organized or related in various ways: inventories of determinants, inventories of results, chain patterns, and axiomatic formats.

Our procedures have been essentially these: As we have tried to abstract from our observations our operational definitions, in effect, we have named phenomena. Then we have tried to define theoretically the

---

[10]The reference here is to conceptual definitions. For research purposes all concepts obviously require valid operational definitions. Obviously, obtaining valid operations is also an exceedingly difficult issue in methodology.

new term we have coined or borrowed. As we wrote down our conceptual definitions we found that they usually contained some terms already in our growing glossary and some new terms. Ultimately we found our way back to our "undefined" primitive list. While this process has a circular quality to it, it seems to us to be the essence of a theory. Ultimately the glossary becomes larger and larger as it becomes more all-embracing [11] As an illustration of our theory-building we present an example growing out of a concept we have called "personalized interaction." The reduction proceeded this way:

1. By personalized interaction we mean the interaction between the teacher and a single pupil.[12]
2. Interaction—a minimum sequence in which the behavior of one or more persons follows another.
3. Behavior—a primitive term, the things people do.
4. Person—a primitive term, an individual.
5. Teacher—an encumbent in a role in the school in which an individual attempts to change the learning of another, the pupil.
6. Pupil—a role in which one is expected to learn.
7. Role—a pattern of activities, interactions, and sentiments bound together by a group belief.
8. And so forth.

As is evident, the list of concepts grows and grows. We have tried in our glossary to account for all the terms we have used. In this manner we have derived more and more complex concepts. They are relevant and related to our other concepts.

In general we have tried to develop concepts which Zetterberg calls "variates." These conceptions are susceptible to quantification in greater or smaller amounts; they represent continua. They also fit within a functional or propositional theory rather than in a descriptive schema or taxonomy.

As a further step, we tried to find in our data the antecedents and consequences of the conception. This led us into forming hypotheses with concepts already in our theory, as well as creating new concepts. The new ones had to be defined conceptually, as we have just indicated, with "personalized interaction." As we sketched out our propositions we found we were drawing diagrams. For instance, we have hypothesized that an increasing amount of personalized interaction leads to increased pupil satisfaction, increased pupil esteem for the teacher, a more highly differentiated role structure in the classroom, and increased clarification of learning barriers. In addition, we hypothesized that pupil satisfaction and pupil esteem for

[11]The reader is urged to consult continuously this glossary for explicit definitions of concepts. While we try to define each new term when it is first used this becomes difficult on occasion.

[12]On an observational schedule our tentative operational definition of this concept involves a minimal two-step sequence. 1) teacher-comment to an individual pupil and 2) pupil-perception or response indicating awareness.

the teacher lead to classroom control and that clarification of specific barriers to pupil learning leads to enhanced pupil achievement. Similarly we hypothesized several antecedents affecting the amount of personalized interaction; these included administrative organization (intact or split-level classes), teacher personality structure of liking children, and staff norms regarding teaching styles. In short we have what might be called a miniature theory of personalized teacher-pupil interaction. We diagramed the hypothesized relationships in Figure 1.2. The concepts were all within the broader theory included in our glossary.

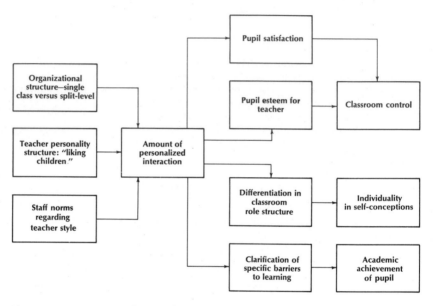

Figure 1.2   A miniature theory of personalized interaction.

Stated in a more axiomatic form, we have ten hypotheses that constitute the basic postulates of our miniature theory of personalized interaction. They are listed below:

1. As organizational structure shifts from a single class to a split-level class the amount of personalized interaction decreases.
2. As teacher-liking of pupils increases, then the amount of personalized interaction increases.
3. As staff norms increase in intensity and crystallization and decrease in range of tolerable behavior regarding personal interaction, then the amount of personalized interaction increases.[13]

---

[13]This proposition has been elaborated more intensively to illustrate the additional complexities introduced by taking advantage of Jackson's (1960) conception of the structure of norms.

4. As amount of personalized interaction increases, then pupil satisfaction increases.
5. As amount of personalized interaction increases, then pupil esteem for the teacher increases.
6. As amount of personalized interaction increases, differentiation in classroom role-structure increases.
7. As amount of personalized interaction increases, clarification of specific barriers to learning increases.
8. As pupil satisfaction and esteem for teacher increase, then classroom control increases.
9. As differentiation in classroom role-structure increases, individuality in self-conceptions increases.
10. As clarification of specific barriers to learning increases, then academic achievement increases.

This small illustration suggested ten propositions serving as postulates. The number of theorems open to test is considerably larger. For instance, personalized interaction should be related to each of the more distal consequences, three testable theorems. Each of the three antecedents of personalized interaction should relate to each of the four immediate consequences and to each of the three more distal consequences, a total of twenty-one additional theorems which would be testable hypotheses. Less apparent theorems include the interrelationships among the consequences themselves, for example classroom control and individuality in self-conceptions. Later, as we present additional concepts, we hypothesize further interrelationships, which increases the complexity of the theory and hopefully presents a more valid map of the reality of the classroom.

Zetterberg argues that several important values arise from this kind of theorizing. First, "a theory can be used to provide the most parsimonious summary of actual or anticipated research findings" (p. 161). In our research the relationships are hypotheses; they reflect what we believe existed in this case. As we have said several times, they need verification through quantitative research in the laboratory and the field. Second, "a theory can be used to co-ordinate research so that many separate findings support each other giving the highest plausibility to the theory per finding" (p. 163). In effect, each piece of support accents the plausibility of related aspects of the theoretical structure. Third, "a theory can be used to locate the most strategic or manageable propositions for testing" (p. 164). Without question, some concepts have more readily available and valid indicators than other concepts. As one has the more general theoretical picture, one's research tactics can be made more flexible and presumably more productive. Finally Zetterberg argues, "a fourth virtue of theory for the researcher: a theory provides a limited area in which to locate false propositions when an hypothesis fails to meet an empirical test" (p. 166). As theorems do not stand the test of carefully drawn data, the specific postulates that are in error can be excised or reconceptualized. The total theory is not dissolved. In this way "negative results" can contribute to the cumulative enterprise.

While Zetterberg (1965, pp. 159–166) argues that each one-step relationship becomes a postulate and each two-step relationship becomes a theorem and that one need only test empirically the end points to verify indirectly the postulates, we have less confidence in this degree of formalization and verification. However, verification can proceed more systematically by obtaining valid indicators of each concept: for instance, measures of norms based on Jackson's return-potential model, attitudes via an MTAI, and class organization through a questionnaire. The amount of personalized interaction can be obtained from frequency counts in direct observation. Pupil esteem for the teacher should be obtainable from questionnaires, and the degree of differentiation of role-structure of the classroom from observation or modified sociometric instruments. Similarly, operations can be devised for other parts of the model; our intent here is to show how the theory can be moved from the formulation and development stage, in which we have been engaged, to the verificational stage of tested propositions. As such results are obtained, we believe that a potent psychology of teaching will become available. We feel that such concepts as personalized interaction, pupil-esteem, differentiated role-structure, clarification of learning barriers are important and largely unanalyzed concepts in the field, and that effort would be well spent in their clarification and extension. At that point educational psychology and principles of teaching should escape some of the twin evils of "good data about insignificant issues" and "abstract proverbs and maxims" instead of carefully limited propositions.

C H A P T E R   T W O

SCHOOL BEGINS

THE BEGINNING

As with many institutions which have a recurring rhythm, the public
schools have a ritual for beginning the school year. City School System is
no exception. On the Tuesday after Labor Day the entire corps of teachers
meets in the downtown auditorium for an inspirational talk by the president of the school board, an analysis of the meaning of public education
today by a superintendent of schools from a nearby city, and a rapid-fire
stream of announcements by the local superintendent. These formal arrangements possess a content and style that help characterize the context of the
classroom of our study and consequently have importance for our analysis.
The field notes summarize these events.[1]

> We went upstairs to the balcony to a full house—literally all the seats
> to the top rows were filled shortly after we came in. The program . . .

[1]The field notes are quoted almost verbatim. We have used only minor editing to
achieve clarity.

began with a brief comment by the superintendent that the first three items, the anthem, the pledge, and the invocation, would be taken in order and that we all were to rise at the same time and stay standing until the third item was over and were all to sit down together. Again,[2] I was not surprised but reawakened to the clipped, business-like, autocratic, if you wish, approach of the superintendent. In machine gun-like fashion he started the proceedings.

The president of the Board of Education gave an impassioned plea for education for all children. He gave an angry rebuttal to the criticism by the Citizen's Committee concerning Board integration policies. He commented briefly on the quality of the school system and on the history of the school system as it related to the integration question. He was strikingly critical of the fact that many of the critics did not know the facts of the situation or they would not be protesting as they were at the present time. He reviewed the Board's unanimous policy. (LMS—Several Negroes are on the board.)[3] One of the items he commented upon was the fact that no teacher would be coerced in her teaching assignment. This brought a wave of applause in the auditorium, particularly from the white teachers and especially from the older female white teachers who clapped vigorously and at length. At the close of this speech the applause seemed to break upon racial lines with strong support by the white teachers and mild to no support, what might be described as a "cool reception" by the majority of Negro teachers whom I could see as I scanned the auditorium balcony.

The superintendent of schools from the neighboring city gave a brief talk on the topic, "Why Teach?". One major point that he made, which seemed to me at the time to be critical, was that a contemporary objective of education that had arisen in recent years concerned the survival of the nation and of the culture. He compared and contrasted this briefly with prior broad objectives of the public schools—the early social reconstruction during the 1930s, the education for individual development, the education for economic welfare, and so forth, which had been rallying points for other generations and other periods.

After a brief intermission, the local superintendent briefly gave a resumé of the issues pertaining to general school activities—such things as buildings, meetings, difficulties with strikes, and items of general interest to school personnel as a whole. He did this in his rapid-fire manner, hardly taking time to swallow a gulp of water before clicking out another set of facts and another array of information concerning achievement and the general quality of the job being done by Big City teachers. He introduced a bit of humor at the conclusion, commenting that since we were getting out early at 11:30 he wanted everyone to be very careful going down the steps, that generally one person sprained

---

[2]I was acquainted with the superintendent and his approach.

[3]Most of the interpretive comments made at the time the field notes were written were initialed and bracketed.

his ankle and at least three fenders were bumped in the general rush of traffic out of the auditorium.   (9/3)[4]

Following this portion of the beginning-of-term ritual, the teachers scatter to their several schools.

THE WASHINGTON SCHOOL

As we drive across the city and into the Washington School neighborhood, the litter and debris scattered on street and sidewalk characterize the physical locale of the school. This impression becomes clearer as one realizes that the lot behind the school belongs to a trucking company. The front of the school opens onto a major truck artery, which masks the sounds of the factory across the street. Later, from Mr. Geoffrey's room, we can see a warehouse and a closed and decaying nightclub across the back lot. Still later we will hear, especially with the windows open, the piercing factory whistle calling, in rhythmic bursts, various supervisory personnel to return to their offices from the production parts of the plant.

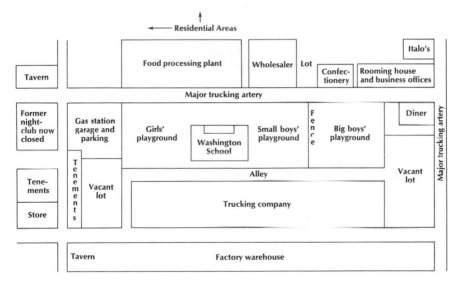

Figure 2.1 Washington School and its immediate environs.

One might eulogize Big City, as Sandburg does in "Chicago," as a hog butcher, a tool-maker, and a player with railroads; or one might lament the contrast with the pastoral, open quality of the green, campus-type schools in the county suburbs. For our purposes we present a map, Figure 2.1, of the school grounds and the neighborhood. The field notes stress a contrast:

[4]Throughout the field notes, these parenthetical numerals denote month and day.

> As we walked into the back entrance of the building, I was struck by the way the floors glistened with wax. Everything was polished. Most of the construction and refurbishing of the summer had been cleaned up. The building seemed to be all set for another year of school.   (9/3)

In time, as we will note, the neighborhood creeps in upon the school, the contrast blurs, and the school approximates the community more closely.

During the first hour after lunch, Mr. Geoffrey visits briefly with his closer friends among the faculty, particularly as they wander by his room. Mainly, however, each teacher seems to be attending to the minor record-keeping and supply-gathering chores. Those with whom Mr. Geoffrey chats are from the second floor, and mostly, but not exclusively, from his end of the building.

THE FIRST FACULTY MEETING

At 1:30, the formal aspect of the ritual begins again as each elementary school in the district, including Washington, holds its first faculty meeting of the year. The field notes capture the reactions:

> Several aspects of the general meeting at 1:30 in the old library room are worthy of note. First, the principal very obviously was in charge of the situation; he directed the meeting, made the bulk of the comments, solicited questions, and left no doubt in my mind that he, in effect, saw his position as one of "running the school." If I had to put a label on his behavior, I would describe it in terms of accepting the responsibility of bureaucratic authority, rather than expressing personal authority. A second general observation concerned the seating arrangement in the meeting. All of the male teachers sat farther away from the head of the table, around another table, as a separate sub-group. This segregation by sexes seemed to be one of the basic dimensions of the school interaction—no one greeted it with any surprise or seemingly with any hostility—it seemed to reflect the fact the men liked to be with the men and the women liked to be with the women. Earlier Geoffrey had commented about the male teachers' room and the gossiping of the women teachers. . . . A third observation in the teachers' meeting was the general reaction of the staff to Geoffrey. The comments from several of the women teachers, mostly joking, some concerning his weight, and so forth, indicated that he was held in high esteem, particularly by Miss Carr, Miss Donora, and Miss Eagle.
>
> The principal spoke at some length about several issues; one of these was the transportee problem, and the fact that the school would have bussed-in pupils and teachers for the first time this year. He made it very clear that his position was that these pupils and their teachers were members of the Washington School and were to be treated as such. Apropos of much of the controversy concerning the transportees, the

Board's position on the administrative difficulties of integrating these children, other than bringing them in intact classrooms, as is done, seemed supported by one of the comments of a transportee teacher who said that they might have difficulty making out their lunch tickets by 9:00 because sometimes the busses didn't run true to schedule. In effect, she seemed to be saying that there were difficulties in getting to school on time. As an outside observer, it seemed to me that this comment in part vindicated the administration's more general position concerning the intact classroom approach. The principal talked a bit about the fact that there had been very little vandalism during the summertime, in spite of the fact that Geoffrey counted at least seven windows that were cracked or broken wide open in his second floor room (which is not above a playground). The principal commented on discipline problems and seemed to be saying several contradictory things: One, that every school has some problems; two, that children are children everywhere; and three, that there were some unique satisfactions in teaching children from less privileged areas. He commented that he was ready and willing to help them with discipline problems, but he did emphasize (and this should be cleared up in later conversations with Mr. Geoffrey and other teachers) that he expected teachers to tell him what they had already done about the problem before they brought the problem to him personally. One possible implication was that most problems are supposed to be solved by the teacher and not brought to his attention.   (9/3)

Other details concerning the building are communicated. The teachers make only a few comments. After forty minutes the teachers filter back to their rooms. The ritual contains one final element: teachers must stay until 3:30. The school day, for which they have been paid, does not end until then. Mr. Geoffrey returns to getting his room organized. As we shall see, he generally leaves most of the book-distribution items and room decoration until the children are present. This freedom provides an easy tempo for conversation with faculty friends and for the introduction of the observer to significant members of the faculty. Miss Holt is treated with humor and flattery. "She's the traveler, the second in command formally, and informally the first in command." Mr. Gennep and Mr. Geoffrey discuss local athletics, both amateur and professional. They raise the possibility of attending an out-of-town State University game this fall. Some of this exchange seems to be precipitated by Mr. Geoffrey's having earlier searched for a radio. He borrowed Miss Carr's and thus was able to listen to the ball game. Mr. Gennep had been a thought and a step behind. Gennep is in and out of Geoffrey's room several times during the afternoon. (Part of his in-and-out behavior reflected a strong friendship as well as his desire to keep abreast of the game.) A few comments about summer experiences and school gossip complete the major conversational topics. At 3:30, the staff leaves. No one is encumbered with books or materials.

THE PUPILS ARRIVE

District policy states that pupils attend for half a day on Wednesday. At 8:37 A.M., after the appropriate bells, the pupils come in quietly and take whatever seats they desire. At 8:40, Mr. Geoffrey and his colleagues in the hall at the head of the stairs disband their small group and enter their respective rooms. The notes capture the tenor of the first few minutes:

> Geoffrey sits quietly at his table in the front. Looks them over and smiles. Starts attendance and roll. Makes brief comments of recognition: "New hairdo?" (to one of girls), "Anyone know whether they have moved?" (about an absent pupil), and so forth.   (9/4)

Shortly thereafter an episode occurs in which he asks a child to go to the board and write his, Mr. Geoffrey's, name. The child errs. The other children are reticent about volunteering to correct the error. Individually Mr. Geoffrey identifies children by name and finally persuades one to go up and correct the misspelling.

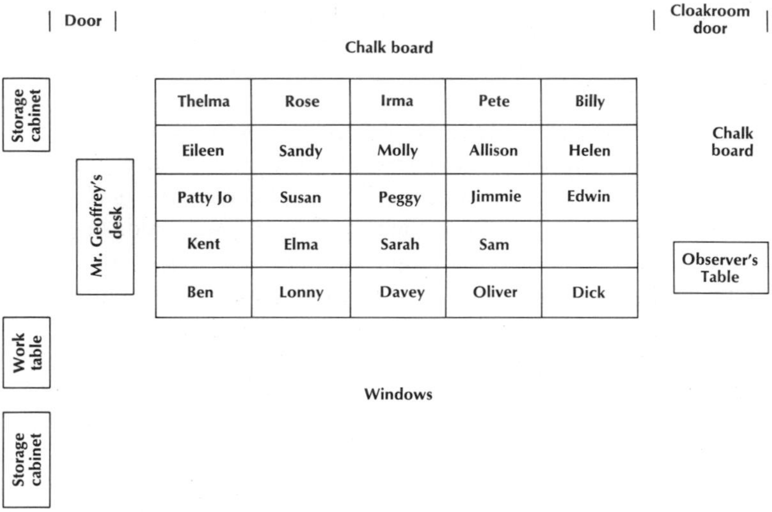

Door		Cloakroom door

Chalk board

	Thelma	Rose	Irma	Pete	Billy	
Storage cabinet	Eileen	Sandy	Molly	Allison	Helen	Chalk board
	Patty Jo	Susan	Peggy	Jimmie	Edwin	
Mr. Geoffrey's desk	Kent	Elma	Sarah	Sam		
Work table	Ben	Lonny	Davey	Oliver	Dick	Observer's Table
Storage cabinet						

Windows

Figure 2.2   The initial seating assignment.   (9/5)

At 8:52, in a quite direct manner, he comments, "Let's talk about rules. Allison, how about gum? Do I like it? Do I like to see people chewing it?" Allison, who "accidentally" came in chewing gum, answers "No," walks to the wastebasket, and disposes of her gum. In the next *7 minutes* Mr. Geoffrey briefly outlines the class rules: First, if you leave the room, you must ask permission and you are not to ask to leave in pairs. No looks of misunderstanding occur. Almost before he finishes that item, Mr. Geoffrey focuses his attention on one boy and comments, "What time does school start, Sam?" which is followed quickly by "If you're at Rhodys[5], when are you to be in the yard?" Sam replies as expected. Mr. Geoffrey asks "Questions?" There are none. Then abruptly he says "Attendance; unfortunately I see some who don't like to be here." He then comments that a note excusing absence is needed. It should be from an adult and not from fellow students. The pupils react and he counters, "Some of you smile; do I hit home?" The discussion continues through borrowing materials, time for talking and not talking, pencil sharpening, seating, and homework. In conclusion, Mr. Geoffrey, with Billy's help, defines reputation: "Ways you behave." He indicates that it is possible to wipe out reputations and start with a clean slate. Finally he asks "Questions?" There are none.

In the episodes of attendance taking and rule establishing the teacher's behavior might strike an outsider as characterized by clarity, a knack for singling out individual pupils and observing something unique, different, or momentarily appropriate about them, unhurriedness, and frequent use of the noun "permission." The children are quiet and reticent. They get the point. They seem to know Mr. Geoffrey.

At 8:59, Mr. Geoffrey begins to distribute books. He explains the routine: everyone must have a number and all of one's books must have the same number. He asks for "strong boys" as helpers. No one volunteers immediately, then with a real twinkle in his eye, he comments, "I guess I've got lazy boys again this year." When he comes to number 13, he comments, "Sam, I'll give you the lucky number. You're not superstitious, are you?" This evokes a general discussion of superstition. Each child walks up for his spelling book. Later, Edwin and Jimmie help pass out books. As the numbers are called, children seem only half alert. They don't show any hostility or what might be called passive resistance. A general inattentiveness and withdrawal from the environment characterizes them.

At 9:22, a new boy, Lonny, arrives. Mr. Geoffrey tells him to take a seat. The book-passing continues. Sandy begins to chat with the girl behind her. A continual byplay exists as the teacher describes the two history books, the number of books they will have (in response to Sandy's question), and so on.

A teacher interrupts briefly at 9:39. Shortly, Mr. Geoffrey is attending once more to the events of the morning. He explains occasional desk inspections. "I expect to find them neat." He asks for volunteers for sharpening pencils and picks two of several who raise their hands and who haven't helped in book passing. He sends them to a table out in the hall. As the rulers are passed out, he asks, "What is this?" Billy replies, "Ruler." "What are its uses?" evokes "Draw and measure." The other possible uses,

[5]The confectionary across the street.

hitting and fencing, are suggested with humor and clarity. "Don't have it out unless you have genuine use," is Mr. Geoffrey's final comment. This is followed by similar remarks concerning erasers, that is, "Don't bite off a piece and throw it."

At 9:50, with most of the books and supplies distributed, Mr. Geoffrey turns to the series of minor activities necessary for the smooth functioning of the group—"certain jobs that must be done in the room." He assigns these jobs according to the twin criteria of volunteering and special skills necessary for the activity. He comments, "Best attendance and best handwriting usually get the assignment job. Molly, how's your handwriting? Pretty good?" She goes to the board. Billy is picked to pass out the chalk and erasers. Molly stumbles in writing "chalk and erasers." Sam spells chalk. Kent and Lonny correct "eracers." Mr. Geoffrey urges the children to speak louder as they contribute suggestions.

At 10:00, two older boys, former students, poke their heads in the door. Mr. Geoffrey acknowledges them, and for a moment talks with them. He then proceeds to select monitors for adjusting shades, obtaining supplies and audio visual materials, distributing library books and paper. Molly continues to have difficulty spelling proper names and nouns, for example, librarian. Mr. Geoffrey calls on volunteers to help with spelling. One boy appeals to his dictionary. Mr. Geoffrey commends him—"I see one boy who has a dictionary out. You had better get used to using dictionaries." After settling the supply room helpers, Sam, Dick, Oliver, and Davey, with a "You'll be able to help out every couple of weeks," and a "You won't run off and play baseball at noon?" Mr. Geoffrey neatly disposes of Molly who has had a provisional trial at the board. "We still need someone for the assignment board. Sandy, you get up and let's see your handwriting. . . . All right, we'll give that assignment to you."

At 10:15, just before recess, he comments. "You all know where to go at recess. There will be no afternoon recess. Behave yourself in the yard. Nothing is worse than having you brought to me by another teacher for nonsense."

The bell rings. "Girls line up." They do. "Boys line up." They do. Shortly they all file out.

The recess, for Mr. Geoffrey, brings a brief interlude of conversation and a coke. Over the last few years the male teachers have developed a retreat of which they are extremely proud (Room 10, on the second floor). To their knowledge, few fifty-year-old school buildings are so well off; it contains a collection of facilities—toilets, wash basins, lockers, couch, icebox, and a table. When the men want to smoke, retreat, and so forth, this is the place.

At recess, the cokes come from the icebox. The conversation with Mr. Arnold and Mr. Gennep, who have gathered there also, is brief and centers on the facts and rumors of the morning. Mr. Gennep has only

15 children, out of 29 for whom he had cards, plus two new registrants. Concern and complaints center on possibilities of "split classes."[6] We are back in class by 10:35.

The children return at 10:37, and by 11:03 a new girl, Helen, has arrived, one set of history books that will be used later is collected back from the youngsters, a good bit more informal conversation among the children has begun, the children who want to shift to other seats have changed, one more humorous and individualized interaction has occurred. Mr. Geoffrey asks, "Can everyone see and hear?" Oliver mutters something. Mr. Geoffrey retorts, "Oliver, I'm talking about having your eyes open." Then, a moral, complete with blackboard illustrations is drawn. It centers around skipping rocks at the lake and sitting straight so that the words don't skip over. The children slouch a little less.

The formal academic work of the morning consists of a paragraph written about experiences of the summer. "I want a sample of your writing habits . . . write a paragraph or two on something you did this summer. This is not to grill you, but to see your penmanship and how you write a sentence. It should fill all of one side." Mr. Geoffrey gives additional instruction on procedures and encourages use of dictionaries. The field notes indicate the reaction:

> Response is a quiet settling down to task. Occasionally a pupil asks permission to go for a drink. Pupils occasionally speak quietly to one another. Businesslike. (9/4)

In the teacher's schema this exercise indicates the vacation is over and provides a sample of work ability better than a formal achievement test.

In twenty minutes, the papers are passed forward. Billy, as instructed, collects them across rows. Another boy horns in, Billy hesitates, and Mr. Geoffrey says clearly and emphatically, "You, no one else!"

The remainder of the morning involves miscellaneous activities, messengers coming in with notices, and comments on unfinished business— such as one on firedrills directed to Sam. "Don't play with the alarm . . . when it rings we go right out. . . . No talking or dawdling." Included also, in response to a question, are references to the bookmobile, the need for a library card, and the twenty book reports, ten each semester, that will be required. Other questions continue the light repartee; Sandy, for instance, doesn't see why Mr. Geoffrey should have a radio in his cupboard if they, the pupils, aren't allowed to have one. Mr. Geoffrey, with humor, invokes the age difference as the criterion. They, the teacher and the children, make a seating chart. Several boys go down to the storeroom and Oliver clowns as he comes back. Other business odds and ends are concluded.

---

[6] Split classes are combinations of two or more grade levels, for example, half fifth and half sixth, or half sixth and half seventh.

Mr. Geoffrey's lunch is a sandwich at Italo's Restaurant around the corner from the school. A number of other teachers eat there the first day. A walk through the neighborhood modifies its image. While the predominant tone of the homes reflects age and wear, considerable variation exists. A few with painted bricks, small, fenced-in yards, and a concern with cleanliness could be characterized as lower-middle class. At the other extreme are some unoccupied homes with doors ajar and windows broken out. A few occupied homes in nearly the same condition also exist. The majority need some to considerable repair.

At 1:00, Mr. Geoffrey's afternoon begins with housekeeping and assistance from Allison, Helen, Sandy, Edwin, and Jimmie. The work is pleasant, conversational, and contains much joking and humor. Occasionally a teacher stops by.

BEGINNING ACADEMIC WORK:
TEACHING THE 3R's

The school directive says that Thursday is a half-day and that Friday begins the first regular day. Mr. Geoffrey plans accordingly.

The pupils file in at 8:37 on Thursday. The teacher-pupil interaction follows the same easy pattern of yesterday. Geoffrey asks, "How about opening a couple of windows back there, boys?" Three respond with alacrity. He comments to a girl about being absent yesterday. He moves Sam so a new girl won't be "lost among the boys" and with a look and a brief comment he quiets Billy's friendly gregariousness. He is called out abruptly to talk with Peggy. On the way to school one of the teachers had seen her getting into an unoccupied car. Peggy, on the contrary, had said that she had bumped into it and the door fell open. Mr. Geoffrey has been involved at the perceiving teacher's request. By 8:44 he is back in class and Elma meets him with "I need some books," to which he comments "I am aware of that." The 8:45 bell rings. Edwin and Sam help put books away in response to Mr. Geoffrey's request. The new girls, Sarah and Elma, who arrived this morning, receive their books. Mr. Geoffrey tells Billy "I made a mistake on the erasers and chalk." He requests help in the form of thumb-tackers for hanging book dust jackets. "Need boys . . . it's difficult for girls to climb up." At 8:57 Miss Holt comes in to borrow a desk. The next entry (9:01) in the field notes reads:

> I've been displaced from my table in the rear by boys hanging up book folders around the room. The past ten minutes have been full of busy activity. All but six children (all girls) have been fixing up the room. Through all this, Mr. Geoffrey has been walking around the room as a supervisor, giving directions, commending the work, and generally keep-

ing the activity progressing. His behavior fits neatly the Kahn and Katz[7] differentiated role of supervisor. He hasn't placed a book on the shelf or thumbed a tack.   (9/5)

The activities move smoothly. Davey helps by tacking a border of letters around the room. As he puts up the alphabet he errs in the sequence. Mr. Geoffrey jokingly chides him. Several of the boys chuckle over this. Miss Eagle's entrance and request for "some strong arms" produces an immediate volunteer, Edwin. Such episodes blend so smoothly that they can scarcely be called interruptions.

At 9:15, Mr. Geoffrey announces that reading groups will be assigned tomorrow, that book reports are due every two weeks, that some of the pupils may go to groups other than the remedial reading teacher, Miss Eagle's, group, and that "depending on how busy Miss Eagle is" some of the pupils may have a reading test tomorrow. His last announcement states, "Today I have several little tests of my own."

Spelling

Mr. Geoffrey sends Susan to Mr. Gennep's room for a sixth-grade spelling book. Then, "Sandy, will you tell everyone how I want the papers headed up?"[8] She replies that one's name goes first in the upper left-hand corner. Edwin, then Allison, indicate the remaining items. As they do this he checks around the room. He then tells the pupils "Go back to the side where your name and date are, skip a line, and number one through ten."

At this point Miss Norton brings in some books and the girls who have been putting name labels on the ball point pens return and catch up on the spelling papers. Mr. Geoffrey asks "Everyone caught up?" They have. Then, "Fold your paper. Put a number eleven across from number one and go down to number twenty, then stop." A few comments are introduced about sixth-grade spelling books which all the children have seen. At 9:29, the dictation begins. A word is presented, used in a sentence and pronounced a second time. The notes suggest several interpretative comments:

> Kids are quiet and behave in what looks like and probably is a well-practiced routine. Mr. Geoffrey walks about the room. Sentences are humorous, simple, local, and personal. (9/5)

> For example:
> "*Leather.* A great many shoes are made of leather. *Leather.*"
> "*Pickles.* When I have a ham sandwich I like to have some pickles. *Pickles.*"
> "*Alphabet.* I hope you all know the alphabet by tomorrow—Davey."[9]

[7] R. L. Kahn and D. Katz, "Leadership practices in relation to productivity and morale" in D. Cartwright and A. Zander (eds.), *Group Dynamics*. Second Ed. New York: Harper & Row, Publishers, 1960
[8] The notes do not indicate instructions to the paper monitors or their response. Presumably Rose and Allison handled this.
[9] This is an allusion to Davey's error earlier in putting up the alphabet.

These procedures continue through the twenty words of the lesson. There is no apparent pupil-copying. At the close of the dictation, Mr. Geoffrey indicates that he will use varying procedures for scoring papers. Sometimes each pupil will score his own; on other occasions they will trade; sometimes he will score them himself. Today he utilizes what will come to be the dominant mode, trading papers. Each child hands his paper to the one behind and the pupil in the back brings his to the front of the row. He describes this routine carefully. Once this is settled he calls on Allison to spell "thread." She does. He indicates that a check mark is to be inserted if the answer is correct and a cross (x) if incorrect. And "Please, please, *please*, no large checks!" (He draws one.) He then calls on Pete to spell the second word. From this point on he takes volunteers: Kent, Sandy, Davey, Oliver. Later to both Allison's and Kent's volunteering he comments "You've had one"; however, on number thirteen he comments "Sam, how do you spell tardy?" Sam retorts "I had one," to which Mr. Geoffrey counters, "I'm giving you this one special." After this, several volunteers, Sandy, Davey, Kent and Jimmie, all receive second opportunities. Finally, "vacant" is misspelled and he goes down the row looking for the correct answer.

Table 2.1
Distribution of spelling scores
on initial dictation test.

Score	Number of Pupils
20	I
19	
18	I
17	I
16	I I
15	
14	I
13	I
12	I I
11 and below	HH+ HH+ HH+

At 9:53 he tells the children not to return the paper but to count the number correct and to put that figure at the top of the paper. The results are shown in Table 2.1. The papers are now returned to the owners but Mr. Geoffrey indicates that he wants them returned to him after the children have a chance to see how they did. He answers questions about several words, then asks "How many would I say is good?" The pupils guess at 15 to 19. The notes then capture verbatim most of his comments:

> "Perhaps we should briefly speak on how well I expect you to do. Better!! If you've gotten 10, then 11, 12, or 13. If you've gotten 17 then 18 or 19. If you come in reading at fifth grade then better. All don't do the same in arithmetic . . . . Don't look at your neighbor and say 'I'm stupid.' Do better than in the past."   (9/5)

From the discussion, really a monologue, he moves to the question of promotion. Once again the field notes capture most of Mr. Geoffrey's comments:

> "I'll speak frankly. In May you take tests on reading, spelling and arithmetic. You must make a certain level on those. They are not set too high. That's not all. The most important thing is doing your work for me. Let's have no nonsense on not doing work. Book reports . . . Assignments. See me if in doubt . . . If you fall behind you will never catch up . . . Do your best and do it regularly." (9/5)

The class listens attentively to the statement.

Reading

With a few minutes of time before recess he turns to his notebook containing cumulative records and begins assignment to reading groups. This occurs simply and directly—if not abruptly. The field notes quote Mr. Geoffrey as follows:

> "No reason not to assign you to a reading group now. Sam, would you come up to this board please. Write 1. Molly, you write 2 and Allison, you write 3. Assign to certain groups. Couple of weeks may change you." (9/5)

Table 2.2
The initial assignment to reading groups.

Group 1	Group 2	Group 3
Susan	Allison	Irma
Oliver	Ben	Henry H
Jimmie	Thelma	Billy
Dick	Susan	Sandy
Davey	Kent	Pete
Edwin	Molly	Rose
Sarah	Lonny	Patty
Helen		Elma
		Peggy

Table 2.2 shows the constitution of each group. Lonny, Sarah, and Helen, the new children, are assigned on the evidence from class performance and the information card accompanying their transfer into the class. The bell for recess rings. Mr. Geoffrey indicates "These groups are where you start. They are not final. You may go up or down." He calls the girls to line up, then he calls the boys.

After recess, Mr. Geoffrey returns to reading; this time, however, he begins with outside reading. He indicates that he will select the first book with each child. Within their grade level limits, the remainder of choices will be theirs. Hardly has he made these announcements when Miss Norton comes in (10:41) and he goes out momentarily to talk with her in the hall. Upon his return he begins to distribute books individually on the appropriate level. He explains the classroom library card system to the whole class and to Susan and Rose, the room librarians. Shortly, all of Group I have books. At 10:50, Miss Holt comes in, talks with Mr. Geoffrey for a moment, and they step out in the hall.

> While this conversation goes on, almost all of Group I who have books begin reading. The rest converse quietly. (LMS—This is a most interesting piece of activity. There's been no prodding or imploring about "getting to work." No "closeness of supervision" in this sense, beyond the initial statement of requirements.) (9/5)

At 10:53, Mr. Geoffrey comes back into the room; the book selecting begins again; Kent volunteers to take a message; and the low group continues, slowly, to make selections. Mr. Geoffrey does not hurry them but makes suggestions and raises possibilities. At 11:07, Mr. Geoffrey presents a dittoed sheet with lists of books; Group III continues selecting; he comments, "Come on, people, let's get going. We want to begin class tomorrow." After looking at the list, Sandy comments, "Mr. Geoffrey, these are baby books." He quietly admonishes her, "Work hard and . . ."

Miss Holt interrupts these activities at 11:15 when she comes in with a note. While Mr. Geoffrey reads, she quietly but completely surveys the room and its activities. After this interruption, Mr. Geoffrey finishes going through books, their numbers, and who is to read each. The fact that some of the books must be borrowed from another room creates some difficulties. To the comment, "Mr. Geoffrey, I've read all these" he responds, "I'll check your records and you can read others." He warns, "When you finish, read others on your sheet, not any old book. I don't want to catch any of you on levels 6 and 7 reading others."

With this accomplished, he comments that he needs help after lunch in the supply room, that he had planned to put it off but the Principal wanted it done today, and that he's looking for volunteer helpers.[10] The remainder of the morning, from 11:22 on, everyone is busy: some read, some work on reading sheets, some help with library books, and some, the talkers (Sandy, Thelma, and Rose; Allison, Helen, and Edwin) converse. Mr. Geoffrey helps organize the bookshelves around the numbers from the levels sheets. The interlude continues with breaks only when a messenger returns, and when Mr. Geoffrey comments (at 11:50) on Sam's sitting idle, "Now let's not get into any bad habits; I expect you to be busy." At 11:55, the library workers are disbanded and desks returned to place. At 11:56, the bell rings and Mr. Geoffrey comments that he will see the helpers after lunch and the remaining pupils in the morning at 8:30, smiling. Before he has an opportunity to ask the children to line up, he speaks to

[10]Each staff member has at least one school-wide "chore"; Geoffrey handles the teacher supply room.

Sandy about her talking. She retorts, "I don't have anything to do." With a grin he finishes the interplay, "I'll see that you always have something extra." The girls line up, then the boys.

FRIDAY: THE FIRST FULL DAY

This morning, as usual, Mr. Geoffrey "checks in" at the office. The formal purpose is to pick up his keys. School policy requires that each teacher leave keys to his room, desk, and cabinets in the office when he leaves the building at night. This requirement prevents the confusion of forgotten and lost keys and, if a teacher becomes ill overnight, enables the substitute to move easily into the teaching responsibilities. Occasionally difficulties arise between the custodian, who keeps the keys in a locked cabinet, and the teachers, who in his view arrive "too early." From Mr. Geoffrey's point of view, the latent function of the check-in is more social and informational. Mrs. Effingham, the clerk, is gregarious, talkative, and a good friend. This morning there is joking centering around Geoffrey's chiding Miss Donora, a first-grade teacher with whom he works in the supply room, because of her failure to show up for their joint storeroom activities yesterday, and the fact that he is *her* assistant in this chore (she has been teaching 10 years at Washington School). The unspoken conditions that make the comments humorous and gentle are that they are good friends, she is conscientious, and also quite shy. Mrs. Effingham enters easily into this conversation as a full participant. Miss Peters and Mr. Miller[11] observe. Brief conversations and some planning complete the morning pre-school activities.

By 8:37 the pupils are in. The morning odds and ends of adjusting window shades, an individual problem or two, lunch count, and so forth are handled. Through all this a few of the youngsters—Sam, Dick, Oliver, Sarah, Lonny, Davey, Kent, and Ben—sit quietly and read, behavior that will become a very stable part of the social structure of the classroom. At 8:39, Mr. Geoffrey comments, "You've had a nice vacation, now it's time to get to work. Take out the little notebooks that I gave you . . . ." He has them count ten pages from the back and label the page "Spelling." Interruptions then intertwine with direction giving, books arrive in the arms of a boy, several girls act as messengers, and Miss Holt comes in briefly.

Book Reports

Reading is important in the Washington School. Supplementary reading and book reports are a part of the language arts emphasis. This activity begins with, "Now turn to the front of the notebook and at the very top

[11] Mr. Miller is the student teacher who spent the semester at Washington School.

write 'Book Reports'." Mr. Geoffrey then evokes a discussion of the elements
required in an acceptable book report. Together, he and volunteers produce
a list:

1. Author
2. Title
3. Publisher
4. Date of publication
5. Where published
6. Level sheet number

The sequence is the teacher's; the items have come from individual pupils.
They suggest also "fiction," "nonfiction," "setting," and so forth. He indicates, "That's right, but they come later." He has them write these items
in their books. Edwin and Billy return, and they are helped by Jimmie and
Peter. Eileen receives instructions—"Eileen, make sure Sandy gets what she
missed when she comes back."

At 8:50, slips of paper are passed out and each child writes the appropriate information for his current library book. Irma's book is at home.
To his question, "What do we do with library books?" several children
respond, "Bring them in the next day." He then picks a book from the
shelf and with a grin to Irma, comments, "This one is especially for you."
From the field notes the following interpretive statement is drawn:

> Once more the humor and personalizing approach to the children; I
> don't have the feeling of a benevolent autocrat; rather an interested
> adult.   (9/6)

At 8:55, he checks around the class, gives help where needed,
and "okays" where correct. The notes contain several observations and
interpretations:

> Allison perplexed by "illustration." Sarah responds to "What is an illus-
> tration?" (LMS—Her responses are able and correct; she is giving answers
> toward best-student criterion. Yesterday, she was the only one with
> twenty words correct.) In 7–10 minutes Mr. Geoffrey has interacted with
> every child in the class. (LMS—His style is both total-class instruction
> and every-individual instruction.)

After a few minutes of instruction on level numbers he explains that
the level six books are at the bindery and that they "must trade around
and rely on the kindness of Mr. Gennep and Miss Norton." He then indicates that the first reports will be given to him orally and individually. He
next develops a discussion which brings out:

7. Fiction—nonfiction
8. Setting
9. Main characters
10. Plot
11. Did you like it? Why?

A number of episodes occur that seem important for developing understandings and interpersonal relationships. To Edwin's response of "True" for fiction, he comments, "I'll let you reverse yourself." The discussion brings out "biography" and Mr. Geoffrey asks, "What do you call it when a man writes his own story?" Sam responds, "Autobiography." He defines setting as, "Where and when," plot as, "What the story is about," and indicates they should try to get another person interested but not necessarily tell the conclusion—as in a murder mystery. Dick, Lonny, and Edwin make the major contributions to this.

After distinguishing again between oral and written, Geoffrey indicates he will check them on each of these points on the first report. The lesson ends as follows:

> "All right Sandy, let's get the assignments up. Let's use this board (east side at front). First book report due. What does 'due' mean, Oliver? September 11. That means that each of you will be ready with this much written out, 1–6, and ready to tell me the rest, 7–11. If you have any questions come up and see me." Goes back to Oliver on what does "due" mean. Dick responds, "Due means deadline." Mr. Geoffrey continues, "Keep list of books read . . . . Second page of notebook . . . . Questions? Don't fall behind. That's next Wednesday. Today's Friday."

Spelling

At 9:27, spelling begins. The notes capture most of Mr. Geoffrey's initial comments:

> "The last ten pages you have marked 'Spelling.' Now turn back to that page. For spelling there is an assignment to be done for every day. It's short. Or at least what I regard as short. Similar to last year's. Some of you mentioned skipping around. This year we'll go straight through. One unit each week."

They move to the first unit on page 2.

Parenthetically, we should note the structure of the spelling book.[12] Each of the thirty-six units contains a week's spelling activity. Usually twenty words, centering on some language arts theme or principle, are listed and introduced with a paragraph of commentary regarding the theme and a pictorial illustration of the main point. Each unit contains two main sections, "Learning your words" and "Using your words." The former varies practice activities from week to week. The latter contains sections, "*A*, Know your meanings," "*B*, Lift your language" (a more general language-arts activity), and "*C*, Use your dictionary." Each unit has a brief "Don't miss the easy ones" section, with examples such as "to, two, and too," and a brief "An interesting word is . . ." section which explains that good-by is a contraction of God-be-with-ye, for example.

[12]W. Kottmeyer and Kay Ware, *Basic spelling goals: 7.* New York: McGraw-Hill Book Co., 1960.

Mr. Geoffrey teaches the materials presented in Unit I, page 2. He clarifies "compound words," the theme, and talks about the picture and its meaning, an iceberg = mountain of ice. He then illustrates with the first two words "within" and "throughout." He reads the introductory material and explains necessary items. Then he picks volunteers to read through the list of words: Sam, Dick, Davey . . . and on around the room. Occasionally he checks the meaning of the words.

He outlines the spelling routine and notes on the blackboard the major recurring assignments. Sarah volunteers the correct answer to his question on the meaning of "definition."

> Due Mondays—Definitions
> Due Tuesdays—Sentences
> Due Wednesdays—Learning your words
> Due Thursdays—Using your words
> Fridays—Test

Words that are missed on the Friday test are to be put in the notebook.

The lesson concludes at 9:45. The notes once again contain interpretation intermixed with observations and near verbatim quotes:

> (LMS—Geoffrey builds in flexibility for himself. The work is due on the days specified but may be checked later in the week.) He raises strong issue about inadvisability of doing one lesson while class does another. "Woe unto you who . . . ."

> "Why have eight, nine, ten empty pages in back of book? . . . for the words you missed . . . like to see a bunch of blank pages. First job when you get your spelling papers back from me is to write the missed words there . . . . Why are you frowning? Don't worry, there'll be more. Whenever I hear groaning I'll assume that you don't have enough to do and I'll double the assignment. I don't like groaning. This morning I'll be generous and give you plenty of time. You may have until recess to do your spelling or book reports. This is the time to see me if you have questions. Sharpen your pencils . . . ."

The remainder of the morning, until recess at 10:15, the children are working on spelling. A variety of dyadic teacher-pupil interaction occurs, initiated by either the teacher or an individual pupil. "I need a couple of alphabetizers" brings volunteers, Eileen and Susan. "Anyone going to the dime store over the weekend?" Irma is. "Buy me some safety pins." He follows this with the admonition, "When you borrow, return. . . ."[13] Davey indicates that the date on the board hasn't been changed. Sandy must do it. Elma is permitted to sharpen her pencil. Oliver volunteers for messenger duty. The children are all working. A messenger comes in with a note.

---

[13] As garments fall apart pins are used for repairs.

Another one comes in for the pencil sharpener.[14] Mr. Geoffrey asks for a volunteer to erase the board. Billy responds. The notes contain a question:

> (LMS—Considerable pupil activity regarding chores. Usually on volunteer basis which seemingly capitalizes on any pupil's need to get up and stretch or move about when he gets restless. There is a beautiful hypothesis here regarding which teachers do most of the chores themselves. What are the system consequences of doing few or many?)   (9/6)

Language Arts

When Mr. Geoffrey returns at 10:39, 7 minutes after recess is over, the children are all busy working on spelling or book reports. Fragmentary field notes convey the essentials of the introduction to the language lessons:

> "Take out *Words and Ideas*[15] .... Let's speak frankly about language . . . it will give you more difficulty than anything else. . . . Papers will come back six, seven or eight times . . . . Why is language important?"

> Enters into discussion of importance of language . . . jobs, applications, driver's test, directions, select movie, driver's license—written test. "Could you get along this weekend?" Illustrates with "ain't." Better job, improving ourselves, sounds better to others, Who'll get the job? The people who can speak, write, and read correctly . . . I'll start correcting the language that I think can be improved. Makes a distinction between "here" and "out there."[16] "I won't be around to rap you on the head with a pointer" (teases Sandy). Acknowledges his lack of control "out there."   (9/6)

From this discussion, he moves to a consideration of a chart hanging high on the south wall. Assignments and problem areas for the seventh grade in oral and written language arts and grammar are contained there. Mr. Geoffrey explains these briefly. His comments flow easily and naturally into a discussion of the text, the authors, table of contents, and chapter 1: entitled "Sentences." He asks, "What do you expect to learn about sentences?" The question sparks several volunteer responses referring to parts of sentences and correctness of sentences. The speculative and hypothetical possibilities do not expand, spiral, or cumulate into fantasy, playfulness, or higher-order abstractions. This discourse is brief and functional and moves into the materials presented by Pollock and Rounds.

With expression, Mr. Geoffrey reads page 1. He pauses on the concept "gesture," as he has with many other words in the past few days, asks for its meaning, and clarifies the responses he obtains. The lesson continues on pages 2 and 3. The substance is "Complete Thoughts" which leads into

---

[14] This child is from Miss Holt's room. He or one of his classmates will be involved this way for most of the semester. Procuring a pencil sharpener is sometimes a difficult job in a large public school system.

[15] T. C. Pollock and R. W. Rounds, *Words and Ideas*. New York: The Macmillan Company, 1960.

[16] "Out there" refers to home and community.

a definition of sentence . . . "a group of words that expresses a complete thought," and into a series of exercises requiring the children to take sentence fragments and make them into complete questions and declarative sentences. The notes contain several interpretive comments:

> (LMS—(1) As he proceeds with the lesson, the brunt of the teaching falls on the text. Need a statement of psychological learning principles underlying a textbook and traditional teaching. (2) Kinds of illustrations—reflect categories in social systems and learning schemes.[17] (3) Teacher proceeds by taking each item in the text and asking for volunteers or occasionally calling on inattentive ones. Always by name.)   (9/5)

Shortly after 11:00 A.M. he explains how written work should be done. This is also the topic on page 4. "Correct Form for Written Work." This leads into a language arts assignment that contains several elements: (1) The exercises on page 5 will be due tomorrow. (2) Sandy informs him that tomorrow is Saturday. (3) He responds with a joke. (4) He reads the directions to the exercise. (5) He completes the first item with the pupils. (6) With humor he comments on the two groups of exercises: "We'll do both. I don't want to deny you anything."

As the class begins work, he has Sandy put the assignment on the board. She doesn't know what a colon is and this provokes an explanation. He moves about the room checking, correcting, and explaining specific items with individual children. This movement up and down the rows evokes an explanation of reasons for wide aisles. As the children finish their work some take out library books, others work on spelling, a few talk quietly, and some volunteer to help him with posters and other chores. A series of announcements, for example, concerning U. S. Saving Stamps and delay in physical education scheduling, are interspersed with these activities. Just before noon Mr. Geoffrey comments: "Remember, there is school this afternoon. Let's have no Friday afternoon vacationers. Did I strike home? Come back on time, please."

At 11:58, the bell rings. The girls and then the boys line up. Mr. Geoffrey evens the two lines so that there are no stragglers. At 12:00, they file into the hall with Mr. Geoffrey leading. His class follows sequentially the priorities of rooms 1 and 2. Rooms 4 and 5 fall in behind. Such an equilibrium began on the first day, continued all semester, and, from reports of teachers with many years of tenure, has been a part of the social structure for many years. When the pupils reach the first floor, some continue to the school cafeteria, others go out the front door and home. Teachers take turns supervising in the cafeteria and on the playgrounds.

---

[17] Mr. Geoffrey made no comment on the Colorado-type camping and trout fishing picture on page 1. The text author's verbal illustrative material on sentence fragments seems chosen from a wide base, for example, two dollars a pair, bad accident, saw a flying saucer, and so forth.

Afternoon Announcements

After lunch, at 1:05, Mr. Geoffrey "enters into some genial banter[18] over the loss of the afternoon recess." The loss of recess follows a directive from the principal and illustrates the influence of broader school policy on the classroom. The Washington School received this year, for the first time, several busloads of children from an overcrowded Negro area of the city. The intent was to lower the interaction between the groups in the hope of preventing overt conflict and incidents. The loss of recess was presented as general policy in many of the schools for the upper grade levels.[19]

In this instance, several children argue that they should be out of school at 3:20 instead of 3:30 since they have lost their 10 minutes of recess. Mr. Geoffrey counters with a plan for "collecting minutes" that are wasted or idled; "You'd be here until 4:00." This evokes a series of "Oh, no" responses. The banter terminates when Miss Eagle comes in regarding testing and grouping for reading. The class maintains its flavor of excitement and high feeling and Mr. Geoffrey reminds them that they are not to talk while he is busy with a visitor.

Arithmetic

At 1:11, arithmetic begins. Mr. Geoffrey's introduction replicates his approach to language arts as he comments on the text's publisher, author, and place of publication. Continuity with their book report format is also established. Before he can obtain answers to "Why do we have arithmetic?" a messenger comes in. Mr. Geoffrey reprimands Rose for chatting while he is busy with the messenger. As the students give reasons for arithmetic there is a general giddiness among the girls and there are requests for boys to raise the shades (more light) and windows (more air). Finally Mr. Geoffrey asks, "How many of you can do without arithmetic?" In keeping with the playful tenor of this afternoon session, many of the children raise their hands. Mr. Geoffrey gives them a long stare. He pinpoints Sam: "Sam, how many shoes do you put on in the morning?" In rapid-fire order he asks: "Who else had a hand up?" "Sandy, how would you know when to get to school in the morning?" He tries to conclude, "All right, let's learn a little bit," but must squelch Susan's giggle before he begins reading on page 4 at 1:21.

[18] As we will develop later, our definition of banter involves a minimum of three statements (pupil, teacher, pupil) and must involve humor.

[19] The following year, recess was reinstituted. The Negro pupils were no longer transported, and the faculty, through the clerk, exerted pressure on the Principal. He was reluctant but they desired an afternoon break. He met their wishes

Chapter I
Our Number System

bear

Seven

When we write the word <u>bear</u>
or draw the picture on the
board, we are not putting a
bear on the board.

When we write the word <u>seven</u>
or the figure 7 on the board,
we are not actually writing the
number seven itself.

Number Names, Figures, Numbers

To help us think about the numbers of things, about
quantities, amounts, and sizes, we use <u>number names</u> and <u>number
figures</u>.

Eight, fifteen, and so on are not numbers. They are number
names just as Tom and Mary are persons' names. Neither is <u>8</u> nor
<u>15</u> a number. They are number figures. Numbers are not marks
on paper. Number names and figures stand for numbers. The
idea of number (how many) is in our heads.

1. Jack said, "If we consider <u>8</u> as
the number itself, then half of <u>8</u> may be
<u>0</u> or <u>3</u>." Is he right?

2. Why are these answers wrong? Did the person confuse
the ideas of number names, figures, and number?

<u>a</u> Take <u>3</u> from <u>43</u>.   Answer: <u>4</u>
<u>b</u> Add <u>3</u> to <u>8</u>.   Answer: <u>38</u>
<u>c</u> How many <u>6</u>'s in <u>66</u>?   Answer: Two
<u>d</u> Write a number larger than <u>4</u>.   Answer: <u>4</u>

Figure 2.3 The initial page of the arithmetic text.
H. G. Wheat et al, *Row-Peterson Arithmetic.* New York:
Harper & Row, Publishers, 1959.

Chapter 1 begins with a review discussion of number names, figures,
and numbers. Mr. Geoffrey stresses the concepts as he reads the material
and works through the examples from the text. We have inserted a copy of
a part of page 4 as Figure 2.3 to picture precisely the content, for the next
hour contains a curious kind of discontinuity of teaching, interruptions,
supervisory attempts, pupil difficulties, and so forth.

At 1:24, Mr. Geoffrey makes the statement, "The next few pages are
going to be a review of arithmetic. Those who know it can take a test . . ."
He then notices that Elma has been shuffling a pile of papers and says,
"Elma, what is that pile of papers on your desk?" This is the first really
stern behavior on his part, and he follows it with a clear, forceful explanation of the proper place for assignment papers: (1) with him, (2) at home
for themselves or their parents, or (3) in the wastepaper basket. They are
not to remain in or on one's desk. He reads on. Page 5 is a discussion of
"Our Number System." In the first paragraph the word "compound"
appears, that is, "Beyond ten we use compound names, each of which is
related to the name ten." Mr. Geoffrey refers back to the morning spelling

lesson in which the unit was built around "compound" words.[20] He reads through page 5, "Our Number System," and carries on an interpretive dialogue with the text as he explains the content to the children. In the course of this, Edwin drops his pencil and Mr. Geoffrey gives him a look. He continues in similar fashion with page 7, "Place value in the number system." Concepts such as quantity, number, and place are emphasized, illustrated, and taught.

Miss Eagle interrupts the lesson at 1:38. She wants Sarah, Lonny, and Helen, the new pupils, at 2:45 for ability testing. Mr. Geoffrey reminds the pupils to "take your pencils" and Miss Eagle, in her characteristic rough-and-ready way, adds, "And bring your brains."

Mr. Geoffrey finishes page 6 and introduces the discussion of "Large Numbers" on page 7 by referring to a picture of the earth, the moon, the distance (240,000 miles), and twenty billion letters, forms, and reports the government produces each year. Specifically the picture's legend states:

> Our government spends billions of dollars in creating and handling some 25 billion letters, forms, reports, and notices each year. Lay them end to end, and they would stretch from the earth to the moon 13 times. (Wheat, and others, 1959)

The field notes indicate:

> Raises questions with girls about distance from earth to moon. They just do not see the point. Finally Lonny responds correctly.   (9/6)

He calls on several pupils, Sam, Edwin, and Elma. Sam reads and Edwin goes to the board to write the figures which show the number 475. The class checks the answer. To Elma, who has kicked her shoes off, his next comment is, "Elma, that means you have to keep your shoes on. We'll wait." In the meantime, the paper monitors pass out small sheets of paper. He does problem (1b) six thousand, five hundred three. Next he calls on Molly: "Problem (1c) Molly. Now don't look at me that way, child, just go up and do it." The notes capture the next few minutes:

> Errs with "1,200,000" instead of 1 billion 200 thousand. Banter with girls about their neutrality (over correctness of Molly's answer). Eileen to board. "Sandy, go to the board and answer (1c). We want no shrinking violets in here." Gives Sam a look to quell a growing snicker. Molly returns with another try.
>
> | | | |
> |---------------|--------|-------|
> | 1,200,000 | Molly | |
> | 1,200000 | Eileen | |
> | 1,200,000 | Sandy | |
> | 1,200,000,000 | Molly | (9/6) |

He then asks everyone to write (1c) on his paper. A messenger interrupts at this point (1:52 P.M.) and while Mr. Geoffrey sorts through a film of

[20] Parenthetically, we might add that none of the spelling words was a number.

cards at his desk, several pupils, Pete and Billy, Davey and Sam, and so forth compare answers. Shortly afterwards, Mr. Geoffrey walks about the class and nods yes and no to each pupil according to his written answer. He re-emphasizes "place" meanings and then develops an extended illustration around 987, 654, 321. After this he returns to (1c) and has Molly, Billy, and Eileen go to the board and redo their problems. The notes catch an additional point:

> With humor to counteract their embarrassment he tells them he will keep them up there even though it is embarrassing. (9/6)

He has everyone try (1d) eight million, nine thousand, forty-seven; he checks papers as he walks around the room. Thelma: 8,900,047, Allison: 8,009,047 (she checked with Edwin before) and Billy: 8,000,000,947. All go to the board to write their answers. Mr. Geoffrey humorously mimics the television program as he comments, "Will the real one stand up?" He goes back to his chart and the extended illustration. The three pupils start reworking their answers. While Thelma is at the board Miss Holt comes in and Jim and Pete are sent out as messengers. Billy goes to the board and changes his answer. Molly is called on for (1e) nine hundred and one million. She writes 9,000,100, and Mr. Geoffrey calls her back to correct her answer. They then take up problem 2 in the text, "Copy these numbers, pointing them off in periods. Then read each number." He directs, "Read the first number loud and clear, Davey." In rapid order Dick, Sandy, Elma, and Allison are called on. There is some humor at Allison's expense for she is at the wrong place. She retorts in kind.[21] Mr. Geoffrey has her go to the board. At 2:25, he selects two additional items from the teacher's manual. They spend a few minutes on 2,575,400,000 heart beats. Mr. Geoffrey introduces some banter and admonishes Thelma for not writing an answer by complaining "I'm not too happy when there's nothing down." The lesson concludes with several "mental arithmetic" problems, such as 2 plus 3, plus 5, divide by 2 and subtract 3. He informs them that beginning Monday they will have a few of these problems regularly.

While Mr. Geoffrey passes out the history books to a pupil who had not received copies and has them numbered and filed, the other pupils sit or talk quietly. Before they begin, Mr. Geoffrey asks if he gave them an arithmetic assignment. He checks his book and comments, "We'll stop there and not have an assignment . . . . I'll let you off this weekend."

Social Studies

At 2:47, he introduces the history text.[22] He indicates they will start in the middle and later move to their other book, *America's Story*. Besides a discussion of why the book might have a title including the word "back-

---

[21] The notes don't contain her verbatim comment, but there is the interpretive statement, "She fires right back."

[22] Edna McGuire, *Backgrounds of American Freedom,* New York: The Macmillan Company, 1953.

grounds," Mr. Geoffrey comments that many pupils find history the least interesting subject, but that he would try to make it more interesting. The lesson continues as Dick is called upon to begin reading on page 250. This is Section 4, "Ancient African Civilizations," of Unit Four, "Growing through the middle ages."[23] The dialogue of text, teacher, pupil, begins as Dick is helped by Sam in pronouncing "Phoenicians" and as the concepts of "continent" (in contrast to "island" and "peninsula") and "civilization" are explored. Elma contributes the names of most of the continents. Sam reads the second paragraph. Allison defines civilization as "people who are decent." Davey and Dick try. Someone suggests, "People who live together in a certain town." Edwin reads the definition from the glossary in the back of the book. They conclude on "way of life of a large group of people." Allison, Edwin, and Sarah all read. Mr. Geoffrey pauses on 740 B.C. in the sentence, "About 740 B.C. an Ethiopian king conquered Egypt." Dick responds to Mr. Geoffrey's question that B.C. means "Before Christ." He quizzes them on "A.D." and many of the pupils miss. He draws a simple

time line, 740 ⎯⎯⎯⎯⎯⎯⎯⎯⎯⎯ 1965, and asks them how long ago it was. Dick contributes, "It's long ago and hard to tell." Edwin suggests, "Subtract 740 from 1965." Sarah says, "Add." Mr. Geoffrey then raises a discussion around a coin which was dated 63 B.C. He asks if it's real; he criticizes Allison for talking out loud; and then comments that he would throw the coin away as a fake. When he asks why, Sandy comments that they didn't use B.C. that long ago. When he asks why, she says she doesn't know, and Mr. Geoffrey leaves the problem as an unanswered question for them to puzzle over. Just after he begins oral reading of the history text, Miss Eagle interrupts the lesson once again to talk briefly with Mr. Geoffrey. The section on Ethiopia is finished by Jimmie, Allison, and Sarah, who is the best reader so far (in the observer's judgment). The lesson concludes with a brief map exercise, which begins with pupils identifying Ethiopia and North America and ends with their identifying the continents and oceans. Pete's, Billy's, and Davey's inability to find Asia provokes a comment from Mr. Geoffrey, "Do I have to call on a girl?" Several girls have trouble finding the various oceans and Mr. Geoffrey rebukes Allison for speaking out, "It's wrong."

The Day Closes

At 3:23, the activity shifts from history to what might be called the daily terminal ritual. This involves the cleaning of individual desks, the chalk boards, and the room, and the putting away of books, chalk, erasers,

[23]The earlier units: "Learning to live together" (the Stone Age), "Developing civilizations" (Egypt, Babylonia, etc.) and "Living around the Mediterranean" (Greece and Rome) had been studied in the sixth grade.

and paper. The ritual includes directions from Mr. Geoffrey: "Clear your desks except for what you're taking home . . . Remember you have a book report due Wednesday . . . There's been too much speaking out during the lessons, only one person should answer at a time; raise your hand and everyone will have an equal opportunity . . . School is business; come back on Monday ready to work." The day almost concludes with his command, "Girls line up," then "Boys," but a good bit of chatter occurs and he tells the boys to return to their seats. The girls continue to chatter and he has them return to their seats also. He comments, "If that were a test, you'd fail. In leaving I want you to be quiet. Try boys first this time." He evens up the two lines, and has the girls come up to the door behind them. With humor he comments, "You don't have to hold hands as they do in the primary grades." He speaks briefly and privately to Allison. The pupils file out into the hall and wait their turn to follow the higher grades down the stairs and out of the building.

C H A P T E R T H R E E

CLASSROOM PROCESSES: THE DEVELOPMENT OF SOCIAL STRUCTURE

The general educational psychological literature abounds in research centering on classroom social structure. While most educators use sociometric data as indicators of a usually undifferentiated construct of structure, our observations lead us to an analysis in slightly different terms. The issues with which we will deal center not only on differentiated structure but also on process, the development of structure. Essentially, we want to analyze the system in action and we want to focus on the teacher as he attempts to intervene (guide, if one needs a more positively-toned word) as a special member of the system. From its inception, the research had a strong orientation toward understanding the sequence of events centering on the teacher's coping with the children, and the planning and strategy that lay behind the coping. Equally, we were concerned with the changing press of events, the teacher's perception of those events, the thinking and altered action that followed upon these perceptions. The aspects of social structure that we differentiate at this point are: roles, belief systems, norms, subgroup interactional structure, and activity structure.

PUPIL ROLES AND BELIEF SYSTEMS

For our purposes we will define a classroom role as a complex pattern of activities, interactions, and sentiments.[1] In this sense it is an abstraction we have found useful in analyzing classroom groups. A belief system can be called, roughly, a common perception by members of the group. We would distinguish it from a group norm that contains an evaluative element, that is, what group members ought to do. In many situations norms and beliefs overlap dramatically. Also, in most groups the roles and the belief systems complement each other. Interdependencies exist, for belief systems frequently pertain to roles, and roles come about partly because the belief systems exist. We have been trying to build taxonomies of the roles and belief systems.

Monitor's Roles

If we distinguish, superficially for the moment, between the roles Mr. Geoffrey builds consciously and directly from those he builds unconsciously or at least indirectly, then we can order several aspects of the first day. The "jobs" in the class consist of librarian, assignment recorder, chalk and eraser monitor, and distributor of paper. Deliberately he sought to develop ideas that certain kinds of activities and interactions were required if the room were to function smoothly. He tried also to establish individuals as incumbents of the roles. For illustrative purposes we can return to the "keeper of the assignment board." When he tried out Molly and then settled on Sandy, he commented explicitly on the behavioral requisites of the role, "Best attendance and best handwriting usually get the assignment job." In Figure 3.1 we have tried to diagram the events of the episode.

This first model should be read in this fashion. On the vertical axis we have represented three classes of variables: Mr. Geoffrey's personality and behavior, the behavior of two individual pupils, Molly and Sandy, and group variables—belief system and sentiment. On the horizontal axis we have broken time into seven steps. At time 1, Mr. Geoffrey announces the specific demands of the assignment role—good attendance and good handwriting. At time 2, Molly volunteers and there is the beginning belief system that persons must be adequate to the task. At time 3, Molly's performance is not adequate—although up to this point the criterion has not been specified—spelling ability. At times 4 and 5, we hypothesize that this creates dissonance[2] between Mr. Geoffrey and the class. This, in turn, leads

---

[1] Activity, interaction, and sentiment are three elements of human behavior conceptualized by Homans (1950) and used by him to analyze group functioning. Our special uses of the terms are in the glossary.

[2] The simultaneous existence of cognitions which do not fit together. This concept, as developed by Festinger, leads to a condition where the person makes an effort to make the cognitions fit better, dissonance reduction. (Festinger, 1960, p. 214).

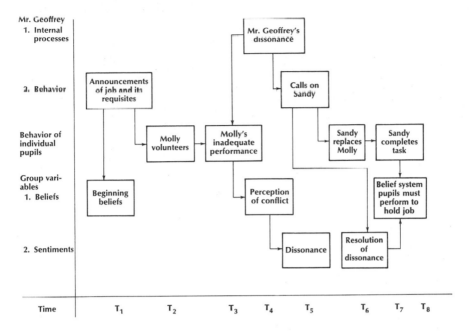

Figure 3.1 A process analysis of the development of monitor roles and belief systems.

to Mr. Geoffrey's request for Sandy to go to the blackboard. The replacement of Molly and the reduction in the dissonance is followed at times 7 and 8 with Sandy's more adequate performance and the stabilizing of the belief that there is such a role as assignment monitor and that it must be carried out by someone adequate to its demands.

The Role of Pupil

During the first morning, Mr. Geoffrey, in a brief 7 minutes, sketched out many of his ideas of the pupil role. In effect this was the first gambit toward formulating a belief system regarding rules among the pupils. Ultimately it was his hope that the belief system would become stabilized as a group norm. For our analytic purposes, this raises several additional aspects of a more overarching model. Lying behind Mr. Geoffrey's verbal behavior regarding chewing gum in class, leaving the room, arriving on time, doing homework, and so forth is his own personal schema of the nature of the pupil role. The model we have presented in Figure 3.1 must be extended now with another set of variables, the cognitive map or schema system of the teacher. Similarly, we need a category of phenomena to handle the "quickness" with which the pupils got his point. Analytically this could fall into categories of prior group beliefs and individual pupil schema or ideas.

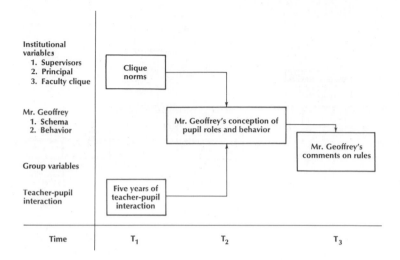

Figure 3.2 A process analysis of Mr. Geoffrey's behavior regarding classroom rules and pupil roles.

Where does Mr. Geoffrey's point of view come from? Our data suggest that two sources predominate, the 5 years of give and take in teaching at the Washington School and the belief and normative systems of a clique of teachers with whom he shares the second floor of the building. Figure 3.2 depicts these sources. Although extended discussion of the model will be withheld until later, we would comment on two implications. First, his experience at City Teacher's College in a teacher-training program was considered unreal and inadequate for the demands of the job. Second, anyone who attempts to change his classroom behavior must come to grips, theoretically and practically, with the informal social structure of the faculty, the cliques within the school. Innovations in curriculum, methods of teaching, pupil-teacher relationships often flounder, so it seems to us, because persons interested in educational change do not understand, or else they ignore, the implications of the variables in this model.

Continuing the analysis of the role of student or pupil: "You've had a nice vacation, now it's time to get to work," says Mr. Geoffrey on Friday morning, September 6. For those pupils who have not recognized the verbal cues on the preceding days, the meaning has now been made clearer. Those who still don't understand will be informed later—on a number of occasions.

Initially, at least two possible and nonmutually exclusive interpretations of the developing belief system seem open: (1) learning should be going on all the time, and (2) learning is work. In support of the first proposition are an array of illustrations—learning to spell his name, "Mr. Geoffrey," and learning the meaning of such concepts as superstition, reputation, illustration, and autobiography. In a sense, all kinds of unknowns become legitimate targets for learning. The teacher's expectation is that pupils should acquire the relevant knowledge. This value is translated into inter-actional episodes of questions, answers, approval and disapproval, which lead toward a clarification of the item or concept.

The second and more emphatic view which Mr. Geoffrey represents is that "learning is work." Also there is the correlated phenomenon that "pupils are workers," that is, they are in the class to work. The following illustrations connect several improbable areas: first, in developing the moni-tor roles, one pupil raised the question about messengers. Geoffrey's response was, "Leave that open for anyone who gets his work done." Second, in discussing promotion, he said, "That's not all, the most important thing is doing your work for me. Some of the assignments are difficult. Let's have no nonsense on not doing work . . . . Do your best and do it regularly." Third, on Friday morning, the first full day, he commented, "You've had a nice vacation, now it's time to get to work . . . .," and finally, on Friday afternoon he commented, "School is business. Come back on Monday ready to work."

The immediate alternatives that seem open to the teacher are that academic activities are fun (gamelike), interesting (intrinsically attractive), important (for a variety of purposes), difficult or easy, and so forth. Sketch-ing out the possible consequences of these points of view, while hazardous, also seems enlightening. It raises the basic question of the immediate con-sequences of pupils who have an apathetic if not hostile attitude toward school. Presenting the "reality" of academic activity joins the issue directly rather than masking it by presenting a conception different from that held by the pupils. The congruence suggests, for the immediate moment, under-standing and communication. For the long term, however, this suggests that little change, or possibility of change, will occur. We will discuss this issue analytically at another time in terms of possible strategies of change in teacher-pupil activity. The point we wish to emphasize is the help the model gives us in thinking about changing the social structure of the classroom.

The multidimensionality of the pupil role with its complex relation-ships to Mr. Geoffrey's goals for the pupils is indicated in the discussion which concluded a spelling test. As we noted before, Mr. Geoffrey answered questions about several words and then asked, "How many would I say is good?" The pupils guessed between fifteen and nineteen correct words out of twenty, and he stated the one thing he wanted pupils to do—better.

> "If you've gotten ten right, then next time get eleven, twelve, or thirteen. If you've gotten seventeen, then eighteen or nineteen . . . . Do better than in the past." (9/5)

From this discussion, really a monologue, he moved to the question of promotion, stressing that the children should do the work assigned. The class listened attentively to his statements.

A final aspect of the role of pupil, which was stressed in this first morning and reiterated throughout the semester, concerns the responsibility of the child to his individual teacher. Recall Mr. Geoffrey's statement: "You all know where to go at recess . . . . Behave yourself in the yard. Nothing is worse than having you brought to me by another teacher for nonsense."

While this defines clearly that a major sin occurs when a pupil needs to be reprimanded by another teacher, it indicates latently a need for the analysis of the staff relationships and the manner in which teacher-teacher interaction is mutually dependent upon teacher-pupil interaction. In effect, pupils "belong" to a teacher. If they don't behave, questions are raised about the teacher's classroom control and his adequacy for carrying out the role of teacher. These subtleties are conveyed by Mr. Geoffrey's notes for the first week of school:

> In his own room, when a teacher must admonish, correct, or punish a child who misbehaves, he may do this as he wishes. He may even ignore the situation. But if another teacher brings him one of his students who has misbehaved, he *must* do something, and it must be fitting. Frankly, at times, this may be a pain in the neck.

> Also, pupils do belong to a teacher, but if they don't behave, this does not necessarily cause questions to be raised regarding the "owner's" classroom control. The critical thing is the owner's reputation. If he has a reputation for lack of control, then this is a shrug of the shoulders and a "Well, what do you expect." But some teachers (for example, Miss Holt) have excellent classroom control and yet their kids can raise hell elsewhere—playground, gym, and so forth. *This in no way* reflects upon that teacher. Rather it raises her status—after all, she can control those problems and I can't. Also, one *might* ask if the very fact of her strong control of students under her thumb might not have some bearing on their behavior while in someone else's hair. No, I would say that a student's bad behavior while absent from his owner casts no cloud upon that teacher. A teacher is judged by what happens in his teacher-pupil interaction, which is 90 percent of the time. He is not judged by what his kids do in the 10 percent of the time they are away from him.

> My comments are also made to the students in order to try, feebly perhaps, to make the job of the teacher on duty easier and to cut down on the amount of time I have to spend out in the hall after recesses.

With the isolation of the belief-system construct, we have continuing interests in the processes by which such a construct is established and the nature of the content of the belief. In an early language arts lesson, the children have been reviewing the use of the dictionary—the sequential character of the alphabet, guide words, and the content of the dictionary.[3] As the children wrote the guide words on the board, Sarah asked about the word "trachery" that Eileen had put on the board. Geoffrey sent Eileen back to correct it, to make it "treachery." The observer wrote a comment which later received corroboration time and again:

> This seems critical also. Without fanfare, Geoffrey always sends the erring one back to correct his or her own mistakes. Implicit rule—if you don't do it right you'll do it again.   (9/10)

The consequence of this belief system emphasizes doing tasks carefully and correctly. The process seems rather simple—at least at first blush—that you please the teacher by getting the correct answers the first time and you save yourself the public embarrassment of several trips to the board. Embarrassment, in this class, also has its complexities. First, Geoffrey almost never humiliated a child for an error in his work.[4] Second, the children showed a variety of signs of discomfort when they had difficulty with an oral presentation at the board. Third, on a number of occasions, Geoffrey made interpretive comments indicating his awareness of their discomfort and the need to continue trying if they were to learn the knowledge or skill at hand.

While we took few measures of learning, the learning process seemed slow and difficult from our direct observation. The tutorial procedure involved in boardwork, "cues, trial, feedback, and trial," has many precedents and much support in learning theory. Careful experimental work seems necessary to isolate the potential inhibiting effects of the emotional reactions in a public performance on the child at the board, and the value of the vicarious experience for the observing children at their seats.

The argument we would make is that belief systems about the pupil roles in academic activities were being built in a less conscious but latently similar manner to the deliberately developed monitor roles we have just described. The model is viable in that it provides a possibility for including alternative conceptions of academic activities.

Sex Roles

The development of social roles around the sex of the members was slightly more subtle. Boys are boys and girls are girls, and later, as we shall see, overtones of "vive la difference" occur. Most obviously, boys hang wraps on one side of the cloakroom and girls on the other. Lines for dismissal are by sex. The records are replete with, "Girls line up . . . Boys line up . . . ." More subtle aspects occur when "strong arms" are needed by Mr. Geoffrey or by other teachers. When he needs ". . . thumb tackers?

---

[3]The reader should note the implications for our "Ability Problem" discussion in Chapter Seven. These seventh-grade children have difficulty with important skills.

[4]Later we will describe incidents wherein kids who "didn't try" felt his wrath.

Boys . . . it's difficult for girls to climb up." (9/5) And a new girl who is surrounded by boys receives Sam's seat so she "will not be lost among the boys." The teaching and learning here seem to fit our analysis of roles as patterns of activities, interactions, and sentiments which reflect or coincide with group beliefs. Mr. Geoffrey subtly interacts in ways that suggest, clarify, and support the formation of the roles and the related belief systems.

The Readers

As we indicated in the field notes:

A few of the children are reading—Sam, Dick, Oliver, Helen, Lonny, Davey, Kent, and Ben.   (9/6)

Similarly on Monday:

8:33   Observer in the room as pupils come in today.[5] Boys in first. Minimal conversation. Kent drops gum off. Sam, Kent, Ben begin reading.   (9/9)

With little coercion, except for the comments about book reports, and with little positive reinforcement, these children began what became a very stable mode of behavior. When not pressed by assignments and when time was free, as in the first minutes of the morning, they spent their time reading. This aspect of the student role raises a number of questions about nonteacher and nonclassroom sources of social structure. We will contrast this with the differences in the pupils who arrive after the "Days of Indian Summer."

INDIVIDUAL ROLES

Teachers and children are hardly conscious of the most subtle aspect of role development. It is seen in a later situation where the teacher wonders why a particular child behaves as he does in class. The antecedents of the role are so elusive, transitory, and appropriate to the momentary situation that their contribution to the development of the role remains hidden.

The Court Jester

Within a month, Sam had developed a special role of court jester. He shuffled about the classroom in a Jackie Gleason style. Physically he was heavy set and wore his hair uncut, and his beltless bluejeans hung low on his hips. On occasion, he gamboled tardily into class with a smile and a big "Hi, Mr. Geoffrey." Once, after loudly volunteering an answer to a question, he responded to a "Raise your hand, Sam" with both arms waving vigorously. In a tense situation he had a ready quip; he freely

---

[5]In contrast to standing at head of stairs and chatting with the teachers.

entered and exited in a banter or tête-a-tête relationship with Mr. Geoffrey. As an illustration we present an episode from the afternoon of September 18. Geoffrey has just been involved in a skirmish with Pete and Allison (see later in the chapter that episode in the analysis of Pete's role). The activity shifts from spelling, where Sam had begun being playful, to history.

2:45 Geoffrey starts on history. He has Sam find Jerusalem, the exact point where the lesson ended before. Sam, with a flourish, finds it (several had helped him before lunch). Geoffrey, in his perennial one-up game with Sam, then draws down a map of the world (in contrast to the previous map of Europe and the Mediterranean) and reasks, "Where is Jerusalem?" Sam counters, with a twinkle, "Can I peek?" (on the original map underneath). Geoffrey, solemnly and with a twinkle in his eye, says "Yes." Sam picks up a corner of the map and peeks. After a moment he finds it and asks for corroboration, "Is it right?" Geoffrey indicates "Yes."

Here was a boy who behaved very differently from most of the other children. The role in this instance was quite functional, for it brought fun and lightness into the class and provided Geoffrey with a challenge and an occasion for his own quick humor. But in many instances such a role can be detrimental to group purposes. Three weeks after the beginning of school we were puzzled about Sam's evolution. When we went back and carefully analyzed the notes, we were surprised to find what had happened.

An important fact is that Sam is a pupil who failed seventh grade last year with Mr. Geoffrey. He did little or no work. On the first day this year Sam had been teased sympathetically about possible tardiness and being at Rhody's Confectionary before school. Next, he had been given book number 13 and was involved in teasing about superstitions. Thirdly, he was called on to help Molly spell "chalk." Fourth, he volunteered to help in the supply room and was teased with the others about running off to play baseball. And fifth, he was pinpointed humorously regarding the fire drill. He had been extended five invitations, far more than any others (only Sandy and Billy were singled out with any frequency and they alternately took special roles). Day by day such interaction accumulated into a role and a related belief system.

The second day contained several more instances of Mr. Geoffrey's public attention to Sam. One of these seemed particularly significant; it occurred during the spelling lesson as the papers were being corrected. Each pupil was entitled to one chance to respond. The teacher had made this clear with references such as, "You've had one" to both Allison and Kent. Mr. Geoffrey gave to Sam the word "tardy" and received the retort, "I've had one." He, Mr. Geoffrey, then commented, "I'm giving you this one special."

Sam also has a high degree of skill in repartee. Few of the pupils could respond with the "wise humor" appropriate to the context. In addition, he responded well to termination cues from Mr. Geoffrey. Banter contains these fundamental attributes.

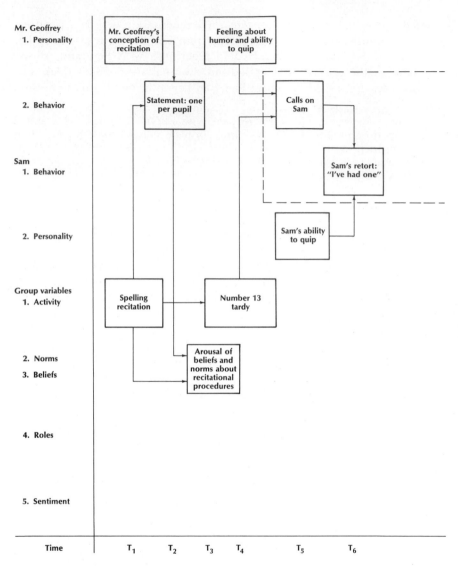

Figure 3.3   A process analysis of an interactional episode between Mr. Geoffrey and Sam and its implications.

We should comment further about the teacher's role in this instance. We had not realized, until we checked the names of the pupils who had been given opportunities to answer and compared them with the names of the children called on after Sam's second turn, that the next four pupils called upon had also given one answer before. In the space of a few minutes, Sam's role had been extended, and the teacher had built another subtle

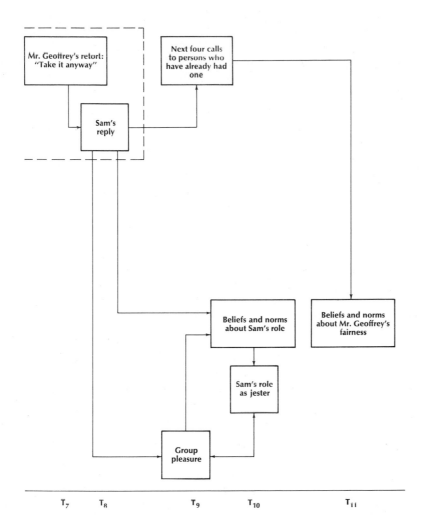

aspect of the pupil belief system regarding his own role—he was fair and equitable.[6] Figure 3.3 contains the sequence of events. Additional insight is provided from comments made by Mr. Geoffrey:

[6]This kind of subtlety and complexity in the teacher's behavior is returned to in Chapter Four.

Teaching at Washington School can have a deadening effect on a normal, live, somewhat eager individual. To work day after day with pupils whose aspirations and abilities are so typical of the culturally disadvantaged child—aspirations and abilities that need no description in these comments—is to court frustration and defeatism. Even what appeared in the beginning to be sensational after a while becomes commonplace.

The teacher in question suffered as much as any other in this environment. As a relief, he sought some humor and life in the children with whom he worked. Sometimes this could be found—as it was in Sam, Sandy, even Elma. Not to capitalize on this would have been a waste of natural resources.

Sam and a few others made it possible to inject joking and bantering into the classroom. It made it possible to smile. It made possible teaching in a personal and, I would hope, kind way. The teacher could treat some pupils as individuals (noneducational sense) rather than as a mob of dirty, sullen children. Some pupils, such as Sam, *responded*. One of the most discouraging aspects of teaching in a slum school is the lack of response from pupils. The teacher works and works, and at the end of the day leaves tired and irritable. This feeling comes from the continual effort to get these students to respond—in any acceptable way. To have them respond in humor, within bounds, is a most acceptable way. At least they are *alive*.

I do not deny that the consequences may be subject to question. I really don't think the teacher thought much of consequences. I believe he thought more of finding life in the body than in what way the body, once awakened, would behave.

This, of course, leads to the question of teacher personality. When faced with frustration and failure other teachers may follow different courses to get through the days.

The Nonworker: Troubled and Troublesome

Pete's role has two interesting characteristics: It was both changing and unchanging. During the first week he did nothing. Later he fought with Geoffrey. Ultimately he fought with Mr. Inman, the Principal. But throughout he seemed to be fighting most seriously with himself. His story seems worth telling.

The observer saw him this way on September 30th:

Pete is a very short boy, the smallest in the class, I think. He wears his hair in one of those very wild duck-tail fashions, the top combed forward and the sides combed back. He has a reputation among the teachers of being a "sneaky kid." He is perhaps the one child in the class with whom Geoffrey has not got along and whom he does not like. He presents one of the most complex mental health and management problems imaginable. First, he does literally no schoolwork or homework. The kind of truce that Geoffrey seems to have made is, "if you sit there and keep your mouth shut and don't bother anyone, I won't bother you either." Second, even though he is the oldest child in the classroom, or at least one of the oldest, he has one of the lowest achievement records in the class. He can't do much above third or fourth grade level. Third, his attitude generally is "I can't, I won't, and you can't make me." Early in the semester Geoffrey treated him like everyone else in the classroom in regard to assignments and in his interaction with him. From the outside it looked as if Geoffrey didn't want to be caught in the trap, on the one hand, of demanding work from a kid who had considerable difficulty with it, and who was going to refuse to do it, and, on the other, of allowing this kind of demonstration to generalize to the rest of the classroom. Geoffrey seems to have taken a third alternative, to make a clear discrimination that Pete is different from the rest of the class. Therefore, Pete hasn't really affected anyone in class except perhaps Billy, although this is debatable. The other kids realize he is not doing anything; they realize also that the same treatment isn't applicable to them.

A further important fact and perhaps the most important lying behind Pete's behavior, and Geoffrey's behavior also, is the fact that Pete will be sixteen this December and will be quitting school at that time. Geoffrey's general notion seems to be to write him off; he's not worth the trouble for the 3 months. Although I haven't talked with Pete about this point, it seems to me that his behavior is indicative of the same thing. "I'm not going to be here very long, you're not going to fail me, and there's nothing you can do to hurt me." It's a standoff relationship that the word "truce" probably fits as well as any other. Pete's classmates typically treat him as atypical. Only in Billy has he found anyone who seems to consistently regard him as a friend or to interact with him more than minimally. This may be partly a function of the seating assignments and most certainly it is a function of the difficulty that both of the children have with academic work and in relating to the other kids in the classroom. Most of the kids, when passing by, ignore him. Some occasionally make a comment; Allison is one of these. In the "around-the-room-recitation" Geoffrey generally skips Pete. Whenever he calls for volunteers, Pete never offers except for some kind of physical chore to be done in the classroom such as opening or closing windows. For this Pete will volunteer and Geoffrey will occasionally ask him to do it. In other aspects of the classroom, Geoffrey does not go out of his way to be extra friendly or extra punitive to the boy, and Pete seems to sense this and live within this general framework. The specific illustration I have in mind is the freedom to go to and from the room for drinks. Pete comes and goes in this regard without any special difficulty or special favors.   (9/30)

Three-and-a-half months after Pete left, Geoffrey wrote in brief summary fashion his reactions to the boy:

Pete: A complete mess all of his years in school. Had unhappy home life, resulting both from a more intelligent and obnoxiously arrogant older brother and an apparently cruel father. The father had left. The boy was completely obnoxious to me. He could never look or act pleasant, and had been a source of trouble in the school until his suspension. Whatever ability he had was directed toward nonsense, sometimes showing genius there. Probably his character has been shaped

> beyond hope by his environment, especially the family, and the mother is a most unhappy woman in trying to deal with him. He stays out of serious difficulty with the law, and it seems he did find some satisfaction in a special boy scout or similar organizational group outside the school. Hope he finds help there before it is too late.   (2/15)

As we try to understand Pete's role in the class and Geoffrey's decision-making and action, it seems appropriate to begin by culling Geoffrey's references to Pete during the first few weeks. The initial entry is on September 9th, less than a week after school began:

> Has done little or nothing. He can't do much. Is no behavior problem yet. Has been a serious one in the past, and it is a minor miracle that he has survived this far in the school. I talked with him briefly regarding what he was doing, or rather, wasn't doing. Had him read a short passage of a book to remind myself of his ability there. He stated he will quit school on his sixteenth birthday. I told him okay, but to behave himself in the interim.   (9/9)

The salient elements are the ever-present reputation and record a child carries with him. Reputation as we have used the term is a part of the group's belief system, in this instance the staff's, or an individual's conception, in this instance Geoffrey's. The reputation provokes an initial image, a set of predictions, and a set of potential responses on the part of the teacher. As this point Geoffrey's gambit is a brief talk about his behavior, academic and nonacademic. Pete's counter implies that Geoffrey has little ultimate power, for Pete will quit school when he reaches his sixteenth birthday later in the semester. We should note also Geoffrey's attempt to corroborate the low ability dimension of Pete's reputation.[7] Presumably this has a functional quality in gauging work demands and also in protecting himself in confrontation with parents or supervisors regarding the boy. If the teacher knows from personal experience and can say "I read with him," he has irrefutable evidence with significance, in personal debate at least, beyond the .01 level.

Geoffrey's second comment includes other pupils as well as Pete:

> Behavior: Some students are getting a little friskier. Amount of work will be increased and time will be utilized better now that gym schedules are in and reading schedule will soon be available. Allison continues true-to-form, and Pete is beginning to get restless. Sandy, Thelma, Eileen, and friends will probably whisper, or try to, at any time for any reason all year. Since their conduct will in general be good, they will draw only gentle reprimands. Allison, Pete, and a few others may need stronger language in order to settle them down. Among the others is Elma and her friend, Susan; the latter will be okay if Elma stays in line. She is beginning to seek the limits, to test.   (9/10)

Geoffrey's category of "behavior" refers to the range of non-goal-

---

[7]This provides also another illustration of "preparation for contingencies" to which we refer in Chapter Four.

oriented activities and interactions that occur in most elementary class-rooms. Note the distinctions in his thinking concerning the social structure. Sandy's clique has been identified and labeled as "good." Allison and Pete precipitate a state of readiness that amounts to "greater disturbance gets sterner reactions." Hypotheses have begun to form concerning Elma, Susan, and their interdependency.

The observer, too, has had impact on the system. Geoffrey has been reluctant to be as punitive as he sometimes sees himself being. Geoffrey himself admits this in his notes:

> When problems arise in class, such as Pete's behavior, the fact that an observer is there seems to affect my behavior to a greater degree than normally. Starting tomorrow, conscious though I may be of what he thinks, I am going to behave as I normally would, or as close to that as I can. (9/11)

The next two days add to the developing sequence. Geoffrey comments on "discipline." Pete is a central figure:

> Pete M. has exhausted my patience. His flagrant flouting of room rules will not be allowed. While tearing up his arithmetic paper on which he was working during history may seem somewhat extreme, it was more for the effect on others than on Pete. It shows others that I mean business on this rule, and thus had to be carried out suddenly and without moderation in order to make the necessary impression. That he says he won't do it over is of little consequence. He won't do much anyway, so the lesson would really be ineffective as far as he is concerned. However, he will conform to rules to best of his ability or out he goes, at least to some other room. (9/12)

The observer recorded the paper-tearing episode in this manner:

2:50 Raises cain with Pete regarding arithmetic lesson that Pete has done in history class. Geoffrey tears up the paper and throws it away. He tells Pete the assignment is due tomorrow. Pete makes a comment. Geoffrey says "Don't talk back to me." Pete sits silently. Through all this the "page, squire, knight" history sequence goes on. The reading is alternated between pupils and Geoffrey.

2:55 "Do all people live that way? No!" Geoffrey introduces briefly "The Life of the Peasants." Oral reading continues. Oliver races out to monitor duty at arrival of matron. (His job is to take the wastebasket out to her.) Reading continues.

3:02 A messenger enters and requests encyclopedia *"D"* for Alton's room. Geoffrey obliges and then finishes reading the chapter. He begins exer-

3:03 cise (on p. 282) called "Word Ways and Thought Teaser No. 1." He answers procedural questions on lesson. Paper is passed out. Geoffrey takes Pete out in the hall for a long lecture and discussion.

3:07 Geoffrey returns. Pete remains outside. Everyone is working except Irma. Billy takes a long time getting organized.

3:17 Geoffrey goes out to the hall and talks again with Pete. Everyone is working. Billy is lackadaisical. Several are "racing the clock," trying to finish their assignments.

3:18 Geoffrey returns. (9/12)

Geoffrey's speculations about Pete and his continuing interaction are reported briefly in the next two comments from his notes.

> Absences: seven in the morning, six in the afternoon. Pete M. is probably truant, primarily because of the Thursday incident. Two have gone to the "country." (9/13)

> My free gym period was not so free. Mrs. Matthews came and related troubles that have led to Pete's trouble. I'm afraid the value of her coming will be ephemeral. (9/16)

> A request that Mrs. Matthews made to me to help Pete by moving him, and the continued whispering and nonsense among Edwin, Helen, and Allison, and also Thelma, Sandy, Eileen, and Molly, convinced me that seats should be assigned to separate these and others. I would also like to save Susan from Elma. I did not mean to do it so soon, but now thought it best to do so before bad habits became firmly entrenched. The usual complaints and nonsense ensued, but there was not too much. Seats will be changed again in a few weeks to a different pattern, and then again. (9/17)

He sees Pete responding through truancy to the disciplinary measure. Also, the intercession of the parent has occurred and Geoffrey's belief is that the effects will be ephemeral. Nonetheless he takes one line of action open to him and congruent with the parent's request. He changes the seats of the children. In his eyes this will facilitate changes of several sorts within the classroom. Later we will speak of multiple threads in classroom episodes and the ringmaster phenomenon as the teacher tries to handle the several strands.

The conference with Pete's mother, Mrs. Matthews, occurred in the classroom. The observer had been sitting at his table across the room and continued working. The notes he took are recorded below:

9:32 Pete enters with his mother for a conference. Geoffrey very directly lays it on the line. "He's done absolutely nothing for me. I know he's behind." He explains the paper-tearing episodes. Rules are rules which he illustrates with a traffic example. Pete feels that they don't apply. Gives Pete a chance to talk, but doesn't let him alter the circumstances about Pete's error in doing an arithmetic assignment during a history lesson prior to the paper-tearing episode. Mother explains part of the history of the problem: parochial school, working schedules of mother, other family problems, and father's sickness. Mother enters into discussion of glasses, and so forth. Geoffrey explains the fact that Pete was promoted because of age, but that he gets no special privileges. Geoffrey explains that he has not pressured Pete, even when he doesn't know the answers. However, Geoffrey states that Pete must do what he can and he must behave. Geoffrey asks the Mother if that is too much (LMS—obviously it's not and she is backed into untenable spot). Mother raises concern about work at home and Geoffrey quizzes about when he is in at night, his club activities, and so forth . . . He raises question with Pete if "that's not too much." Pete agrees it is not.

9:43 Geoffrey excuses Pete. Mother talks on about jobs and the other boy at home. She discusses difficulty in getting jobs and alternatives to turn to. The mother is concerned about future schooling. She realizes that he "plays hooky."

9:48 Geoffrey stands up to terminate the interview. She gets up and they walk out; they continue talking in the hall.

Afterward Geoffrey comments to me that Pete's father has been in and out of the home and now is gone. The father threw lye in the boy's face a year-and-a-half ago and Pete has had eye troubles ever since. Apparently it occurred on purpose. The father allegedly cheated the boy out of some summer work money, also.   (9/16)

Later in the same day the observer noted:

3:10 Last 15 minutes for assignments.

Pete has done practically nothing all day today except talk to Molly. This occurs in spite of his mother's visit earlier in the day. (LMS—incidently, Geoffrey told the Principal, Inman, that Pete's mother had been here. He clears his lines of authority for actually Pete's mother should have gone to the office first, and Geoffrey should have taken her there. Inman commented that she has a heart condition.)   (9/16)

For two days Pete's behavior remains constant—he does no work. The growing belief system about Pete among the pupils is apparent in Allison's behavior.

11:10 Geoffrey gives a language test. Test 3, p. 26. "Hope no one is afflicted with R. E.'s—Roving Eyeballs." Everyone but Pete seems to take the test seriously—working quietly and steadily. There is no discernible copying.

11:20 Cheerful Allison goes about the room collecting test papers, passing out new papers, giving everyone a big smile.

As she comes to Pete she pauses. He raises his head from resting on his desk and gives her a blank look. Without batting an eye, Allison goes on to Helen.

On September 18 Pete again becomes the center of attention. The field notes capture the incident.

2:15 Geoffrey begins arithmetic assignment. Geoffrey comments, "Three talking boys: Edwin, Dick, and Davey each 'asked' for an additional arithmetic assignment. (If you have time to talk, you have time for more work.) Anyone else want one?" There is considerable interplay. All (except Pete) are engaged in good humor.

A fracas occurs that involves Pete and Allison; Geoffrey quizzes Pete about the content of their conversation. Pete says across the room, "She said for me to kiss her butt." Geoffrey didn't hear it immediately and Pete repeats. Geoffrey finally has him come to the desk. He repeats his comment. Geoffrey sends him from the room. A few minutes later Geoffrey asks Allison to come with him into the hall. They engage in a discussion. While this goes on there are a number of snickers—none of shock or indignation. Geoffrey and Allison return.

2:35 Spelling starts and goes on without a hitch. (LMS—Frustration level in spelling is quite low.) Everyone is cooperative and interested in the

> humor of the material. Geoffrey is relaxed and casual. In homework, Sam is back in joking relationship. Allison is quietly working. Pete has not returned. Participation by teacher and pupil is easy and appropriate. (9/18)

On the evening of the same day Geoffrey recorded his comments about more general issues of discipline and noted that Pete continues in his "nonwork" role.

> Afternoon: Extra arithmetic is assigned to those who act up, talk, and so forth. Education textbooks say assignments should not be used for punishment. However, I attempt to keep all working on subjects. I attempt to get them to read library books, and to use time with some constructiveness. The gambit is that students so talking must have plenty of time to do additional work. Perhaps some will take more care with assignments, and others will start to do them. Exhortations from supervisors to "instill motivation," are fine, but not here. Pete, incidentally, does no work. He is simply removed from the scene. Another departure from "good" classroom organization and management![8] (9/18)

The notes in October take on a different flavor. The "aggregate," a number of disturbed children, have arrived. Pete becomes seriously involved in difficulties with them. The context has changed. Geoffrey doesn't have a pupil like Sam to lighten the load. Some of the particulars of Pete's difficulties with Timmie and with Joe K., of his contagion into disciplinary episodes with Leonard, will be sketched in the later discussion of the new group of children who arrived in October after the closing of a room in the school. The teacher's notes for October are full of comments such as:

> Leonard and Pete are throwing objects; Pete is sent to the hall, Leonard to the office.

> Fireman comes in for discussion (during Fire Prevention Week); there is nonsense and incessant chatter. Pete and Joe K. are sent to the hall.

> We don't have a movie today because of nonsense; Pete, Joe K., Alan, and now even Harry are involved.

> Something must be done with Pete M.

Two final entries in Geoffrey's notes regarding Pete read as follows:

10/31 Pete has been given a temporary suspension by the Principal and is absent.[9]

11/1 Mrs. Matthews came in this morning with Pete. We discussed readmit-

---

[8]Geoffrey and Smith had a friendly and humorous running dialogue on how the "good teacher" who knew the "principles of teaching" would have handled these episodes "much better."

[9]When a temporary suspension is given, the parent(s) of the suspended child must come to the school within three days and discuss the matter with the Principal. If the parents do not appear the suspension becomes permanent and the parents go through certain procedures, as specified by the Board of Education, to get the child admitted to another school. *Almost* always the child is readmitted when he and his parents, or one parent, appear within the three day period.

ting him in the room for the last six weeks until he is sixteen. However, Pete, upon being called into the office for consultation, acted in an arrogant and insolent manner, so the Principal gave him his walking papers.

The story ends. A complex role developed and was played out in the classroom.

Breaking the Spiral

Our analyses of Sam and Pete have accented the multiple factors within the child, the teacher, and the interaction which we hypothesize precipitated the development of special individual roles. In the first instance the spiral seemed to produce consequences positive to the classroom, the child, and the teacher. In Pete's case the spiral was negative, a vicious circle that seemed progressively to create more difficulty for Pete, Geoffrey, and the classroom as a whole. A brief glance at a third boy, Lonny, and at an episode of interaction suggests the subtle threads eliciting positive, negative, and neutral development. Toward the end of the first month Lonny was described in this manner.

> Lonny is, as I recall, a boy new to the school this year. The difficulty in making that recollection indicates quite clearly that he has found a place in the classroom. My first observation of him was of a socially alert but hostile boy who was looking for trouble. It seemed true then and it seems true now. Initially his contact with the other children in the class centered heavily on Davey, the boy who sat on his right. Now recently in the shake-up of seats he has been placed near Sandy. This really brought him to life, for he is one of the several boys now who are continuously teased by her. He is interested and responds in kind. He doesn't sit back in class in a sulking way as much as he used to, he is much more animated. While he has never totally blown up in class, on one occasion (and this is in the field notes, I think) Geoffrey asked him, as part of a lesson, to carry the coffee cream jar across the room. Lonny carried it across the room but slammed it down on the desk. Geoffrey refused to be disturbed and ignored the action. Academically Lonny's work seems average or low average for this class. Being on the school patrol has given him some contacts and privileges along with Edwin, Davey, and Dick.   (9/23)

After recess during the morning of September 19th, the observer was alone in the room with the children. Mr. Geoffrey had been on yard duty and had not returned as yet. The field notes capture some of the fun surrounding the cockleburrs that had ripened in the field next to the boys' playground. Our central interest, however, lies in Lonny and Geoffrey as they carry out a brief but potentially significant episode in a language arts lesson.

10:30 The kids are back from recess, Edwin throws a cockleburr at Sandy. She brings it to me. Edwin asks—"You won't tell Mr. Geoffrey?"

I laughed and said "No." Pete squirts Billy with Elmer's Glue-all. Irma told me of her infant brother who died last summer. She was worried about whether he had been "cut up," apropos of earlier science discussion on dissection,

10:45 "If I could cry I would," says Geoffrey as he begins the return of the language test papers. Slowly and dramatically he takes up each item in the test.

Sentence No. 3: "Tom had brought hamburgers and rolls." Illustrates "action" by having Davey bring the pencil sharpener. Then, "Who brought? Did the hamburger bring Tom?"

(LMS—Sometime it might be desirable to tape one of these.)

As the lesson goes on, this seems to be one of the few times that there is strong latent hostility. Lonny shows it in the coffee-carrying illustration. Jimmie misses a question after long elaboration. There are a variety of sullen looks (Edwin, Davey, Elma). Only a few (3) score over 70 (Shirley, Dick, Irma) "Miserable," "Terrible," are Geoffrey's comments.

11:05 Mr. Geoffrey tells the children to begin homework lessons on the board.

11:07 Once again Geoffrey's lack of emotional vindictiveness comes through as Lonny asks to go to restroom. He is permitted without a comment or a glance in spite of his strong attempt to provoke Geoffrey in slamming down the coffee jar with an insolent air. (LMS—He's out a long time. It is now 11:17 and he is still not back. This allows him time to cool off as well.)

The homework lesson is once again a mild probing, quizzing, and helping session. Geoffrey is directive but gentle here.

11:17 Introduces exercise requiring kids to construct a sentence using the word "apple." He then has five kids go up and underline subject once and verb twice.

11:18 Lonny returns.

11:20 Geoffrey expresses mock anger over the neglect of the verb "were." "What do you see in the sentence that's *always* a verb?"

11:23 Geoffrey skips Chapter 2, "Conversation and Making Friends." This material borders on human relations content. He picks up verbs again (p. 49), Chapter 3: "Verbs."

(LMS—Beyond the human relations content it raises, this material might have provided more interesting examples of some principles for review.)

(LMS—Lonny is in good humor again.)

11:28 Mr. Geoffrey makes the assignment.

11:33 History. Right at this moment Lonny has a book report ready. Geoffrey brushes him off until this afternoon.

(LMS—At this time and moment this seems unfortunate.)

11:48 Lesson terminates. Homework is assigned: No. 2 in "Selftester" and No. 1 and No. 2 of "Thought Teasers" (pp. 3 and 5).

(LMS—Geoffrey's freedom in allowing kids to come and go needs more analysis in total system. Safety valve for group as well as individuals when negative sentiments build up.)

(LMS—Statement on mental health of kids. Number who look unhappy is huge.)

The elements we would accent are several. First, this kind of interaction occurs in scores of instances, daily, weekly, through the year. Most teachers, we believe, are so caught in the flow of events that they are hardly conscious of any one episode. Second, Geoffrey's behavior illustrates patience, impersonality, and lack of emotional response. This seems in great contrast to the positive emotion and fun involved in sparring with Sam and the frustration in the running battle with Pete.

Conclusion

The monitor jobs, the nature of being a pupil in Mr. Geoffrey's class, the fact that one is a boy or girl, and the clowning of one pupil are superficially quite disparate events. We have formulated them in more analytic terms and indicated some key similarities. At least two other important individual roles were discussed in similar terms. One of these concerns "the troublesome role" and the other concerns the "no work" role. In the former, several children were constantly in conflict with Mr. Geoffrey. In the latter, several children literally did nothing but sit through the semester. In Pete's case, he played both. It is our belief that these students and their roles are made more understandable through the kind of analysis that we have endeavored here.

THE INITIAL TEACHER ROLE: ESTABLISHING CONTROL

Frequently teachers refer to a phenomenon which they label classroom control. Most educational psychology discussions do not make clear what teachers mean by this term. Instead they move into discussions of discipline problems, mental health outcomes, and terminological confusion centering on "democracy" in the classroom. The thesis we wish to state is quite simple: classroom control refers to the relationship between teacher direction, usually verbal, and a high probability of pupil compliance. If we separate teachers into those who have control and those who do not, then we have situations where pupils acquiesce and follow orders or they do not. The dichotomy may be thought of as a continuum. We may raise the question concerning compliance by the total class, various subportions of the class, and individual pupils. Further, we can subdivide according to situations ranging from the imperative of the fire alarm to chewing gum. And we may distinguish between responses to direct commands by the teacher and responses mediated by an activity suggested or imposed by the teacher; for example, does the child answer questions and carry out exercises in spelling as these were outlined and set in motion three weeks before? Finally, an array of antecedents and consequences of this multidimensional phenomenon can be investigated.

Grooving the Children:
Achieving Clarity in the Role

Mr. Geoffrey saw this problem clearly and in quite simple terms. He acted upon the conception in a manner that we have called "grooving the children." Specifically, during the first few days he gave literally dozens of orders, to individuals and to the total group, which involved a number of trivial items. For instance, he handled the distribution of books by assigning each person a number, then calling out the numbers of the books from the storage cabinet, and having each child walk up and get his book. Later he modified this with "runners," children who distributed books to those children who raised their hands as he had instructed them. Next, he utilized the word "permission" over and over again. In the field notes, recorded before 9:00 A.M. on the first morning, "Permission phrase appears and reappears." Interestingly, Geoffrey's statements showed situations requiring permission differentiated from those not requiring permission: "If you wish to leave the room to go downstairs, you must ask permission." And later, "For occasional borrowing, you don't need my permission."

Theoretically, we would argue that these interactions moved within the pupil group, toward a belief system: "The teacher gives directions and the pupils follow them." The immediate consequence of such a belief is the additional belief that future order-giving-and-following will occur in the same fashion. This eliminates questioning by the pupils and extended teacher explanations. It eliminates also rewards for compliance as well as punishments for noncompliance. This point is most important for our later discussion of bureaucratic versus personal authority. A more long-term consequence to which we will turn our attention later revolves around the implications for critical and creative thinking that demand that one doubt and question before one acts.

Finally, the development of this belief system seemed to capitalize on several aspects: (1) the requests themselves were individually quite insignificant; (2) they dealt mostly with activities in which teachers are expected to be involved; (3) they were asked of everyone; consequently, to refuse would be to cast oneself in a special light; (4) the situations were cloaked with individual attention, warmth, and humor; (5) they often involved activities such as getting up and moving about, which was a pleasurable alternative to being seated for a long period of time; and (6) many of the requests involved volunteering and special, favorable attention. Some of these points are seen in the following episode:

> "Do I have any good pencil sharpeners?" Several boys raise their hands. He picks two who didn't pass out books. He directs them, "Out in the hall."

Beyond the development of the belief system as a relatively emotion-

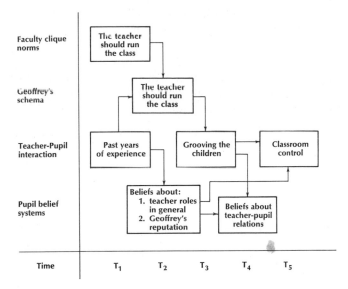

Figure 3.4 A model for analysis of initial steps in classroom control.

less organization of cause-effect relationships, the association with conditions of positive emotion moves toward what we call a classroom norm containing both beliefs and sentiments.

In short, classroom control may be viewed as an important aspect of classroom social structure. In this sense it becomes a goal the teacher strives to reach. Our analysis has suggested that the teacher is faced with the problem of developing such a belief and normative system within the classroom. This time, however, the beliefs and norms center about his own role in the classroom. As we have analyzed our data, we described an interactional sequence, "grooving the pupils" in which Geoffrey gave orders and obtained compliance in a variety of mundane and critical situations. As these accumulate, they develop into belief systems—"this is the way it's done"—and ultimately into normative systems—"this is the way it should be done." Achievement of this goal has a number of potentially positive and negative consequences for further long-term goals. Figure 3.4 contains our summary model.

I Mean It:
Second Steps in Establishing Belief Systems

Most of our examples have emphasized clarity of presentation of those aspects of behavior that Geoffrey wanted built into the belief and normative system of the classroom. Beyond clarity, Geoffrey's behavior contained an "I mean it" quality, which one might interpret as a threat or as a statement of cause-effect relationship. Our interpretation suggests that the teacher's performance needs analysis for implications in establishing the social structure of the classroom; in other words threats must be distinguished as to whether they suggest cause-effect consequences that may or may not be punishing, or those that reflect punishment per se. The former seems evident in Geoffrey's interaction with Susan:

> "Who's been eating sunflower seeds?" Susan says she has. "Don't dine on them in the school room. I'll confiscate them. Who knows what confiscate means?" (Keep them.) "Anytime I collect food you'll be lucky to see it again." Geoffrey moves about checking papers. (9/10)

Following Through:
A Third Step in Establishing Beliefs

Although we have used this illustration in indicating the "correct work" belief associated with pupil roles, we find that it illustrates beautifully the connecting link between dimensions of teacher performance, things a teacher does, and a major consequence or function of his behavior, firmly supporting the developing belief system. What we call "following through" is another dimension of teacher performance. Its meaning lies in the combination of an earlier statement of intent, frequently a warning or test situation, as in the sunflower seed episode, and now a demand that the pupil behave in accord with the rule. In a way, the simple behavior of Eileen's walking to the board carries considerable import for the classroom system:

> Few questions about letters. Sarah asks about "trachery," Geoffrey sends Eileen up to correct and to make it "treachery." (LMS—This seems very critical also. Without fanfare Geoffrey always sends the erring one back to correct his or her own mistakes. Implicit rule—if you don't do it right you'll do it again. Expand and interrelate.) (9/10)

A similar situation occurs with Sam. At approximately 11:25 during a language arts lesson:

> "How many are through? Those who are please wait patiently and quietly. Sam!" Geoffrey walks around the room, gives Allison a look. Stops to talk to Sam. (Can't pick up conversation except some about staying busy, book report. Sam protests that he has finished and is ready to give report.) Discussion—not quite banter occurs between Geoffrey and Sam. (9/10)

Three minutes later:

> "Sam! All right, that's enough. Turn around. All the way." He does. (9/10)

Two minutes later Sam volunteers to go to the board and work a problem.

Geoffrey lets him. Later, as we will see, Geoffrey is not averse to putting further punitive teeth into his demands. The occasions for that kind of behavior are important for our analysis.

The Shift from Beliefs to Norms: Softening the Tone of Classroom Management

If our analysis is correct, that norms must be distinguished from beliefs, and that the distinction involves the incorporation of sentiment into the belief, then we can talk about "acceptance of belief" as equivalent to the concept of norms. Part of the teacher's task is not only to have the pupils know what they "should" do but to be "willing" to do it. In Geoffrey's class, humor seemed to be a major dimension of his performance that carried these implications. Late one afternoon, he received a memorandum from the office regarding some insurance forms to be taken home. In the course of the discussion the following notes were made:

> "Let me have your attention. I have some material for you." Raises accident insurance materials. Indicates parents are to make decisions about materials and not the kids. "Don't mutilate. Stop work and listen. Know what I have done on occasions with someone who wouldn't stop working? Don't guess. Ask someone who knows me." Goes through insurance form carefully.   (9/10)

A similar illustration, which we have already used, applies to "softening the tone of classroom management." It indicates Geoffrey's concern for establishing not only a belief but a norm as well. Many times he seemed to feel the need to make rules and regulations clear. He often did this dramatically. However, when his point was made, he usually softened the criticism and maintained the task-oriented quality of the group through drama, humor, and incidental learning. The records are replete with illustrations of this sort, and the incident with Susan and the sunflower seeds typifies them.

As we have indicated earlier in this chapter, in our framework a belief is a generalized perception of what exists, while a norm is a generalized or group expectation of what *ought* to exist. As Geoffrey made the class rules clear, he was dealing with belief systems; as he tried to build an emotional commitment on the part of the children to these beliefs, he was engaged in the more complex task of shaping normative structure.

A Concluding Illustration

Early on the morning of September 12, Geoffrey engages in the beginning of the day chores and a spelling test. During these activities, he has almost withdrawn his attention from the norms surrounding monitorial roles, and he is artfully clarifying and softening the establishment of beliefs about gum chewing:

8:38   Observer comes in after yard duty. He receives a big "Hello, Mr Smith" from Sandy. Geoffrey in. Banter begins over shop schedule. His comment about somebody not doing his job brings all the monitors (paper, chalk, date) into action. He corrects a schedule and takes attendance. Everyone but Lonny is present.

8:45   After paper is passed and pencils are sharpened, Geoffrey starts with "Name at top; number from 1 to 10 . . . ." Raises question with Dick, "Are you going to make that your permanent seat?" "Yes, sir." He starts spelling test (pop test?). "No. 1, Handsome. You are lucky to have such a handsome teacher." Geoffrey grins, everyone smiles . . . . "No. 2, Warehouse. The Hawaiian Co. stores sugar in the warehouse across the street. Warehouse. No. 3, Coconut . . . . No. 4, Gentlemen."

8:48   Messenger arrives. While handling the interruption, Geoffrey apparently suspects that someone is chewing gum. "I don't have any gum chewers in here?" Sarah says, "No, wax . . . ." Everyone smiles. He generalizes rule to wax, paper clips, paper, and tar.

   Continues through list with humor, local items, maxims of behavior. 5. Iceberg . . . . 6. Throughout. study throughout day . . . . 7. Midnight. no one up after midnight . . . . 8. Backward. There is not a backward student in this room. 9. However. However, there are some students who don't work as hard as they should. 10. Therefore. Therefore, I shall do my best to see that all of you work as hard as you can." (9/12)

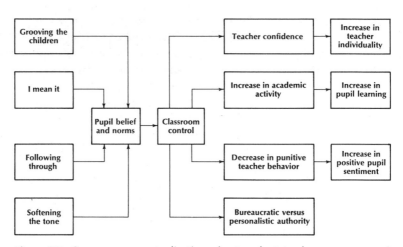

Figure 3.5   Summary conceptualization of antecedents and consequences of classroom control.

THE SUBGROUP INTERACTION STRUCTURE

The social structure of the classroom contains not only a variety of roles and belief systems as we have defined and developed these concepts, but also a series of subgroups. A subgroup refers to two or more individuals from the total who interact more frequently with each other than with the total group. Clique is a synonym. A dyad is a two-person subgroup. An isolate is a person who belongs to no subgroup. In the classroom at the Washington School a part of the early structure was a group of girls we have labeled as "Sandy's clique." The central figures include Sandy, Molly, and Eileen. Peripheral but yet a part of the group are Thelma, Patty, and Rose.[10] Interaction patterns other than this tended to be dyadic and isolated: Susan and Elma, Pete and Billy, Allison and Helen (in spite of her recent arrival), Sam and Oliver, Edwin and Jimmie. The latter two dyads sometimes flowed together and occasionally Davey and Dick joined with them. The isolates tended to be Kent, Ben, Lonny, Irma, Peggy, and Dick.

A number of significant generalizations seem warranted in discussing "subgroup interaction structure." First, the sources of the structure seem to lie outside the teacher's direct influence. Sandy's clique and a number of the dyads were present from the beginning of school. Presumably these were friendships from past years. Second, the phenomenon immediately strikes the observer, for there are children who seem to be together constantly. Third, the high frequency of interaction spills over into a variety of other group phenomena; for instance, they share sentiments, beliefs, and norms. In a sense, the dyads and the cliques are much closer to the latent meaning of a "real" group than is the classroom, for a freedom to join or not, to be accepted or not, seems to lie within the members rather than in a coercing institution. Fourth, in these interactions one sees a good deal of positive, expressive behavior that does not appear in other parts of the classroom functioning. Fifth, when one influences one of the members one has indirectly influenced all of the others. Sixth, when dealing with difficult academic problems involving frustration and failure (for example, below-criterion responses as in arithmetic, page 4, problem 1c), the teacher could keep the group on the problem, emitting responses until the correct one appeared and was reinforced, and interpret in a way seemingly satisfying to all that "it's embarrassing but . . . ." The assumption seems to be one of justice—since all my friends are suffering, I can tolerate it, too. Presumably, isolated individuals would not produce the same reaction when called upon.

Sandy's Clique: An Illustration

On the first day, as our seating chart noted, a group of children, most of whom had come from Mr. Alton's class, seated themselves in close proximity. (See Figure 3.6). This group of girls we have called "Sandy's clique," for she was the most outspoken member in interaction with Mr. Geoffrey. (Later observations suggested that Eileen and Molly were the

---

[10] Later we will develop the changes in this group as children moved from the school.

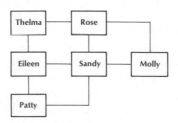

Figure 3.6 Seating arrangements of Sandy's clique.

closest friends and had the highest rank in the clique. Sandy, however, was the member with high social visibility.)

Both the early development of the clique and its early visibility to the observer are suggested, for on Monday morning, September 9, the notes indicate, "Clique of girls come in together." The behavior, or the observer's perception of it, had stabilized.

After two weeks of the semester, the observer taped brief summary statements about each of the children. The instructions he gave himself were these:

> Now, after two weeks of school, it seems appropriate to comment on the classroom from the point of reference of individual children in the classroom. I will try to give brief thumbnail sketches of each of the children as I have seen them from the corner of the room. I will do this by going around the room in the original seating chart that Geoffrey had for the classroom and, in effect, try to catch the flavor of the first set of permanent geographical positions. As I think about it at this moment, the points of reference probably will be the individual's relationship to Geoffrey, and the individual's position in the group. This latter point refers to the developing idea of the social roles of pupils in a group and might help to clarify the ultimate status of that point of view. (9/20)

The early comments on the half-dozen children who became the clique are these:

> In the first row, first column of the classroom, is Thelma. She is reasonably cute, attractive, wears glasses. Not noticeably different in any physical characteristics. Slight build, medium height. In the first seating chart she was full-fledged member of the clique of girls centering around Sandy, who was geographically located a little more centrally. Only recently, since the move of Oliver next to her, has she interacted with any frequency with the boys in the classroom. She and Geoffrey seem to have a very good working relationship: she volunteers for academic as well as nonacademic matters; he often will chide her, for instance, about not speaking loudly enough, and on one occasion he told her that she would have to stand in front of the room and present her answers if she didn't speak more loudly. On one occasion later he reminded her of this fact. To this kind of chiding she reacts quite shyly and bashfully in a sweet sort of way. She lived in the community even

before she began school. She seems to have stable, well-developed friendships with Eileen, Sandy, Molly, and more recently she has responded to Helen, one of the new children in the class.

She is not bright, and at best a low-average student in this class. A point I would make here is that although she does not fit the aggregate of able boys who carry the brunt of the correct class discussion, she is not as hopelessly inept as Peggy, Elma, Billy, and Rose. Some of this may be bias because of her pleasantness and cooperativeness.

Eileen, who sits behind Thelma, probably is the prettiest girl in the class. She also is quite demure and shy; she seldom speaks out in class. As mentioned earlier, she is part of the clique of girls and seems well accepted by them. I have had very little personal contact with her, in contrast say to Thelma, who has talked with me on several occasions. Geoffrey's reaction to Eileen seems to be that she is "just another pupil in the class." (This is my evaluation of his behavior and not his own statement, and is not intended to carry negative implications for either him or Eileen.) She too has considerable difficulty with schoolwork. She doesn't seem particularly interested in school. I have no clue at this point as to what satisfactions she does find.

The third girl in the row is Patty. She is short, quiet, attractive, but almost a nonentity in the classroom. She seems to belong to no clique in the group;[11] she takes very little part in volunteering, in recitation, and she has a sister in the classroom who also is quite quiet and unobtrusive. Her behavior is not apathetic in the usual sense of anomie, but has more the quality of nonassertiveness.

Rose is another of the quiet, unobtrusive children in the classroom. It was several days before I realized that she also had a sister, Patty, in the class. She is short, as is Patty, but she is considerably overweight. She, along with Allison, are the two cases of obesity in the classroom. The sources of this problem are not clear. (I have not had a chance to talk with Geoffrey about it.) Actually, she performs as a very, very dull student; seldom is Geoffrey able to obtain a deductive answer from her. She seldom volunteers in class and never enters into the byplay and banter that is generally common in his approach to the classroom. She goes to the board and participates in the around-the-room recitation. She usually has difficulty with language and with arithmetic. I don't recall having heard her read.

Sandy is one of the girls in the group most difficult to describe. She is the center of the clique of Thelma, Molly, and Eileen. She is one of the few girls in the class who is actively boy-crazy. This became particularly evident as she was moved during the wholesale seat change. She is cute, flirtatious, pouty. In Nabokov's terminology, she is in the late nymphet stage. She, along with Sam, are the two central foci of classroom interaction with Geoffrey. Academically she is not a strong student. It is sometimes very difficult to tell, though. Her general mode of response clouds all of her specific adequacies and inadequacies. As to academic questions, she has a kind of a "Who, me?" response, and "How am I supposed to know something like that?" (Monday, 9/23)

---

[11] When he first went back to the field notes the observer was surprised to find this statement, for later in the semester Patty was heavily involved.

> Molly is a quiet girl, but she seems to be one of the members-in-good-standing in the Sandy-Thelma clique. More recently, as the desks have been moved, she has developed a very friendly relationship with Sam and Susan. She strikes the observer as an optimistic person, seems to enjoy much of what she is doing, and to be operating relatively free from tension, anxiety, or emotion. Among this clique of girls, she interacts much less frequently with Geoffrey than do the others. She does not appear to be a strong student, although it's very difficult for me to evaluate her academic behavior at this time. As the semester wears on, I see more and more a picture of her importance within the social structure of the classroom. This may partly be a function of my observational opportunities because she is a bit nearer to me than she was before, and may also be partly a result of the fact that she is sitting next to Sam, who is in the center of everything. Physically, she bears a striking resemblance to Jackie Kennedy. I have not heard any of the kids comment about this, however. (As I make this report I am more and more struck by the fact that until this moment, I have not seen her in this light. Part of this may be due to the fact that she does not have the coquettishness of some of the other girls such as Sandy or Thelma. She needs more careful analysis.)   (9/24)

The evidence that subgroups play a special part in classroom functioning is scattered throughout our records. The notes on Monday emphasize the helping relationship in arithmetic.

> Elma looks for help from Sarah's paper. Molly turns around for help. Elma checks Peggy's paper. Helen, Allison, and Edwin check each other out. Pete queries Billy. Sandy, Eileen, Thelma, Rose and, Molly. Mr. Geoffrey looks over records. Quizzes Kent about his library books from last year (Mr. Alton's room).   (9/9)

In general, the individuals from whom one seeks help are class members with whom one has a closer relationship. The clique and dyads fulfill this.

The behavior in class flows out onto the playground and back into class. The notes catch the observer's growing interaction:

> Today while I was on yard duty, before school, at morning recess, and at noon, a number of the children came up to Geoffrey and to me, both together and independently, just to be around and to tell us all their "tales of woe." Sandy's clique is so vibrant, and all of them are so pert and coquettish, that they are amazing to watch. Several of them, Sandy, Molly, and Eileen particularly during the lunch hour, would hang over the fence and call to the boys from Adams School who were coming for industrial arts. The boys would answer back and there would be a brief tête-a-tête, to the mutual satisfaction of all the participants. They would then go into long stories as to how the boys were bothering them and the fact that these boys were nicer looking than the boys from the Washington School. The girls asked me what I thought of rock-and-roll and what I thought of Elvis Presley and innumerable similar items.   (9/26)

At one point the children worked on a geography problem concerning map-making. The task involved drawing a floor plan of the classroom and school. The observer used this as an opportunity to move about the class and visit with the children.

> In class during the geography period I walked around the room talking with the children and looking at the drawings that they were making of the school building. They responded by-and-large positively to my presence and interest. Pete and Billy were particularly pleased because I gave them some help in figuring out their problem, which, incidentally, they both executed very neatly. Much better than you would expect from either one of them alone, much less the two of them together where nonsense between them would intervene. Elma, Peggy, and Susan continually giggled whenever I came by. Neither of the latter two did much on their drawing, presumably because neither one of them knew very much about how to do it, and also because Elma wouldn't let them. Sam and Oliver goofed around and from time to time made remarks to me about how it was going and whose part looked the best. Molly, Patty, and Helen got into problems as they had the school upside down. Part of the pupils had the school rightside up and part of them had the school upside down. We talked about it briefly and they started to erase and make changes that would make it more sensible. (I am not sure how much good I did them there.) In the Eileen, Sandy, and Thelma group, Eileen seemed to be doing most of the work and responded quite positively to my being around. She seems to have gotten over her shyness about me, and she acts more and more like Sandy all the time. She was one of the more forward of the forward out on the playground.   (9/20)

Summary

Analytically we have defined clique as two or more individuals, but less than the total from a group, who interact more frequently with each other than with the total group. While this phenomenon is another obvious distinction, it, too, has important consequences. For instance, it will develop structure and dynamics of its own, which means there will be an integrated network of norms, beliefs, activities, sentiments, and so forth, which will become important influences controlling the behavior of the individual member. From the teacher's position, the clique can provide motivation and reason for the individual child's attention to academic tasks and also a mode of organization for carrying out the necessary tasks. Further, in accenting a criterion other than pupil-learning, it provides important benefits in teacher satisfaction in his profession. We have tried to sketch these relationships in Figure 3.7.

A Special Dyad: Elma and Susan

For several reasons we will comment on the Elma-Susan dyad: they remained in the class all semester, they represent two of the local Negro children and hence a point of contact with the larger group of transported

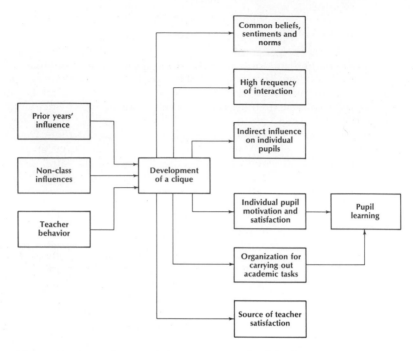

Figure 3.7   Antecedents and consequences of Sandy's clique.

children, and they present special problems to Mr. Geoffrey. Toward the end of September the observer made these summary comments regarding the girls:

> Susan is one of the two Negro children in the classroom. She is very quiet and seldom volunteers. When she does respond to a question, it is usually in such a low, soft voice that it is impossible for me to hear it. Academically her work is very poor. I guess that it would be below the level of Sandy's clique. Physically she presents a very striking picture. She is in the middle of adolescent development, yet she still wears what I would call "little girl" dresses. She is very dark in complexion. She gives a picture of a Negro girl just off the plantation or out of the cotton field. I have no idea how long she has lived in Big City or what her immediate background is. Only on a few occasions have I seen any animated activity on her part. This usually occurs in the line when the kids are getting ready to go outside for lunch or recess. On these occasions she will sometimes josh with Elma and will speak out in a fairly loud voice, with strong components of southern dialect. I recently noted she has responded a time or two to Sam and his buffoonery.   (9/23)
>
> Elma is the other Negro child in the classroom. She is a much more difficult child to work with in the classroom than most of the other girls, for she combines serious low ability and low achievement with considerable hostility. She has little of what might be called respect for or

responsiveness to authority. Scuttlebutt among the teachers reveals a past history of problem behavior in the school. Miss Norton commented on one occasion when a substitute was in a fourth grade room, Elma heightened the process of driving her out. She lay on the desk in the room, cursing and screaming wildly (and quite wildly, according to Miss Norton) so that the noise was heard all over that part of the building. Miss Norton and another teacher with considerable hesitation and the hesitation seemed to be due to the fact that you don't invade another teacher's room—went into the classroom and helped the teacher regain some order in what was going on. Little of this behavior has appeared in Geoffrey's class. Now it is much more a surly defiance. She walks around as if she had a chip on her shoulder. Physically she is tall and well dressed most of the time. Most of her social interactions in the classroom are with Susan. This was especially true before Geoffrey moved the two girls in the general seating rearrangement. She did, however, interact some with Sarah and some with Peggy. She also felt at considerable liberty to borrow answers from Sarah's paper. This seemed especially true after Sarah had done well on the first arithmetic paper or two. Academically her performance is quite poor, although it is very difficult sometimes to accurately judge this for she always has this "I'll do it maybe, if I want to," kind of attitude, which prevents telling whether she is trying or not. This, as well as some of the other summary observations, indicates quite clearly the need to obtain first-hand notes on the actual papers, tests, and homework that the kids turn in.   (9/23)

Isolates

While a number of children interact infrequently with each other and with Mr. Geoffrey, we present as illustration only the brief descriptions of Kent and Ben:

Ben is a tall, quiet, awkward kind of boy. On occasion he will volunteer in class, although most of the time he does not. He doesn't seem to be a part of any special clique within the classroom; occasionally, he will talk with Kent. It wasn't until today that he seemed to exhibit any kind of intelligence at all. This came up in a discussion of the concept, "monastery." He seemed to have a fair amount of information related to monks, priests, and the Catholic religion. Geoffrey has no special interaction with him. There is no banter between him and Ben or occasions for discipline. While I don't have access to Geoffrey's gradebook, my guess is that he gets a fair percentage of his homework in. Only on the regular, around-the-room recitations does one get any impression of Ben's classroom and academic ability. In the ability to identify subjects and verbs in sentences, he's not strong. He has little facility with arithmetic processes. The nature of his reading skills is not clear; I would guess that he reads haltingly

Kent presents a picture very similar to Ben's in class. He takes very little part in the ongoing classroom interplay and banter. Occasionally he and Ben seem to buddy-up as I indicated above. Once or twice on the playground I've seen him a bit more active, but the basic impression I have of him is that while he is not as tall and gangly as Ben, he is also awkward and seems to have an extra-short torso. In class he works along quietly and is not engaged in any kind of disciplinary problem as far as I can recall. He, like Ben and several others, is just there.

A Reject

In some discussions of classroom social structure a sentiment hierarchy—a social rank ranging from high acceptance through neutrality to rejection—is postulated. Mr. Geoffrey's class seemed more describable in terms of belief systems, roles, and interactive subgroups and cliques. As we have noted, some of the children interacted infrequently with Geoffrey and infrequently with the other children; we categorized them as isolates. Several children, and especially Irma, showed high interaction rates with Geoffrey, individually, and in class participation, but minimal amounts with the other children. However, the negative sentiment of the class members toward Irma, which we have called rejection, is the critical aspect of her part of the social structure. The summary statement in the notes contains several observations and interpretations:

> Irma strikes the observer as a vivid example of a preneurotic individual. While she is not an intellectually dull child, at least in reference to this group, there are areas of her behavior that reflect what Dollard and Miller have commented upon as "pockets of stupidity." The best illustration of this is the field notes record of Irma's inability to accept the fact that Canada and Mexico are not part of the United States.[12] She also illustrates the very real and acute problem of a child "earning" her reputation and her social status. The kids view her as kind of an "odd ball." For instance, Oliver's comments, both verbally and metaphorically, indicate that she is different or "nuts." Her social status is indicated by the fact that few of the children interact much with her and most of them systematically either avoid her or "talk right past her." The best illustration of the latter is Oliver and Pete carrying on a conversation right in front of her. She sits between them, and neither one of them seems to know that she is alive. Her relationship to Geoffrey is that of almost complete and utter dependence. As a seventh-grade girl this is very noticeable; she is always up front, asking him "some stupid question." In Geoffrey's words she "drives him batty." I keep wanting to posit an anxiety and conflict hypothesis underlying much of her behavior. Academically her performance on many aspects of the school program is quite good for this class. She often will score well on the spelling tests and on the daily boardwork. (9/24)

In Figure 3.8 we try to view more generically the vicious circle problem that seems to be a special case of the self-fulfilling prophecy: a child

---

[12] This episode was a dramatic several-day encounter in which Geoffrey, the observer, and several of the children were involved in attempts to convince her that Canada and Mexico were not a part of the United States. Some of the details are reported in Chapter Seven.

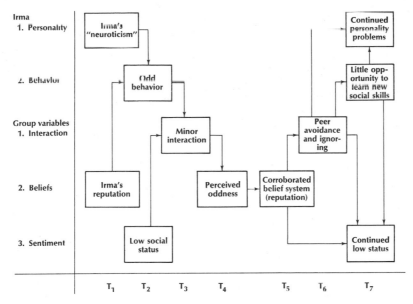

Figure 3.8 A process conception of Irma being caught in a vicious circle and "earning" her status.

has a particular reputation; she acts and interacts in accord with it; and she thereby corroborates the impression. The process locks her in place in the social equilibrium or structure. In her case, it seems critical to note, to hypothesize, a series of personality processes that are "beyond her control" or "neurotically stupid" that indicate an inability to alter her behavior in socially significant ways. As we observed—and interacted with her—this didn't seem to be a simple perceptual difficulty, nor a conceptual problem, for she was intellectually able for this group.

Conclusion: Changing Seating Arrangements

Whenever a social system changes—or is changed—much of the structure and dynamics becomes clear. In this instance the field notes from the day Geoffrey changed the seating arrangement summarize some aspects of the initial equilibrium that had been achieved. We cite the summary observations and interpretations in some detail to conclude the analysis.

> Yesterday, Geoffrey moved the children's seats for the first time since the first day. This 15 or 20 minute interlude, before history, sparkled with fun. The banter and rapport made it difficult to stay in the role of observer. I found myself a vicarious participant. While the students were doing the beginnings of the homework assignment, Geoffrey drew a five-column five-row chart on the front board, alternating the letters B,G,B,G, and so forth. The pupils soon knew what was to happen. The

buzzing began from child to child and seat to seat. Groans intermixed
with laughter and physical movement. Sam engaged in a running commentary indicating that the girls would bother him and keep him from
doing his homework, that Edwin wouldn't have anybody to help him,
and generally indicating how his world was coming to an end. Sarah
inquired, "Do I have to? and Geoffrey quietly replied, "No you don't;
in my class you always have a choice. You can do it or you can leave
the room." She moved over. It might be observed that she gradually is
becoming a full-fledged member of the group. She transferred into the
district this fall and is slowly being acclimated or socialized. Up to
this point, her only major contributions have been, first, as an excellent
student, generally the one with the right answers, and, second, as an
assignment monitor. Only at one other time has she bantered person-
to-person with Geoffrey. (I can't recall the specific details. She may
have been involved in loaning her paper to someone to permit him to
copy the answers. To the outside observer her comments made her
stand out as an individual in her own right who was now a full-fledged
member of the class.) Edwin was quite unhappy about his move, for he
and Helen have become fast friends.

Because there is an extra girl in the room, Geoffrey decided to have
one of the girls next to his desk. He asked if there were any volunteers.
All the girls volunteered. This was done dramatically by asking each of
the girls who might be interested to write her name on the front board.
One by one, and with considerable drama, they all marched up to the
front. Dick started to make a mockery of part of this by walking up also.
Several of the girls got a chuckle out of that. Geoffrey was then faced
with the problem of how to choose one of the girls. He had each of
them write her name on a piece of paper and he, Geoffrey, began to
look for a hat from which to draw the winning name. He prowled around
the classroom and the cloakroom, then inquired of the children whether
any of the men teachers had worn hats that day. He made quite a todo
about the incident. Finally he found a library card box, emptied out
the cards, and put the names in. Next came the basic problem of who
would pick the name out of the box. Many kids were vying for this
honor. As this was developing, Sandy, in a loud and clear voice, suggested, "Let Mr. Smith do it." Her suggestion proved to be eminently
satisfactory to all the class. Geoffrey brought the box around to my
side of the room and with a chuckle in his voice he commented in an
undertone, "If you draw Irma I'll shoot you." With as much TV-show
drama as I could muster I read off "Patty." She was quite pleased. The
history lesson began shortly after this. Oliver volunteered and was
elected to write the names in the checkerboard on the front board.
This he did with a flourish. Flourish in the sense of creating a mild
disturbance through most of it. He had difficulty spelling some of the
names. Thelma, who remained seated up in the front of the room,
would whisper help to him, accompanied by an occasional comment
from Geoffrey that if Oliver couldn't do it he would get someone who
could; Thelma wasn't supposed to be helping him. Unfortunately I was
not in the room during the afternoon to catch the initial by-play concerning the change. This should be filled in later by conversational notes,
from Geoffrey.

I did have a few moments to talk with Geoffrey during lunch about the shift in the room. This shift had come as a surprise to me, although I had a good idea that one was coming sometime in the next week or so. Apparently the level and quantity of interaction helped precipitate the move at this particular time. Pete and Billy were beginning to talk together too much. Billy seemed to be catching some of Pete's "no need to do any kind of work" attitude and point of view. Billy is a "good kid" even though quite a dull boy. Edwin and Helen were more interested in each other than they were in their outside reading and book reports and other lessons. Sam and Oliver and Jimmie also were becoming comfortable with each other. Sandy's clique of Thelma, Eileen, Molly, are constantly interchanging glances, sighs, answers, and nods. Allison also was in the middle of things with Edwin and Helen. The change is not permanent, for Geoffrey commented, "As some of you who know me realize, this isn't forever or for even a semester, only for a while. For you who want to get changed back, the best way to bring that about is to quietly do your own work and show me that I can trust you." (9/18)

THE STRUCTURE OF ACTIVITIES

In the beginning of school the teacher has many problems. From the organization's perspective the key directive for the teacher concerns the establishment of the activity structure. As we have understood sociologists such as Homans (1950), an important part of the social structure of a group is the activity of the group, the transactions of the group with the physical facilities and environment. In the classroom, and Geoffrey's class is no exception, it is the "work" to be done. A major and often neglected part of classroom social-system analysis is the structure of activities. Activity is one of our basic dimensions. As we watched Mr. Geoffrey's class, we found that the children did a "variety of things" and this variety had special patterns. In the words of the teachers and the children, they studied a number of subjects. This simple taxonomy of the curricular areas, reading, writing, arithmetic, and so forth, represents the public schools' attempt to order the "structure of knowledge" that has been accumulated in Western Civilization and to which the growing child must be socialized. In Big City, the school says there are eight of these areas for the seventh-grade teacher and their varying importance requires a set distribution of time.

The organization's official form for activity structure is the "teacher's program." Directions are explicit for each of the three parts of the form. In Part *A* the teacher is instructed to:

> Give the curricular area or subject studied in each period. Show your full school day including recess.[13]

The several columns require the teacher, as we have indicated in Figure

---

[13]These quotes and the following are from the official record forms used by Geoffrey.

Time of day	Length of period	M	T	W	T	F
8:30-8:35	5	⊢————————— Organization ————————⊣				
8:35-9:30	55	⊢————————— Reading ————————⊣ Language				
9:30-10:15	45	Gym	Science	Gym	Science	Social Studies
10:15-10:30	15	⊢————————— Recess ————————⊣				
10:30-10:35	5	⊢————————— Organization ————————⊣				
10:35-11:15	40	⊢————————— Language ————————⊣				
11:15-12:00	45	⊢———————Social Studies ————————⊣				
1:00-1:05	5	⊢————————— Organization ————————⊣				
1:05-2:00	55	⊢————————— Arithmetic ————————⊣				
2:00-2:30	30	⊢——————— Spelling and Writing ————————⊣				
2:30-3:30	60	Music	Art	Music	Art	Health

Figure 3.9   Copy of Mr. Geoffrey's teaching program as filed in the permanent records.

3.9, to indicate time of day, length of period, and subject taught each day of the week.

In Part *B*, the directions read:

> Summarize under the proper area the approximate number of minutes per week devoted to each area as shown in Part *A* of the program. Total each curricular area.

Geoffrey did this. The areas include fine arts (composed of music and art), language arts (which includes reading, language, spelling, and writing), mathematics, social studies, science, physical well-being (including recess and physical education), practical arts (not given in the fall in the seventh grade) and organization. The latter are those minutes at the beginning of each day in the morning and just after recess and lunch when "chores" are to be done.

The final part of the form, Part *C*, operates by implication and assumption. Its directions are:

> Copy the time allotment for each area from the *Superintendent's Circular* or from the *Handbook for Beginning Teachers and Substitutes.*

Geoffrey did this. The form included: fine arts, 180 (minutes); language arts, 520; mathematics, 240; social studies, 300; science, 90; physical well-being, 260; practical arts, 110; and organization, 100.

Interpretively we are saying several things at this point. First, a major part of classroom structure has its origins in the organization's primary purpose—fostering academic learning. Second, some degree of goal displacement occurs with the emphasis on the time allotments teachers spend in each category of activities. The system does test, at regular intervals, the achievement of pupils, but these results are "confounded" by pupil abilities and social-class factors that vary significantly across the city. Third, the implication exists in Part *C* that the teacher's program should be similar to the time allotments in the *Superintendent's Circular.* Fourth, the actual time of various activities varied markedly from the program as filed. For the moment, we would note that the pupils seldom were in the class before 8:37 in the morning and it was almost always 8:45 or later before attendance and lunch money collections had been completed. Also, as we shall indicate further, organizational problems arose all semester. Later we will examine in considerably more detail variations that exist in the heavy 3 R's orientation, especially in language arts, which go far beyond the stated time allotments. Fifth, the teacher has freedom to arrange these areas into the day and week as he desires. It should be noted that his options do not include the time of the year—in the sense of doing the year's work in arithmetic in the fall and all the language arts in the spring. Similarly, limits exist in the degree to which the pupils have a voice in what activities are to be studied. Sixth, within the activity a large number of options exist in the sequence one might use in the presentation or the discovering of

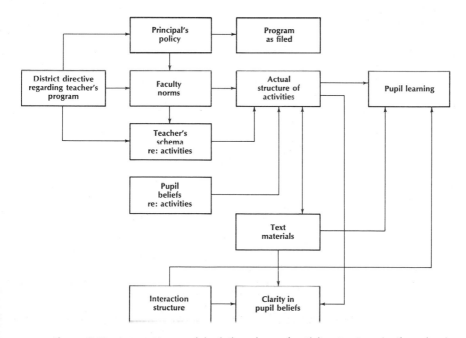

Figure 3.10   A tentative model of the place of activity structure in the school.

the accumulated knowledge. In the Washington School generally, and in Mr. Geoffrey's case in particular, this part of the sequence was determined by the authors of the texts. In effect, Mr. Geoffrey and the children moved through the texts page by page and, usually, problem by problem. Presumably this is one set of meanings to such phrases as "textbook-oriented curriculum," "systematic teaching," "traditional teaching," and so forth. Insofar as the text authors can clearly see their domain, this puts meaning into the activities. Insofar as one follows regularly through the text, this puts a procedural clarity into the activities. Pupils know what to expect. Most teachers at the Washington School believe that this is especially important for children with limited ability, with limited auxillary skills (for instance, use of reference materials and related reading techniques), with limited motivation, and with limited self-control, all of which are alleged to be part of the syndrome of cultural deprivation. These implications are sketched in Figure 3.10.

In short, as the semester began, one of Geoffrey's responsibilities involved the establishment of the activity structure. We might well have phrased this as an important initial teacher role. As our discussion in Chapter Two has indicated, the first few days contain Geoffrey's gambits into the several curricular areas. Prior experience "in school," as well as in the Washington School per se, has long since developed pupil-beliefs and norms regarding the activities to be undertaken. The only novelty resides in Geoffrey's idiosyncratic ways of structuring the activities. As we have indicated, the central office directives and the faculty norms to which he was sensitive made his choices reasonably uniform.

C H A P T E R F O U R

RECONCEPTUALIZING TEACHING

A serious discontinuity exists within educational psychology. The language of learning theory—Hull, Mowrer, Skinner, or other behaviorists—used to analyze the behavior of children cannot easily be used by the teacher to analyze and alter his own behavior. As we see it, the problem focuses on the pupil as an object, a complex of operant and respondent behavior controlled by the environment, a part of which is the teacher. The child's "rationality" and autonomy are minimized as the program and the reinforcing contingencies are accented. The teacher, however, usually is implored to be rational, to plan carefully, to meet the child's needs, and so forth, as though the locus of control lay within himself. The teacher who thinks about his own behavior as a series of operants has difficulty in synthesizing these positions. We believe the issue lies fundamentally in the heart of contemporary social science theory, and we do not propose anything like a basic solution. Rather, we are going to present a way of talking about teaching that has seemed "comfortable" to us at this fundamental level. It has provided a congruence between the experience of observing and participating in teaching and the language available for describing teaching. As we meet the traditional problem areas of educational psychology we will try to rephrase them from this point of view.

DECISION-MAKING:
THE METATHEORY OF TEACHING

Researchers who use the nonparticipant-observer methodology relate insightful experiences when the thesis, which lurks in their data, sharply comes into focus. Insight phenomena have a flashing, startling, and exciting quality to the perceiver, even though they may be slowly shaping to the outsider. To us, a major result in this investigation is the hypothesis that the teacher can be viewed from the model of decision-maker.

As we looked to more general theory on decision-making, we found discussions of fact-and-value propositions, rationality, alternative, subjective probability, consequence, effectiveness, and so forth. Teaching often involves doing or not doing something such as tossing or not tossing a chalkboard eraser to a child as a dramatic illustration of a direct object in language. "Choice behavior" is part of the decision-maker's conceptual repertory. It is also part of the teacher's schema. Lying behind such a choice are the teacher's objectives in language arts for the morning. Objectives are goals and values to the decision-maker. The teacher suspects that such action on his part will startle a few children, provide a concrete illustration of an important concept, and will give him a chance to compliment lightly or tease gently one of the boys for his skill or lack thereof. The decision-maker, conceptually, refers to these suspicions as subjective probabilities. The several events that might occur are, to the theorist, consequences. Later, when the children report such an incident to their friends, within earshot of another teacher, other events may occur that the sociologists call latent and unanticipated consequences.

In addition to throwing or not throwing an eraser, the teacher also may dramatically snap a new Board of Education pencil into pieces, call a child up front and rap him lightly on the head with a flourish, or he may draw humorous stick-figure cartoons on the board. In the theorist's terms, any one of these are alternatives. They, too, have consequences. The consequences have several probabilities as seen by the teacher, and we might phrase his behavior as "subjectively rational." Theorists might attack this illustration analytically with concepts such as *objectively* rational, *organizationally* rational, and so forth.

The observer watched Mr. Geoffrey toss his eraser and break his pen-

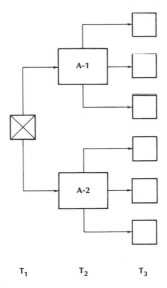

T_1 T_2 T_3

Figure 4.1 An adaptation of a 1953 Bross decision tree.

cil. He talked with him later about the reasons for his actions. We became enthused about this discovery of teaching as decision-making. A number of subproblems began to fall into place.

The Prediction System

Schematically, a cogent analysis of decision-making has been made by Bross (1953). He suggests a model involving a prediction system and a value system. Very simply, in his diagrams the prediction-system choices lead to alternatives, and alternatives to consequences. The consequences have varying probabilities. Although his diagrams do not indicate them, arrows should run from Alternative *A-1* to the Consequences following from *A-2*, and vice versa. The probabilities may be close to zero but they should be indicated.

In addition, his figure should be elaborated to account for latent and unanticipated as well as manifest consequences.[1] Throughout the account in the description of the development of the classroom, alternatives arose which seemed plausible to the observer. On occasion, as these were suggested to Mr. Geoffrey, he would react with an intuitive feeling that this would not be appropriate. As we talked, he would elaborate a variety of consequences that the observer had only partially anticipated. An illustration of this occurred

[1] In another project, *Social Psychological Aspects of School Building Design,* (Smith and Keith, 1967) we made an intensive analysis of this conception.

early in the semester with the concept of "pacing" and the slow speed with which the children were introduced to academic content. The notes capture his reaction:

> His statement concerned earlier experience in which he tried to rush the children (and rush probably would be defined as moving them along faster than they would want to be moved by themselves). Moving more rapidly, in his experience, has often resulted in not getting very much farther in the long run, and at the same time, frustrating everyone, the children and himself, and creating, as a consequence, several emotional problems in the group.

The Conception of the Ideal as an Approach to the Value System

As we have elaborated, decision-making involves what we have called, after Bross, the prediction system and the value system. The latter presented us with a number of difficulties. In most situations requiring a decision it is impossible to: (1) determine the desirability of each alternative, (2) compare these desirabilities and undesirabilities and combine them into a meaningful summary. Among the many reasons for this, the lack of scales with common meaningful zero points and units is among the most important. In wrestling with this problem, analyzing our own decisions, and attempting to order our data, we have found that a model involving a "conception of the ideal" makes a more satisfactory point of departure.

In the vernacular this might be phrased, "If you had your druthers how would you like things to be?" or "What do you see as the optimal equilibrium?" or "What is the best of all possible worlds?" Such a statement implies the following as a minimum:

1. An assessment of the desirable elements.
2. A pattern including an ordering of the elements surrounding their importance.
3. One man's optimal pattern is not another's; that is, it is subjective.
4. The pattern of one system, for example one's job, must be articulated ultimately with other systems, family, "self" as a person, and so forth.
5. The ideal may change momentarily or over long periods of time.
6. The system may be congruent or in conflict with systems of other individuals, groups, or institutions.

In essence, this involves a careful elaboration of an individual's goals. As value premises these are statements of wishes and desires. The ultimate goal, whether it is a well-considered philosophy of life, religious position, or ethical social-political framework, is a statement of first principles, which, because they are first principles, by definition are not derivable from other propositions. Classroom goals and conceptions of the ideal must necessarily fit into this and relate to it with varying degrees of probability. Classroom ideals must also effect a compromise among personal, group, organizational, and community positions.

Combining the Prediction and the Value Systems

In one sense, decision-making involves a very simple judgment as to whether the prediction system surrounding one alternative or chain of alternatives corresponds more closely to the ideal conception than does the prediction system following the selection of another alternative. Obviously, decisions are not that easy.

For example, Mr. Geoffrey had to decide, after a month of school, which children would be sent to the next teacher and which children would remain with him. As he later commented on the decision, the prediction and value elements stand out rather dramatically:

> I decided to send to her the group I had received at the beginning of the year—mostly repeats from Rooms 13 and 14 and new students who had come in. I kept the other natural group—those who had come to me from Room 16. I did this because the group I sent her was older than the Room 16 group, and I felt the seventh-grade group would fit better with the sixth graders than would the other group. . . . the numbers were okay per the instructions from the office. . . . I was sensitive to what had happened the previous year. I chose the simplest way administratively and one which I thought she would have the least complaint about.

And in regard to the complications arising from the fact that several groups of siblings were involved:

> Some of these kids had been together anyway. Since I made the decision by groups I saw no particular reason to make any exceptions. . . . After all, I had both Allison and Edwin together anyway, and she (another teacher) had had both Patty and Rose together. All-in-all, again, I took the simplest way to a decision—by the groups in which the children came to me.

Strategically, we would hypothesize that the process proceeds more effectively when one frames his ideal or value system *first*. By asking for an organized statement of ends, conditioned by the time, place, and circumstances in which decisions must be made, one introduces what is usually called flexibility and rationality. Then, as soon as alternatives are raised at any choice point, one can compute probabilities of an alternative aiding the attainment of a goal or subgoal. One of our next research steps will attempt to verify hypotheses in teacher-attempts to combine prediction and value systems.

Operationalizing the Decision-making Model

The decision-making model has tremendous possibilities in linking conceptually such diverse influences on the classroom as the formal curriculum guides, the faculty peer-group beliefs and norms, and the composition of the class itself, be it lower socioeconomic scale as in Mr. Geoffrey's case or in a class in general, and treating teaching functionally rather than just structurally. To make the conceptual models viable, operational techniques become mandatory. For a long period of time we had considerable difficulty in thinking through concrete ways in which we could implement the model in field research with ongoing classes. While our discovery, if it be that, sounds simple as hindsight, the process of arrival was slow and difficult. The lead we see here combines several elements: First, one must establish several "natural" units in teaching—the lesson, the day, the week, the unit or the semester. It is our belief that the unit will vary with a number of conditions: for instance, Mr. Geoffrey's spelling program had basically a weekly rhythm within which there were also daily regularities. The independent reading, library books, and book reports had a semester unit as the rhythm.

If we select a single lesson in a subject such as geography we can illustrate further. The model requires that the teacher be quizzed via questionnaires or interviews concerning his goals (the value system) and the means (the prediction system) for reaching the goals in the geography lesson. An alternative, which has the beauty of objectivity and ease of access, is to make the age-old "lesson plan" into a functioning research tool.[2] In Mr. Geoffrey's case, as with many experienced teachers, the lesson plans in geography lay in his head, in the text, and in assignments registered in his plan book, which all teachers were supposed to keep up to date.

After selecting the unit and obtaining quantifiable statements of plans and intentions, the third step, careful observation of the lesson—with a move toward reliable quantifiable schedules—would then occur. Fourth, post lesson interviews or questionnaires concerning altered goals and means and cues that suggested to the teacher the need for alterations could be obtained. As a number of teachers in varying situations are studied, verifiable principles should be generated.

Such a mode of research would allow comparisons between school and teacher goals, would begin to clarify our concept of functional equivalents, would move away from an overall "good-bad" assessment in favor of more situationally expressed aims and procedures. It would capture more of the ebb and flow of teaching which many of our analyses have missed up to

[2] Incidentally, the research literature on lesson plans is almost barren. This also provides possible articulation with the volume by Miller, and others, *Plans and the Structure of Behavior*. New York: Holt, Rinehart and Winston, Inc., 1960.

this time as we have focused on what the teacher does independent of his thought processes, and analyses of what he thinks, independent of what he actually does. Such research also provides a means of attacking the problems of inservice education and altering teaching in mutually desirable directions.

Additional Implications

With the model in hand, we began to see a number of additional implications in difficult problems. We entitled these: legitimizing the "What do I do?" question, the best of a bad situation, congruence with teacher schema, model of the teacher training product, and treating children as decision-makers.

The What-do-I-do? question   By legitimizing the "What do I do?" question we mean that for many years, in our experience, teachers have been asking the question, "What do I do with this child, this situation, or this problem?" For as many years, in our experience, psychologists and teacher-educators have parried the question by remarking "It's impossible to respond to such a question; answers aren't that simple." The teachers complain to their colleagues about unhelpful experts. The psychologists and teacher-educators talk to their colleagues about the teachers wanting "something practical," "wanting a push-button psychology," or "wanting recipes."[3] The hypothesis we would offer is that the decision-making model legitimizes the teacher's question. By this we mean, there is basic psychological theory where such a question is not heresy, but in its more abstract form, it holds a central position. For instance, in a literature lesson, what goals do I have? What are the specific ways I can present this material? What probabilities of success exist for changed attitudes? for increased information? for improved reading skills? A research-supported theory of teaching will indicate the probabilities of these relationships.

The Best of a Bad Situation   The best of a bad situation suggests another group of difficult problems faced by the teacher. For example, Mr. Geoffrey was faced with the dilemma of giving or not giving homework assignments. Part of his thinking was predicated on such propositions as (1) These children are academically behind for their age and grade. (2) Additional work beyond class time is necessary to maintain progress as well as to cancel the increasing discrepancy. (3) The kids are apathetic and will do little homework. (4) The parents are disinterested in school and will not support the teacher's efforts. (5) Assignments which are made but not carried out will weaken the teacher's power and control in future situations. As we talked about such complexities in assignment

---

[3] One of the major exceptions to the shying-away tendency has occurred in the efforts of Fritz Redl and his colleagues, especially *The Aggressive Child* (1957).

making, Mr. Geoffrey would ask, with a twinkle in his eye, what would the *good teacher* do in this instance. The decision-model point of view suggests that each alternative or pattern of alternatives has outcomes scalable in desirability as well as probability. On occasion the range is from low- or moderately-undesirable to extremely undesirable. The solution rests in picking an alternative which, while not desirable in some absolute sense, is relatively more desirable than other alternatives. In the teacher's terms, you "make the best of a bad situation." Such an analysis fosters rationality, suggests pertinent research problems, and lessens the load of guilt carried by the teacher. Obviously one must guard against restriction in alternatives considered and rationalization in logical analysis.

Congruence with Teacher Schema   Congruence with teacher schema concerns the consequence of making the model conscious and explicit. When this concept was first raised with Mr. Geoffrey he was skeptical. He found Simon's *Administrative Theory* book not especially exciting. As we introduced appropriate content this skepticism moderated. If it can be established that teachers implicitly operate within this framework then we may have an important vehicle for moving from the "real world" to one we might call, on some grounds, more ideal. Specifically, we are thinking here of long, involved discussions that we have had with students who reject Skinner's image of man as it is presented in *Walden II* and *Science of Human Behavior,* and who have difficulty thinking of classroom problems in behavioristic terms. In November, the observer's notes reflect the early struggle with this point:

> This point now just seems to have arisen of late. It ties in with Wirth's "images of man"[4] concept and it ties in with my own floundering for a conception of human behavior that's appropriate for the elementary school teacher. The model that keeps getting reiterated in the discussions of the teachers and the discussions of the pupils and the threats and warnings, the pleading, the arguing, is almost universally a responsibility model. In effect, it goes something like this: You as pupil are responsible for your own behavior, for getting your lessons, for getting to school, for doing the homework, and so forth. When you don't do these things, then you are liable to certain kinds of consequences that follow directly from not doing these things. You should be able to perceive these consequences, you should be able to plan for them, you should be able to alter your own behavior to handle the contingencies as they arise. This model seems to pervade everything that goes on in the schools. It is the kind of model that the Skinnerian approach has put into considerable doubt.   (11/5)

[4] This reference is to Professor Arthur Wirth's general concern with the varying conceptions of human nature, the images of man, underlying different approaches to educational theory and practice.

If the shifts one is trying to make do not demand reorganization of the basic dimensions of teachers' conceptual systems, the probability for alteration and innovation should be higher. This hypothesis needs evidence.

The Product of Teacher Education   The model provides, for us, a clearer image of the product of a teacher education program and suggests some experiences, role playing, simulation, and successive approximation in classroom behavior, as vital but not currently prevalent. We are planning currently to build situations and problems from our data and present these in our teacher training program. We hope this will have a number of affective as well as cognitive effects upon our undergraduates in the preservice program.

The Child as Decision-maker   Another implication upon which we are working is this—in some contexts Mr. Geoffrey treated the children as decision-makers. He acted with them, both verbally and nonverbally, as if they had choices, for instance, to attend or not attend, to behave or not behave, to do their work or not. They were held responsible, accountable for their actions. He indicated the consequences that followed such choices on their part and which consequences he had control over—that is, which were alternatives in his own repertory. For purposes of the present discussion, we would hypothesize that the conception of the child as a decision maker is a different conception from the child as a product of operant and respondent conditioning. We state this a bit hesitantly for we recently finished an educational psychology text in which we take, in part, a strong Skinnerian bias (Smith and Hudgins, 1964). Also, we are hesitant in that we have not pushed, as yet, the comparison at any length or depth. On the positive side, it helps us integrate two aspects of the counseling and mental hygiene literature. Ralph Ojemann's (1958) "causality training" and E. G. Williamson's (1950) "clinical counseling" attempt to make clients more rational seem closely aligned with the decision-making point of view. Mental health problems, we have argued, are an important dimension of the reality of cultural deprivation in the classroom. Insofar as these psychological positions can be integrated conceptually, they can be drawn upon for help.

Conclusion: Situational Thinking, Process, and the Larger Structure

As we have sketched the prediction system and the value system, we have implied another set of considerations in decision-making. These include situational thinking, process over time, and the larger structure. By larger structure we mean the context in which the problem resides. As we have described Mr. Geoffrey's thinking about the children who would be sent to the next room, the context includes the teacher who would receive the pupils, the formal regulations, the informal staff and pupil norms, repercussions on the children, and so forth. In effect, we are asking for many of the items that would make more specific, complex, and elaborate the prediction and value systems. The benefits of a general theory of teaching arise here, for the necessary aspects and dimensions would be included, tentatively at least, in the general theory.

The concept of situational thinking accents the momentarily important aspects in time and space. For instance, Mr. Geoffrey and one of his colleagues postponed some cooperative teaching plans in arithmetic and geography because they did not want to add another problem to the burden the Principal carried at the moment, for he was busy with a variety of difficult and time-consuming issues. Also, they discussed, in terms of who had made the most demands recently, which of them would broach the subject. While this was cloaked in humor and repartee, it did not veil the intuitive understanding each had for the way the system worked.

Finally, the model stresses a time dimension, and consequently accents processes as well as structure. Each decision rests upon a past and has implications for the future. Related to this aspect of the process is the further notion that forces outside the teacher's immediate control influence the system and, as time moves on, the situation will be different and must be reanalyzed.

ISSUES OF SUBSTANCE: THE BEHAVIOR OF TEACHING

Introduction

Our metatheoretical considerations have been cloaked in the garments of decision-making. This point of view has enabled us to step back and to look at teaching from a perspective of more general social science theory. For us, a second major gain rests in a viewpoint which is more all encompassing than some current models or theories of teaching. Teaching must be seen as an intellectual, cognitive process. What goes on in the head of the teacher is a critical antecedent of what he does. The way he poses his problems, the kinds of goals and subgoals he is trying to reach, the alternatives he weighs as he circumvents obstacles and barriers, the momentary assessment of potential rewards and costs are aspects of teaching which frequently are lost to the behaviorally oriented empiricist who focuses on what the teacher does, to the exclusion of how he thinks about teaching.

What the teacher does, while only a part of a general psychology of teaching, is a very significant part. We would not want to underestimate it; consequently, while it has been helpful to us to have beginnings of clarity in the general language structure utilized in teaching, the "practical teacher" wants the metalanguage cloaked in the day-to-day problems of teaching, the flesh and blood as it were, rather than just the skeleton or the ideas. In this section we present basic concepts and principles from a developing theory. In effect, they become issues and alternatives in the middle of teaching decisions.

When one has a number of concepts at approximately the same level of abstraction, a press develops to group them in hierarchial fashion. Unfortunately, discourse must proceed in serial fashion and some concepts must be introduced before they can be fully defined. Tentatively, we find that the situation and preparation for contingencies have a contextual flavor. By stressing a distinction between the child's behavior in the classroom and his life outside, in the family and the community, Geoffrey was providing a context in which he could work, a discrimination of areas under his control and into which he would introduce relevant influences. Similarly, his behavior, characterized as preparation for contingencies, indicates classical barriers toward goals which he has anticipated and for which he has tentative solutions.

The concepts: awareness, provisional try, ringmastership, continuity, sequential smoothness, pacing, teaching in motion, and shaping all contain ways of looking at the teaching art in process.

At any given moment in the process of teaching, the teacher presents cues to the children which indicate he is aware of the latent meaning of events outside the give-and-take of recitation. In the vernacular, he knows what is going on. Our analysis suggests that this is an important dimension of teaching. Our process conception suggests also that the tentativeness in teaching gambits, the provisional try, is a dimension of teacher behavior requiring further analysis. The oft mentioned analogy that the elementary school classroom is a "three-ring circus" found concrete substance in our data and led us to the dimension we have called ringmastership, the handling of multiple simultaneous facets of the classroom system. The ability to do this without overloading the teacher's capability for adaptation seemed a potent issue in teaching. Continuity seems almost a variant of ringmastership and refers to the degree to which the teacher relates the present events with those that have gone before and those which are likely to follow. Our analysis suggests that this has important, and possibly independent, components of an ideational as well as a social sort. Sequential smoothness, the easy flow of event upon event, and pacing, the number of events per unit of time, add further specification to a broad model of teaching. Teaching in motion, the moving about the room, can foster awareness and perceptions of minimal cues necessary for shaping, or altering, pupil behavior in minimal steps toward significant goals.

Finally, autonomy, skirmishing, banter, and getting-off-the-hook, lambs, tigers, and anger, and individualizing instruction—all these are imaginative methods that highlight the children and teachers as separate entities. When one represents quite different groups—adult versus children, middle class versus lower class, and so forth—a situation is posed which may have elements of incompatible goals and emotional antagonisms. By autonomy and aloofness we mean an independent way of behaving after solicitations for cooperation have failed momentarily. One does not plead, beg, or order. One assumes competence and resources for carrying on alone. Similarly, in verbal interchanges one skirmishes verbally, wages minor action in a manner which permits one's major efforts to remain free and operable. Banter, a humorous jousting, permits a number of potentially conflicting situations to be explored, debated, and resolved without committing either party, the teacher or class, or its representative, (Sam, for example) to a line of action it would not ultimately want. Getting-off-the-hook is a special form of interaction, a dodge which enables one to leave a situation which is rapidly becoming untenable. Geoffrey's ability to vary his behavior from lamblike gentleness and tigerlike ferocity also represents a less than real mechanism, an "as if" type of reaction that appeared in situations where one judiciously does not explore more completely and invade the privacy of the child or when one has grounds for real anger and "plays" it in mock fashion for other benefits. The degree to which a teacher individualizes and personalizes remains a major dimension in a theory of teaching.

As we describe the situations that provoked the concepts, we will keep returning to our common language and will also suggest possible operations that will move the reader to experimental and verificational research.

The Situation: A Distinction between "Here" and "Out There"

One of Mr. Geoffrey's distinctions, "here and out there," states a problem, a resolution, and a whole series of assumptions. Specifically the "here" refers to the classroom and the "out there" refers to the child outside the school, in the home and the community. The distinction was first noted by the observer in the context of language arts. Geoffrey, in trying to improve the verbal behavior of one of the pupils, commented that she should use the correct form of expression in class. He acknowledged that he did not have control of her behavior outside of class, and, in effect, she could do as she wanted there. The specific illustration seemed to raise a fundamental issue in teacher behavior. To explore further, the problem lies essentially in whether the classroom stress in language arts should be one which maintains a sharp distinction that it is to be applied in the classroom but not necessarily out of school. The other side of the argument states that transfer is the most important goal, learning is more meaningful when related, and learning is retained longer. Seldom do classroom-learn-

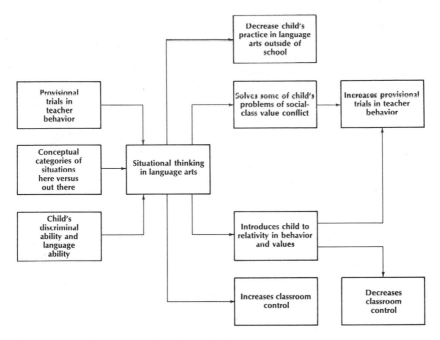

Figure 4.2 Implications of situational thinking.

ing theorists pose the problem as one of personal conflict for the child and the teacher.

One assumption seems to be that the motivational problem is paramount. The child "knows" the right answer but he won't practice it. A fair share of the truth of the matter seems to fall this way, especially regarding such terminology as "ain't," "them guys," and so forth. When the pupils are called on to change their errors they usually correct them readily. In more subtle discriminations the children seem not to "know." This problem becomes more complex as issues of motivation, relevance, and minimal practice and maintenance of skills become important.

A further alternative suggests a middle way. "Teach them that it depends on the situation" is an hypothesis that contains several implications. First, time must be spent developing a conception of language that is not an all-or-nothing, right-or-wrong way of doing things, but a flexible set of conventions applied differentially depending on the setting and purpose. This assumes, of course, that one has a conception of situations or settings that can be conceptualized, discriminated, and taught to the children. It assumes also that the children have the capacities to make these discriminations and to build relatively independent repertories or systems of language habits. The introduction of this kind of relativity into one area of behavior suggests the possibility that other areas are open for subtle discriminations.

When this extends into teacher-pupil relations and classroom control, the clear authority patterns also come open to question. If these are opened for discussion in an institution that draws and holds its members because of coercive legal reasons rather than self-motivation, an interesting phenomenon may develop. In the diagram (Figure 4.2) we are left with conflicting predictions—increasing versus decreasing classroom control—that need careful verificational investigation.

Finally, as we have suggested earlier, the conception of situational thinking is fundamental to our entire analysis of teacher behavior and teacher-pupil interaction. The behavior and the interaction always occur in a context, a situation; isolation of the behavior or the interaction can cause a gross error in the analysis of the process of teaching.

Preparation for Contingencies

While in this monograph we do not propose to analyze the concept of teacher experience, many items of the report seem to specify aspects of this concept. So it is with "preparation for contingencies," the mobilization of time, material resources, and activities to overcome barriers in working toward group goals. A specific illustration of the general point concerns the "safety pin" episode. Sometimes it is difficult to analyze the effects of being an upper elementary teacher, a male teacher, or a teacher of the culturally deprived. Early in the semester (9/8) Mr. Geoffrey discussed the need for safety pins and the problems of "girls who are always falling apart." Part of poverty means having old clothes with missing buttons or faulty clasps. If our inferences from giggles and hurried trips from the safety-pin drawer to the cloakroom are sound, blouses, skirts, and lingerie of lower class girls seem constructed of safety pins. Having one of the girls buy assorted-size safety pins brought benefits throughout the semester. The obvious results were: (1) active involvement of the girls—one volunteered to purchase the pins; (2) useful training in repaying obligations, for they had to replace each pin that was borrowed; and in terms of our general concept, (3) behavior that aided the group to continue functioning by overcoming hurdles that blocked paths to their goals.

If we tried to link this preparation-for-contingencies into more general relationships the model would contain such important concepts as frustration, reduced emotionality, altered perceptions of and sentiments toward the teacher, and reduced disciplinary problems. Additional relationships occur with important concepts introduced later in this chapter, for example, ringmastership and sequential smoothness.

A number of other aspects of Mr. Geoffrey's behavior can illustrate this point: (1) the keeping of careful records, (2) his classroom social structure (the monitor roles), (3) and the structure of activities (the spelling routine). The forerunners of this analysis were in the notes on the morning

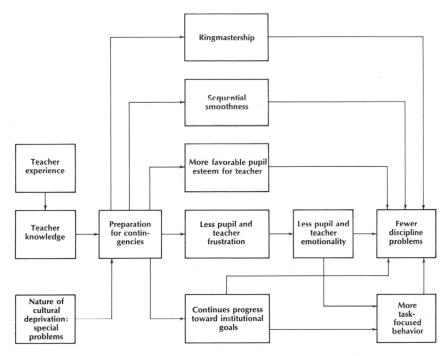

Figure 4.3 Hypotheses centering about the concept preparation for contingencies.

of September 10th. The children were studying spelling by writing sentences using the words when these episodes occurred:

9:12 "I'd like to have most of you finish up in the next 5 or 6 minutes. Check you." (LMS—Individual differences in speed of work handled very neatly by his lengthy earlier procedures of reading book assignments.)

9:13 "All right let's have some of you putting up answers on the board. Allison, Sam, let's just go down the row." Each goes up when the other has finished. Suggests to Allison to move to center board because some can't see. Keeps sequence moving. (LMS—Implicit in both of these comments is elegance in order and nonconflicting interaction. Really problem prevention: no clowning at board and in later protests of "I can't see" type. Suggests a whole line of analyses.) (9/10)

While the points are simple and mundane in one sense (that is, having continuing independent reading to which the children can return when they finish other study, sequencing movement to the board, and keeping all work easily visable), if the conceptualization is sound the implications are far-reaching for the smooth operation of the system.

We present one final illustration of contingency preparation:

10:37 Geoffrey interrupts to caution about book reports. Second one will be due before they all have given the first one. Runs through whole list of those with none. (LMS—This reminder, warning-type of comment, is frequent with him. Needs analysis as a supervisory technique. It activates Oliver for instance to ask for first opportunity today for his report. Identifies kids by name—in terms of personalizing.)

Awareness

On occasion, discussions wander, and as a consequence they provide the teacher with an opportunity to interact in ways he might not have in the formal give-and-take of recitation. Geoffrey has just been interrupted by three messengers; the notes pick up the next episode:

2:43 Back to insurance.[5] Explains (1) twenty-four hour coverage and (2) school hours. Wants parents to sign it, so he'll know they have seen it. Some questions. (LMS—Stupid ones?)[6] Banter back and forth. Several questions seem to reflect lack of understanding of insurance (get your money back). Mostly illegitimate. Talk in banter fashion about every other seat boy-girl. Teases Edwin. . . . "In some cases, where boys want to sit next to girls, certain girls, they won't get to." Geoffrey has difficulty restraining himself to just a grin. Allison has kind of an incredulous "How did he know about Edwin and Helen" look on her face. (LMS—All this is done in good humor—no real sense or threat on either side.)   (9/10)

The notes contain a prior entry at 2:35: "Edwin teases Helen by tapping her on the head with a pencil." While we have no record that Geoffrey saw this, a number of similar interactions were occurring.[7] The point we wish to make centers on Geoffrey's awareness of the Edwin-Helen "romance" and his ability to introduce it casually in the flow of classroom interaction. The conceptual implications are sketched in Figure 4.4.

In some instances, awareness or alertness occurs when the children try, as pleasant mischievousness, to fool the teacher. Susan is "caught" in such an episode early in the semester:

9:53 Billy collects dental cards. "Make sure each student gives you a card." Others start on language lesson. "Any I see talking I will assume want some more work. All I can hear when you whisper is 'Mr. Geoffrey I want some more work to do. Mr. Geoffrey I want some more work to do' . . . . Need an alphabetizer." Several hands up. "Need someone who hasn't done it." Several hands go down, although Susan's does not. "Susan, you have done some alphabetizing." Finally picks Helen. (LMS—Perhaps important: an illustration of Geoffrey's being on top of things.[8] Susan had responded with a sheepish grin (more grin than sheepish) and set about getting to work.)

[5] The school sells accident insurance.

[6] The observer's naïveté raises question as to who is stupid; later interaction suggests a difficult distinction between the children's lack of knowledge and delay tactics.

[7] This is another good illustration of the methodological issue surrounding the "Two Realities" and the implicit "Third Reality." See discussion in the appendix.

[8] Later work may well indicate the importance of discriminating (1) simple awareness, (2) communication of that knowledge to the group, and (3) acting upon one and two, e.g. "being on top of things."

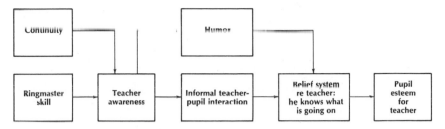

Figure 4.4   Relationship of teacher awareness to pupil sentiments and beliefs as well as its relationship to other aspects of teacher performance and teacher-pupil interactions.

The Provisional Try

Learning theorists, or at least one theorist (Hilgard, 1956), makes extended use of the concept "provisional try." Our conception of teaching as a decision-making process seems to demand such an approach. In essence, much of the teacher's behavior needs to be analyzed as a tentative gambit, a trial that becomes a premanent part of the structure only as it meets certain criteria such as "being interesting," "promoting learning," and so forth. A number of illustrations occurred in Geoffrey's room; for instance, seating arrangements were put in the context of "We'll try it for a while and see how it goes" and "You be the assignment monitor for now." Interestingly, little of the academic learning was construed this way.

The demands that this puts upon the teacher's schema and the group's belief system are interesting in their implications, for considerable fluidity is introduced. The teacher becomes much more of a probing, tentative, flexible—to use a current "good" word—kind of a person. This demands that style always be considered in terms of short-term as well as long-term objectives. This point seems exceedingly important. Conceptually it means that any act of the teacher or interaction of the teacher and pupils has the double reference, short- and long-term goals. It means also that different overt behavior may be interchangeable, that is, functionally equivalent.[9] The problems this poses for measurement and quantification are immense.

The kinds of children, as individuals and as groups, who not only tolerate but thrive on this have not been ascertained. Nor has the more interesting problem been analyzed: How does the teacher with a random aggregate of thirty children shape a pupil-belief system and the correlated interaction structure which must accompany it? Presumably, specifying the outcome will permit experimentation regarding the means. The implications for our general analysis are suggested in Figure 4.5.

---

[9]We borrow this concept from Merton (1957) and raise it in greater detail later in the chapter.

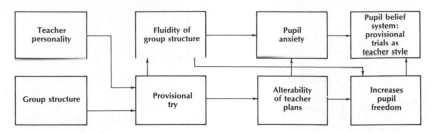

Figure 4.5 Implications of provisional trial in classroom social systems.

The Ringmaster: Multiple and Simultaneous Events in Teaching

In our discussion of "continuity" we suggest that teaching might have varying amounts of interconnectedness with what has gone before and with what will arise in the future. A related dimension we have called the "ringmaster phenomenon." Our intent is to suggest that teaching contains multiple facets occurring simultaneously and that teachers may vary in their awareness and ability to handle these simultaneously occurring strands. In viewing what is ostensibly a language arts lesson, the observer made the following notes:

9:28 "Take out language books. Have volunteers to board. When we run out of true volunteers then I'll select some volunteers on my own." (Billy, Allison, Edwin, Jimmie, and Sam). Allison picks up Edwin's error (both on problem 3). Geoffrey restates problems 2, 3, 4, 5, and 6. Clarifies and they go on. He moves about the room checking papers of those in seats. Usually no comment, an occasional one where there has been an error.

9:34 Billy finishing up. They start through numbers 2–6. Oliver raised a question about a left-out word. Geoffrey says, "We'll forgive him." Oliver jokes. Geoffrey, "The only stupid question is what? . . . The one you don't ask." Finishes No. 6 and corrects Sam strongly by saying firmly—"No tipping chairs. If they wanted them that way they'd put only two legs on." Next group of sentences put on board. Asks Lonny if he's volunteering or just stretching. When he comments that he's stretching Geoffrey goes on.

9:40 While they write, Geoffrey lines up coffee table errands with Edwin and Lucille. Other children watch those at board. A few listen to Geoffrey and a few talk in pairs.

The nature of this particular set of multiple and simultaneous strands demands a set of abilities on the teacher's part. Presumably this set of abilities can be operationally measured by ratings or judgments and presumably this set would influence diverse factors such as classroom effectiveness and efficiency. Figure 4.6 suggests these relationships.

A less complex illustration occurred during a study period on the afternoon of September 10:

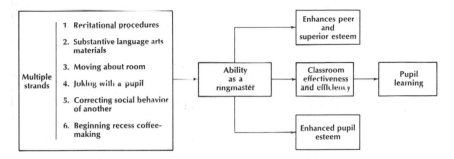

Figure 4.6   Clarification of "ringmaster phenomenon."

Everyone busy. Book reporting, Geoffrey shakes his head, "No," over Billy's report, while keeping eyes on the class.   (9/10)

Continuity

Continuity within social systems and learning has received stress in a number of sources. Mr. Geoffrey's classroom is impressive in this regard. References to past events and probable future events are the denotation of continuity. It seems essential for effectiveness in group functioning and for conceptual learning.

Several illustrations exemplify the phenomenon. In the afternoon of Friday, September 6, the term "compound" appeared in arithmetic. The teacher linked this with the earlier discussion of compound words that was the major topic in the week's spelling unit, thus providing for an extension of meaning that had not occurred in the morning. None of the twenty spelling words was a number word and none of the prefixes or suffixes in "Learning Your Words" referred to numbers. An observational schedule would have to cut across subject areas (spelling and mathematics) and across time (morning and afternoon) if it were to properly attend to the events.[10]

A second illustration occurred within the same Friday afternoon arithmetic lesson. As part of a series of interactions that had moved from banter-responses to social and emotional stimuli (the afternoon recess episode) to the restraining attempts (squelching Susan and Elma) Geoffrey had given Edwin a look for dropping a pencil just as he (Geoffrey) tried to make a point in the arithmetic lesson. Shortly thereafter, as he raised problem No. 1 on page 5, Edwin volunteered and Geoffrey called upon him.

Another illustration is enclosed from the notes of September 10:

1:55   Monitors get paper. Sandy changes assignment board. Geoffrey talks to Elma and Susan about giggling. Irma comes up for book report with

---

[10] Actually a carefully worded questionnaire or interview schedule might pick it up more economically and possibly more validly than direct observation.

only half of it read. . . . Geoffrey gets into mock exasperated argument about impossibility of reporting on half-read book. Calls Sam (loud and clear) to come up for report. (LMS—Earlier this morning Sam had been giving him a bad time about this. Note this as a methodological point regarding free observation in contrast to schedule, especially regarding process.) (9/10)

Perhaps the clearest episode of continuity occurred during a 25-minute arithmetic lesson as Geoffrey tried to teach the concept "approximate numbers." Sandy, among others, has been working and erring at the board on a series of textbook problems. She has been corrected by Lonny at Geoffrey's request, and now she is called upon again. The notes catch the flavor:

Geoffrey comes right back to Sandy who has a real haughty glare about her. Cardinal, ordinal, odd, even, exact, and approximate are reviewed and the class moves on to page 10, "round numbers." Several children volunteer and nonvolunteers are called upon. Sandy is one of the latter. "Sandy, when we count 70, 80, 90, what are we counting by . . . 88 taken to tens is 90?"

The notes continue:

Next item he goes to Susan and comes back to Sandy who now has the concept. (LMS—Beautifully done.) (9/9)

Shortly thereafter he goes into a briefer but similar routine with Allison.

Conceptually the points we would make depend upon the specific content of the continuity. In the case of the "compound words," the consequences should be increased meaningful learning through what might be called "integrative reconciliation."[11] In the instance involving social behavior the phenomenon seems to be a concrete instance of personal attention or "consideration."[12] We have included these hypotheses as Figure 4.7.

As we have indicated, continuity not only weaves an intellectual fabric, it also has impact on the social webbing of the classroom. Early in the semester, Edwin became infatuated with Helen. On Thursday, September 12, Geoffrey becomes involved at recess:

10:17 Bells. Girls up. Boys up.
Spent recess on duty in girls' yard.

Two principles: (1) on child hitting, Geoffrey asks the instigator "why," then gives both a look, and they go on. (2) Helen asks about someone in her desk. Apparently something written on her eraser. She has erased it now. Geoffrey comments to me, "Continual problem with dirty words. If they don't get excited about it I don't either."
10:40 Back from recess. Messengers out. Most kids working.
10:42 "Take out dictionaries please." (LMS—Continuous by-play between Edwin and Helen. He's having a tough time leaving her alone.) Starts lesson.

[11] See Ausubel (1963, p. 80).
[12] See Stogdill and Coons (1957).

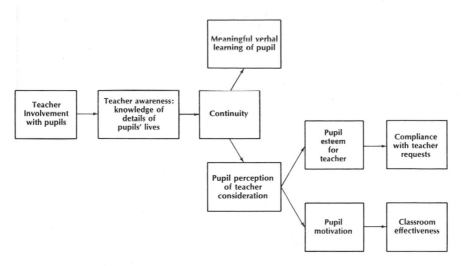

Figure 4.7   Relationship of continuity to the social system.

Reviews uses of dictionary. Meaning yesterday. Today spelling. Molly puts words up. Some correct, some incorrect.

10:51 Everyone still busy. Pete goes up to Geoffrey regarding what Geoffrey called a "Book bug. You find it in a book." Pete saunters back. Geoffrey brings Helen's note to show me (Figure 4.8); "Her head was hurting yesterday morning." Geoffrey comments that you get some idea of the problem. Comments to Sandy about being finished? And talking. (LMS— Problem of "education of masses in a democracy." What should goals be: literacy, take job, legal minimum on social behavior, responsibility for family?)

Geoffrey walks around room. Picks up Helen's oversized eraser and looks at it. Makes comment to her for Edwin's benefit. Then gives Edwin his "hard smile look" which says, "I know what's going on." Edwin verbalizes, "I didn't do nuttin'" with a guilty smile. Helen grins. Later their (Edwin and Helen's) byplay goes on.   (9/12)

While there is continuity in the several episodes of Helen's and Edwin's contact with Geoffrey, the continuity principle also has playground and home aspects to it. The verbatim note from Helen's mother (Figure 4.8) is included to extend the specificity to our example.

Sequential Smoothness

Artistry in teaching has many components, one of which we've called "sequential smoothness." Conceptually it seems to be a dimension of activities and interaction which is heavily under the control of the teacher. The class was engaged in dictionary work and the field notes provide the context:

Eileen finishes four test lists. They work one in class. "Cross out those that spoil alphabetical order."

```
                                          Big City
                                          9/11




Dear Sir
        Helen James is my daughter.
Helen wasn't feeling good the first of this week.
Last night she started her first menistrel period.
She didn't feel well this morning that's why she
didn't attened school today. Helen's father and I
have been seperated for sometime.  I'm working.  If
Helen gets wild.  See that I find out about it.

                  Thank you.

Mrs. Donora James
3834 Jackson

Un 47578 home
Ti 47290 Work
```

Figure 4.8 Letter from Helen's mother.

11:03 Messenger. (Send files on withdrawals.)

All work on this. Including Pete. Oliver volunteers to go up. Sam up to correct. Humorously, "If I'd said some of you seventh graders didn't know the alphabet you'd hoot and holler . . . go to test 3 . . . that's an 's.' Eileen gets carried away sometimes. That's a chubby 's' . . . ." Interaction over spelling and pronunciation of rally, severe, and power.

Allison is writing new lists on the board. (LMS—Geoffrey neatly sequences exercises so that he's on top of situation and chore aspects move right along to be ready. Exercises taken from mimeo or printed set of lessons.) (9/9)

The next morning, another episode occurred which the observer noted and interpreted:

9:13 "All right let's have some of you putting up answers on the board. Allison, Sam, let's just go down the row." Each goes up when the other has finished. Suggests to Allison to move to center board because "some can't see." Keeps sequence moving. (LMS—Implicit in both of these comments is elegance in order and nonconflicting interaction. Really problem prevention: no clowning at board and in later protests of "I can't see type." Suggests a whole line of analysis.) (9/10)

In this instance the concept, "sequential smoothness," is taken as a dimension of pupil interaction. Presumably there should be correlations between sequential smoothness of activities and sequential smoothness in interaction. Similarly, one can seek relations within lessons and in transition between lessons.[13]

On Pacing

Early in the semester, (9/5), while Geoffrey was dictating the spelling the observer made an interpretive comment in the field notes:

Pace continues to be easy in the sense that everyone hears (the words and examples) and has time to think and write his response. (9/5)

A day later this was expanded in the summary observations and interpretations:

One of the first, most important generalizations to come out of the research to this point concerns what might be called pacing. This concept should handle some of the difficulties in the static-dynamic controversy. By pacing, I mean essentially the speed with which new materials, new ideas, new positions were introduced by Geoffrey during the preceding day. One of the most striking features of yesterday's first day of class concerned the relaxed, easy, unhurried approach Geoffrey made in setting up the room. In one sense, all he accomplished yesterday was passing out the books and having the children write a one-page, approximately 20-minute lesson in language. The lesson consisted of one page, really a short paragraph or two, on some experience of their summer. Geoffrey's main intention was to have the pupils actually begin some academic work on the first day of school; secondly, he used this as an indication of the quality of work the children would be capable of doing. His argument to me later was that this particular exercise was a more valid test of achievement and aptitude than the typical achievement or aptitude test.

As a concept, pacing has its "inside" and "outside"[14] aspects. The outside aspects are those open to the observer. They are first, the goals

---

[13] Kounin and others (1966) have stressed the latter as an important correlate of pupil attention.

[14] Methodologically, this seems to be the first explicit reference to the inside-outside label in the methodology which later loomed large.

that the individual seems to be striving for; second, the *ease* with which one utilizes materials to arrive at the goals; third, aspects of the environment that form critical elements in the area between present location and the goals; and fourth, the aspect of time.[15] In yesterday's class these points seemed to be applied in the following manner:

The major aims were to begin to structure the class into some sense of order and semblance of a group. The means were the general activities of getting materials passed out, and establishing rules of the classroom. The aspects of the environment that seemed to be critical were the abilities of the pupils, their prior experiences, and most important, the as yet undetermined aspects of the Washington School: such things as physical education schedules, patrol-boy assignments, and lunchroom duties.[16] Apropos of the nature of the children, I was struck by their inability to handle a variety of simple instructions and academic tasks (problems such as spelling the teacher's name, the word chalk, eraser, monitor and so forth). Geoffrey presented these as problems that had to be solved, and, at the same time, taught several new concepts (for example, superstition).

Briefly, from the inside point of view, Geoffrey's rationale amounts to this: "Part of what I do depends upon how I feel personally. If I feel full of energy, I move much more rapidly. If I don't, I move much more slowly." The second aspect concerns his statement of earlier experience in which he tried to rush the children (and rush probably would be defined as moving them along faster than they might want to move by themselves). Moving more rapidly often resulted in not getting very much farther in the long run, while frustrating everyone, the children and himself, and creating, as a consequence, several emotional problems in the group.

At this point pacing seems conceptualized best as a ratio of amount of activity to time. In the example from the notes, activity is operationalized as the number of spelling words dictated, and time is operationalized as the movement of the hands on the clock. Variations in pace can be observed from teacher to teacher and, with one teacher, from lesson to lesson. Variations can be linked functionally with such concepts as (1) staff norms on appropriate and inappropriate pacing, (2) teacher satisfactions and dissatisfactions in getting "a day's work done," (3) pupil sentiments related to a pace which is too fast (for instance, "I can't finish") or too slow, ("I'm bored") and (4) pupil learning, the ratio of stimuli presented to amount of reinforcement occurring. Finally we would make two general points: the concept is an appropriate one for an applied science in that it is one the teacher can manipulate and alter readily. Second, for teaching culturally deprived pupils, it would seem that "too fast" or "too slow" is a judgment made in relation to pupil abilities. As these have significant limits, the

[15] Note also the conception of classroom processes which began early to differentiate itself.

[16] Some aspects of the program, especially those with special teachers as in Physical Education, became fixed and required planning around.

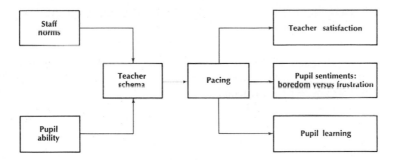

Figure 4.9 Some tentative relationships concerning pacing.

concept is very appropriate. Some of these tentative relationships have been sketched in Figure 4.9; obviously all variables in the system could be interrelated.

Teaching-in-motion

A truism one often hears about teaching advises moving about the classroom rather than sitting at one's desk. The notes contain many comments that Geoffrey often circulated about the classroom:

> Geoffrey moves quietly around the room. Checking, suggesting, urging several to slow down.

> Checks Oliver and indicates that only three out of twelve are sentences, the rest are run-ons. (Oliver had raced through the assignment.) (LMS— The moving about the room has a number of psychological components: for example, picking up Oliver at that point rather than later when there would be exasperation, failure, and frustration on Oliver's part; academic learning; a signal to him and to his audience—Sam and Lonnie—that such behavior doesn't work.)

The interconnections with the prevention of problems, maintaining control, development of belief and normative systems, showing consideration, and enhancing learning seem extremely important, belying the simplicity of the behavior itself.

Shaping through Successive Approximation

Educators and psychologists have long talked about shaping pupils through successive approximation: the gradual alteration of behavior by minimal steps toward a desired criterion. In a general sense, the graded educational program from kindergarten through high school (on through college and graduate school for some) illustrates the concept. In the classroom, however, the idea often is hard to see and even harder to implement. Integral to the general concept are such subaspects as: (1) the desired criterion (goal or objective) especially as held by the teacher, (2) an assumed logical or psychological order or sequence in the area of behavior under scrutiny, (3) an awareness of the pupils' current position regarding the sequence, and (4) some just noticeable differences within the sequences —the minimal steps. These points are relevant for the individual as well as for the composite or group mean.

Textbooks (especially those in arithmetic), tests, review exercises all help clarify one aspect of the institutional attempts to handle the phenomenon of successive approximation. More specifically in regard to the teacher-pupil interaction, our notes capture the continuing problem of Joe K. As we have mentioned in other aspects of the report, Joseph is the boy with the self-imposed tattoos, the boy we described at one point:

> Although I've not seen him smoking, his fingers looked stained with nicotine and my guess is that he's a regular. The dirt and body odor in which he seems to be cloaked on most days is not at all pleasant. (10/21)

This is the boy (among several) who is on probation from the juvenile court, and the boy who was kicked out of his brother's house by his sister-in-law.

In regard to the issue of successive approximation, especially concerning the minimal changes, he went through a period of "really trying," in the observer's eyes. The teacher, who then was busy with others with overt problems, ignored or missed most of these attempts by Joseph. The observer's notes catch part of this:

> He does present a most interesting illustration of the problem in shaping the behavior toward several kinds of goals. He is now currently getting his assignments in, although they are done in a very harem-scarem, lickitysplit manner. One might well make the case that Geoffrey should be most satisfied with the assignments in this fashion. As this is stabilized in a week or two, if it does become stable, then the quality aspect of the assignments should be shifted more in line with what might be done. (In the sixth grade.) (10/21)

As we have raised the concept of successive approximation we have had reference to the gradual alteration of children's behavior to meet a standard. From the teacher's point of view the problem complicates itself in terms of the energy and resources which must be deployed. Early in the semester, Alton, Geoffrey, and the observer were discussing bulletin boards and current events. Alton commented:

> "I'm giving up. These kids just don't read the newspapers. They aren't interested. I was just putting jokes, sports, and violence on the board. The only thing the kids would bring in was an occasional Dick Tracy comic." (9/10)

Geoffrey indicated that he had quit for much the same reason—he was doing all the work. He mentioned one occasion when he brought magazines such as *Better Homes and Gardens,* which one of the girls called "wishing books," and related a game they sometimes played at home — wishing for the items in the pictures. These illustrations indicate (1) the long and difficult job required to reach goals such as interest in intellectual matters, (2) the deep contrasts in home, school, and the middle-class community, and (3) the requisites for increasing the relevance of contemporary social studies.[17] The teacher's limited time and energy compound the difficult choices he faces.

In contrast, Geoffrey attacks the issues in approximating the spelling equilibrium with more success. For example: Monday morning, September 10, the class has arrived. The readers are reading. The talkers begin chatting quietly. Mr. Geoffrey takes care of the usual morning chores. The field notes show his early attempts to shape spelling activities:

8:42 Everyone is busy.
  "First, take out your spelling."
  Messenger comes in.
  "All right, let's see your papers." Looks at and chats with one girl about hers . . . . "What about No. 3?" Moves down the aisles. Interacts non-verbally with everyone and verbally with every other one. "No. 10 is not right." (LMS—Once again the teaching-machine image occurs to me.) "Think . . . . The definition . . . . Where are your sentences?" (To Billy) . . . "Definitions yesterday, sentences today . . . . 'Throughout,' you're talking about as two words . . . like 'baseball.'" (To Edwin) . . . "I like No. 14 (to Dick). Where's your's?" (with feeling, to Pete) . . . . "Who'd like to claim this?" Holds up an eraser, shrugs shoulders. "All right, I said the first lesson we would do together."

8:48 On page 2 he starts quizzing about italicized word. Continues with the text exercise, "Learning Your Words." Sections are due Wednesday ("Learning Your Words"), and Thursday ("Using Your Words"). Friday is the test. "All the assignments will be collected on Thursday." Has Edwin write the first one on the board. (LMS—Once again building clarity in routines.) "Remember that after this week you will do this on your own."

8:52 *All* begin work individually. Elma and Susan make an occasional comment. Pete dawdles along. While Geoffrey checks records, kids are moving in and out. (9/10)

The lesson continues until 9:28 when language begins. In the meantime, Mr. Geoffrey has checked around the room, looking at the paper of each individual child, has had illustrative sentences put on the board, has analyzed these orally with the class, and has clarified the assignment for the next day. In succeeding days the routines of spelling were gradually mastered by the children. Implicitly, the burden of teaching particular words is heavily emphasized in the program of the materials, a point to which we will return later.

---

[17] See our later discussion of African geography, current events, nationalism in Africa, and schoolwide integration problems.

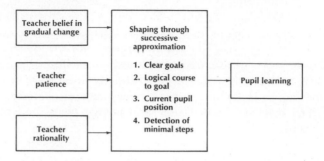

Figure 4.10 The implication of successive approximation in the classroom social system.

Autonomy and Aloofness

In some situations that were outside the commonly accepted province of the teacher's role, if Geoffrey needed help, he would ask the pupils for it. He solicited volunteers rather than commanding pupils to do the jobs. Usually one or more of the children would respond. Occasionally, no one did. This then put him in an interesting position—should he ask again, haggle, plead, beg, cajole, or order? How should he react emotionally— unhappy, angry, flustered?

> Billy and Edwin bring in a small table . . . . Tells Sandy to move assign- ment board sometime during the day, to accommodate the coffee table.[18] Looks for a coffee monitor . . . . No volunteers. "Don't everyone volunteer at once." Oliver suggests that Mr. Geoffrey volunteer. Geof- frey goes along moving material.[19] He *does not* push, ask, or plead. (LMS— This seems very significant. Follow up later in the notes to see how it works out. This is part of his aloofness, powerfulness, or autonomy.) (9/10)

We tried to diagram this meaning in Figure 4.11.

As we look back at the notes we are impressed once again by the ambiguous nature of humor ("Don't everyone volunteer at once") as it enables Geoffrey to repeat his request but doesn't put him in a haggling or ordering position. The second request frequently brings a response, for there are implicit and explicit rewards in monitorship. Not volunteering restricts the individual pupil-outcomes. Presumably an open-ended question or request gives these needs, however diverse and potent, a chance to be satisfied. A social structure based on "ordering" has received considerable analysis in the literature. The implications of a "haggling" relationship upon the social system has received much less analysis even though teachers in their everyday conversation are extremely reluctant to see this as viable.

---

[18] This refers to an interesting thread which was a part of the classroom fabric through- out the semester. Geoffrey, the observer, and a number of the teachers had coffee during recess in Geoffrey's room. The methodological section presents additional aspects of this.

[19] Straightening up the room in housekeeping fashion.

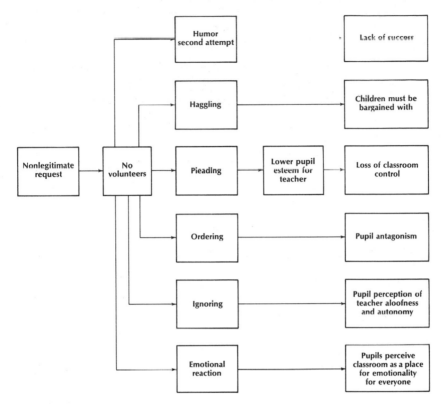

Figure 4.11   Genotypic analysis of the initial coffee-table episode: situation, Geoffrey's potential alternatives, and potential consequences.

Skirmishing

With a slight modification, changing the word "war" to "game," Webster's definition of "skirmish," "A slight fight in war, usually incidental to larger movements," fits a large part of Geoffrey's behavior. Here also we find interrelationships with our concepts of ringmaster, aloofness and autonomy, and awareness:

11:33 Lets them work on assignments. Sam tries to get "rest of day." Oliver comes up for book report. Geoffrey keeps eye on "travelers" around the room. Everyone (only thirteen left) working.

11:38 Edwin has lost his pen cap. Oliver is bothering Sam. Irma is back with Geoffrey; he finally takes her to map.

11:42 Oliver has finally gotten a language paper and copies rapidly and artfully. Edwin still can't find his pen cap. Oliver returns book and paper to Sam. Edwin working.

11:44 "Edwin, did you find it?" "No." "Who has it? Sam?" Interchange between Sam, Oliver, and Geoffrey. "I just want it. No questions asked . . . . I hope no one is playing tricks in here." (LMS—Very interesting

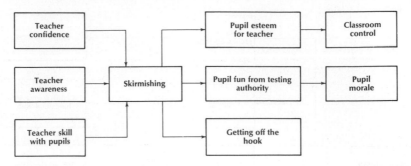

Figure 4.12 Skirmishing as a concept in teacher-pupil interaction.

approach here. Geoffrey *never* gets boxed into demanding. Always artfully probing, doing something, always acting as if he had things under control.) Leaves situation by picking up Sam's spelling, looking at it carefully and quietly putting it down and walking off. Edwin, apparently pacified for the moment, goes back to work, as do Sam and Oliver. (9/13)

Banter

One of Geoffrey's most fascinating abilities was his talent for joking with pupils: Sandy, a clique leader, Oliver, a class clown whom we have not sketched in great detail, and Sam, the court jester, were perhaps the most frequent targets. As the joking involved a two-or-three-step "comment-retort-counter" it became an interaction we have called banter. In Figure 3.3 the sequence enclosed between T_5 and T_8 qualifies as an illustration of banter. The frequency of this kind of interaction seems to have important implications for the "good feeling" or general positive sentiment felt by the pupils. Molly, for instance, felt depressed when Sam left the classroom because "he was a lot of fun." Similarly, banter seemed to

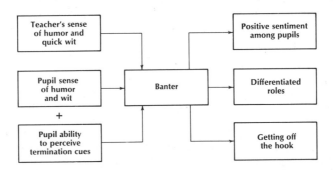

Figure 4.13 Antecedents and consequences of banter in teacher-pupil relationships.

Figure 4.14   Hypotheses regarding the "getting off the hook" phenomenon.

have other outcomes, building differentiated roles such as Sam's and such phenomena as "getting off the hook" which we describe shortly.

Getting off the Hook

Geoffrey had a way of artfully leaving an interactional episode. Partly it may have been a function of not getting too deeply involved or committed to a position in the momentary give-and-take of classroom interaction, and partly it was his ability to find logical or "obvious-to-the-pupils" issues to attract his attention momentarily. Our illustration "skirmishing" contains the observer's remark:

> Leaves situation by picking up Sam's spelling, looking at it carefully, quietly putting it down, and walking off.   (9/13)

As we have indicated earlier, his ability to engage in banter with several pupils, especially Sam, frequently gave him opportunities to elude final phases of a growing conflict.

On Lambs, Tigers, and Anger

Most of the time, as our discussion has intimated, Geoffrey's style is neat, tidy, businesslike and task-oriented. Minor themes do exist as Geoffrey plays out mock anger in a "ferocious tiger" role (as the observer came to call it) and a gentle lamblike or velvet-glove role as well. Occasionally the mock aspect of the ferocious tiger evaporated and Geoffrey was seriously fierce.[20] The difficult analytical problem resides in pairing these variations with the situations occurring at the time. First we present several illustrations, and later we draw our tentative hypotheses. Early Friday morning, after a test, Geoffrey turned to the new spelling words:

[20]The frequency varied from seldom with the first group to frequently after the change in classes at the end of September.

> Reads through list. Talks about pictures. Reads paragraph and asks that
> they read along silently with him. Reading deals with syllables. Raises
> questions about one-syllable words . . . calls on Elma. Raises "everybody
> look" as procedural device. Accented versus unaccented syllables. Goes
> down list of words; picks up accented and unaccented in each. Calls on
> kids around room. Everyone gets a turn. Edwin has trouble on number
> of syllables in "example." Geoffrey, with grin, has him say it, and he
> changes his answer from two to three. Similarly, on the accent Edwin
> says first syllable, Geoffrey says *ex'*ample, and Edwin corrects to second.
> (LMS—This was "lovely" in its fluidity, empathy, warmth. Edwin is a
> big, tall fifteen-year-old repeater and Geoffrey is usually the ferocious
> tiger; he handles him with a gentleness that characterizes a Lawrence
> Durrell type love affair.)   (9/13)

In a similar vein, elementary teachers are urged frequently to be
"patient." The meaning often is not clear. In one language arts episode
we think we caught much of its operational meaning:

> Continues around the room. Billy has trouble with No. 4. Geoffrey stops,
> and they work on it. Asks prompting question. On No. 12, "One of the
> men rose to his feet" Sandy is in trouble. "What's the verb? Can you
> use 'his' in another sentence?" She suggests "rose." What rose? and so
> forth. Works patiently (time, tender tone, simple questions). "Give her
> a little help, Dick!" Goes on. "Questions?" Comments to Alice about
> combing her hair in class.   (9/12)

The precipitating events or situation for this role seemed to be an individual
pupil who was having a difficult time with an academic learning problem
that was embarrassing.

During the first minutes of the first day of the room closing and
change of classes the following episode occurred:

> Quizzes Evelyn regarding her sisters, both of whom are absent. She
> is embarrassed (looks uncomfortable) and he lets her off the hook
> gently, warmly, and with a smile. (LMS—Mr. Geoffrey does not probe
> hard when there is resistance.)

This illustrates very well a recurring pattern in the teacher's behavior.
In glowing terms one might call it "respecting the privacy of the individual
pupil." Or in more analytical fashion one might argue the principle, if you
probe too far or too deeply you put the child in a position of conflict:
"Should I tell or not tell?" If forced into this position, the child loses either
way—the teacher is unhappy if she doesn't answer, or her friends (siblings
in this instance) are unhappy if she admits that they stayed home because
they were tired, uninterested, or for whatever inexcusable reason. The second
significant inference we would make is that Geoffrey's considerate attitude
alerts everyone, the audience and the child being quizzed, and ultimately
the absent children, that while privacy is respected, absenteeism is not
desirable. Mr. Geoffrey's views accent two elements: (1) "Her embarrassment
has given me the answer anyway," and (2) "The more I probe, the more

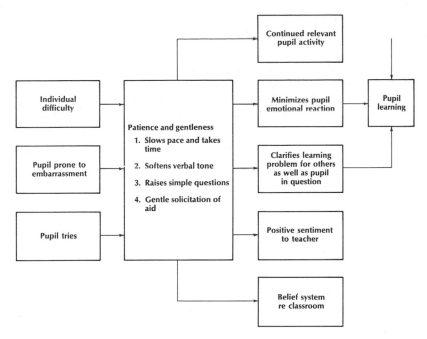

Figure 4.15 Nature and implication of patience and gentleness in teacher-pupil interaction.

the resistance." We sketch this in Figure 4.16. The critical aspect of the decision seems to center on the relative merits of alienating one of the children and making clear the importance of the issue, one which brings severe penalties.

In his ferocious-tiger role, Geoffrey would pace back and forth in front of the class and would roar in mock anger like a wounded, caged animal. Typically, the occasion would be a total group event in which a number of children had made errors in materials that should have been mastered long before. The illustration cited in the map episode[21] and his chiding the class through Sandy typifies this.

On another occasion, during an arithmetic lesson, the class had been relatively "high" through considerable banter and they ran into difficulty with the concept, "addends":

2:05 Interplay with Irma when she asks about checking. "I don't know what I'll do," he says. Interchange over broken chalk, "What do I think of broken chalk?" (from joke the other day). Banter is started. Works on "addends": reads sentence, "The addends may be grouped in any order. My God! What does addend mean!" Starts asking around the room. Gets most of it. Then, "Let's get it exactly, Sarah"—she sings out loud and

[21] See the "Ability Problem" section of Chapter Seven.

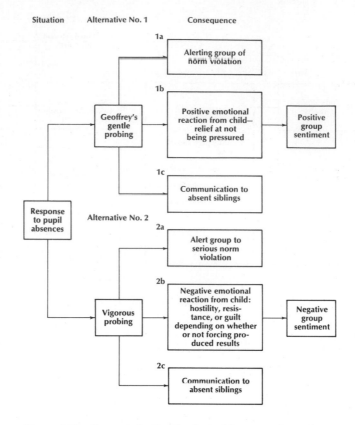

Figure 4.16 Elements in Geoffrey's decision regarding privacy.

clear: "When you add, its the numbers you add together." (LMS—Geoffrey's style, the ferocious tiger blends neatly with his personality.) (9/12)

The "mock" aspect of anger does not show in his developing conflict with Pete, a role we have described in detail elsewhere:

1:53 Collects papers and sends ten kids to board.
1:56 Messenger in.
Chaos in getting to board. Geoffrey straightens this out. Pete comes up about a drink. Geoffrey lays him out . . . . "Not in the middle of a lesson! . . ." Goes through problem. Corrects those in error. (9/12)

And an hour later:

2:50 Lesson goes on. Raises cain with Pete regarding arithmetic lesson done in history class. Tears up paper and throws it away. Tells him assignment is due tomorrow. Pete makes a comment. Geoffrey says, "Don't talk back to me." Pete sits, finally. Through all this, the page, squire, knight, sequence goes on. Reading alternated among pupils and Geoffrey. (9/12)

We report a final episode which contains several of our elements. The class has been reviewing dictionary usage and Geoffrey has moved toward an assignment when this episode occurs:

> "Who'd I say could have a list, Edwin?" Several boys (Sam, Oliver, Dick) indicate that it should be Billy. "Edwin next time."

10:59 Interchange with Sam. Geoffrey takes on ferocious-tiger role regarding assignment. Assignment has been gone over. He has individuals redo. Here he accents with loud voice and vigor: (1) syllables, (2) accent, (3) mark vowels. More banter. When Sam doesn't do much besides sit and grin (with Oliver) he motions for him to go out into the hall.[22]

11:04 Numerous interactions, explanations, assistance, by this time.

11:05 Everyone busy. Some talking (pupil-pupil) back and forth but all task-relevant. Geoffrey back at task entering data onto calendar.[23]

11:08 Geoffrey checks around.[24] Dick asks Geoffrey, as he pauses, about silent vowels. Geoffrey goes immediately to the board with the comment to the class, "I told you I would mark silent vowels." He strikes these off:

comment	intensive
floral	family
proper	disgrace
cosmetic	pastel
magnetic	incriminate

11:12 Sam to Geoffrey, ". . . drink of water?" Geoffrey immediately says yes. (LMS—Beautiful testing by Sam and response by Geoffrey . . . the "stop-go" behavior to run situation but no lasting spite; for example, he could have refused Sam and as a consequence rubbed in his displeasure. Not so though.)[25]

Individualizing Instruction

Theory and practice in teaching accent individualization of instruction as an important element of instruction. In our experience the concept is used loosely—sometimes to *contrast* with traditional teaching, sometimes to suggest varieties of instructional materials, and sometimes to illustrate teacher-pupil interaction. Our purposes suggest the need for sharply defining these usages and arriving at more discriminated usage. To this end we propose the term "personalized interaction" to deal with a phenomenon which involves a minimal two-unit episode:

[22] As we indicated, this was a standard disciplinary technique at Washington School.

[23] Although the observer missed it, this is probably when Geoffrey spoke to Sam in the hall and brought him back to the room.

[24] This is the "teaching-in-motion" concept.

[25] This is our point regarding bureaucratic authority.

Pupils	8:40-8:42	Reading: small groups 8:40-9:00 Geoffrey mostly with sixes	9:01-9:06 Geoffrey in and out	Reading			9:32 Science
				sevens 9:07	sixes 9:23	Others back 9:28	
Thelma		13			9	1	7
Kent		1			6		8
Eileen		1		6		4	3
Ben		7			4		2
Sandy		8			8	1	18
Oliver	1		1	6			6
Rose					1		
Jimmie				5			3
Elma			2		out of class		
Lonny		3					2
Irma							2
Dick		1		11	1	1	51
Molly		3			1	1	3
Davey					out of class		
Peggy	1		1		out of class		
Pete							1
Susan		6					3
Sam		3	1	19		1	37
Sarah		1	3	6			3
Edwin	3	3	1	10	1		6
Helen		2					3
Billy						1	11
Allison	1	11	1			2	18
Patty							1
Nonclass pupils		2	2	2			2
teachers	1						

Figure 4.17 An informal attempt at quantification of amount of personalized interaction.

On occasion more units may be involved:

Beyond the fact that the episode may vary from two to several units, another dimension seems important, the relative cognitive or affective components. For instance, early in September the children have been told and discussion has occurred regarding the organizational format for book re-

10·15-10·37 Recess	10·38 Language	11:08 Assignment	11:16 History	11:55 Assignments Patrol Boys out
	14	2	11 (out at 11:40)	
	14	2	5	
	11		7	
	8		1	
	13	2	17	1
3	4		7	2
	4			
	7		1	
	comes in 11:06		(11:30 lunch)	
2	8	2		
1	13		5	
	22		49	
	3		(11:27 lunch)	
	absent			
	1 (comes 11:06)	3		1
1				
	10		3 (11:30 lunch)	
2	9	1	13	1
	8	1	18	
	11	2	5	
	6		1 (11:30 lunch)	
	17		3 (11:30 lunch)	
out until 11:00	3	5	14	1
	5	3		
			4	

ports. The following personalized interaction occurred and a brief interpretation was made:

8:50 "Now when you've finished copying, write these six things for your library book." Questions Irma regarding book left at home "What do we do with library books?" "Bring them in the next day" (from Bill and one or two others). Geoffrey gives book from shelf to Irma. "This one is especially for you." Grins. (LMS—Once more the humor and personalizing of approach to the children; I don't have the feeling of benevolent autocrat, but interested adult.) (9/6)

A few days later, September 10th, the observer was struck by the same phenomenon in a spelling lesson:

Mr. Geoffrey starts around the class. He comments: "People, don't forget, an italicized word may go before or after." (LMS—A simple inter-

action count on an individual (teacher-pupil) basis would be astound-
ingly high. Already this morning he's been around the room twice.)[26]
(9/10)

Finally, on September 24, the issue overwhelmed the observer and
he made an informal quantification attempt. Personal interaction (verbal
and nonverbal contact) was defined this way in the notes:

> This represents an attempt to obtain quantification of all interactions
> with *individual* pupils, by recitations, discipline, and nods. The purpose is
> not to record *who* is receiving personal attention, but to measure the
> *amount* of contact between teacher and pupil, both at Geoffrey's initiation
> and the initiation of the children. The focus is on the one to whom
> Geoffrey is attending. When he shifts his attention to another person,
> that pupil's perception of his attention defines the personal contact,
> the interaction between them.   (9/24)

While we would raise considerable question ourselves about the reliability of our coding, the 767 contacts in one morning, even granting appre-
ciable error, is a startling phenomenon. Although teachers vary in their
capacity for personal interaction, the kind of personality structure that can
tolerate and even seek out such relationships seems an important dimension.
Perhaps this is part of the significance of the statement: "You've got to like
children, if you are going to teach them." The summary scores are in
Figure 4.17.

In an earlier paper (Smith, 1965) reporting on some of the data, a
more extended point was made concerning the concept of functional equivalents. One illustration of this concept involves individualized instruction.

When the observer first approached the classroom, he carried a host
of the current dichotomies: traditional versus progressive teaching, textbooks
versus units, class recitation versus individual work, and so forth. Fairly
early in the semester he was struck by several recurring events: first, the
teacher was a textbook teacher. By this he meant the bulk of the program
focused on moving steadily and systematically through texts in spelling,
language arts, arithmetic, and so forth. The notebooks are replete with
statements describing the activity and interaction in dealing with the
arithmetic problem on page 5, then page 6, then 7, and so on. In spelling,
the weekly units consisted of definitions, use of the words in sentences,
special exercises, and so on. We can pin down concretely the activity of
any day during the semester. But after having said that he was a textbook
teacher, the larger truth is missed if more is not explained. For instance,
recitations varied from calling on pupils in sequence up and down rows,
or calling only volunteers, or nonvolunteers, or even calling on pupils
who looked confused. Occasionally this produced some high humor. As we
have indicated early in the semester, the teacher checked a spelling test

[26] This refers to Geoffrey's recitational procedures.

by calling on pupil volunteers. He had turned down several volunteers with the comment, "You've already had one." When the group came to the word "tardy," Mr. Geoffrey called on Sam. Sam immediately retorted, "Oh, I've already had one." Mr. Geoffrey then commented "I'm giving you this one special." Later when we went back to the note books we found that the next four pupils called upon also had received one earlier in the list. The humor introduced in this episode was not atypical. The notes contain recurring episodes of banter, a tête-a-tête interaction in which the teacher and one or more pupils exchange witty remarks. The teacher's behavior involved a tremendous amount of "circulation"; he was on his feet moving continuously from pupil to pupil.[27] This circulating behavior was punctuated with yes's, no's, nods, more vehement expostulations, questions as to sources of answers, and explanations of difficulties.

In summary, by calling the class a "textbook-oriented class" one misses the more important point that the pupils are receiving considerable individual and personal help with their learning activities. Functionally, the class is equivalent to many aspects of programmed learning—carefully sequenced materials, active pupil responding, and immediate reinforcement. Or, functionally, the class is equivalent to many more informal learning situations wherein humor, pupil volunteering, and individual attention are the keynotes.

This kind of argument—functional equivalents and inequivalents— suggests that we must settle some of the implications of varying levels of abstraction. When one says that two concrete and different procedures have something in common or two supposedly similar events are different we are engaging in the not so simple, but time-honored process of concep- tualizing. At its best, this can move us in the direction of cumulative and more analytic tools that are the essence of any scientific inquiry. At its worst it can move us toward a cynical reductionism—all theories of teaching are "really" theories of psychology and as every psychologist "knows" all psychological theory is "really" physiological.[28]

As we have been saying, at one level, "many roads lead to Rome," the conception is a very simple truism. At another level of analysis, our theory in education makes distinctions that do not exist, or it does not make distinctions when they do exist. This spills over in our research methodologies also. The current vogue in the analysis of teacher behavior seldom taps the interdependencies and functional equivalencies in homework assignments and textbook materials, which may stress attainment of informa- tion while the teacher stresses intellectual skills or vice versa. The teacher may stress information and leave the skill development to carefully drawn homework questions, projects, or text assignments. The concept provides an

[27] We have reference to our "teaching-in-motion" concept introduced earlier.
[28] Stephens' (1960) conception of spontaneous schooling has overtones of this.

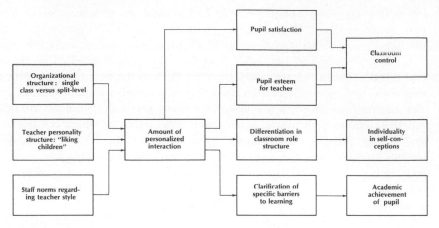

Figure 4.18 A miniature theory of personalized interaction.

additional implication that suggests items to which the innovator who wishes to improve teaching and learning in slum schools or elsewhere might attend. Merton comments:

> As we have seen, once we abandon the gratuitous assumption of the functional indispensability of particular social structures, we immediately require some concept of functional alternatives, equivalents, or substitutes. This focuses attention on the range of possible variation in the items which can, in the case under examination, subserve a functional requirement. It unfreezes the identity of the existent and the inevitable. (Merton, 1957, p. 52)

The unfreezing of the existent from the inevitable opens the discussion of a multitude of other ways, new means, and innovations that can accomplish present manifest ends as well as other latent and desirable objectives.

In summary, although we have not carefully analyzed aspects of the initiation of interaction, the positive or negative quality (from pupil and teacher point of view), and the more general context (a broad program of learning activities continuing), we propose in Figure 4.18 several hypotheses relating to the consequences of large amounts of personalized interaction.

CONCLUSION

Much of our effort has been spent in reconceptualizing teaching. The fundamental conflicts in psychological theory are nowhere more evident than in the ways psychologists talk about teachers and children. We have been persuaded to a "metatheory" which has its basis in decision-making. While the full implications of this are far from clear, we have found the point of view helpful in organizing our ideas. In turn, this point of view has helped us to see more clearly the dimensions of teacher behavior and performance, as the teacher implements these, as alternative means for reaching particular objectives. The weighing of alternatives in a particular situation, the social skills involved in teacher-pupil interaction, and the repercussions upon the individual and the group seem to strike at the heart of the "process problem" in teaching.

As we look at the behavior of teachers, the concept of "situational thinking" seems especially important. It seeks to relate provisional trials in teacher behavior, the teacher's conceptual categories of situations "here" versus situations "out there," and the child's discriminal ability with such implications as decreasing the child's practice of what he has learned in school in outside-of-school behavior, solving of some of the child's problems of social-class-value conflict, introducing the child to relativity in behavior and values, and increasing classroom control. The solving of some of the child's problems increases provisional trials in teacher behavior. The introduction of the child to relativity in behavior and values also would have this effect; however, it also can lead to decreases in classroom control.

Hypotheses centering on the concept "preparation for contingencies" bring the elements of teacher-knowledge and experience and special problems of cultural deprivation into relationships that hopefully lead to fewer discipline problems and more task-focused behavior in the classroom. The concept of "awareness" speaks to the teacher's ability to interact in ways not predictable in formal lesson plans. This is, in a sense, related to the "provisional trial," tentative gambits that become a permanent part of the teaching process only when successful.

The multiple and simultaneous events that occur in teaching have been described in "ringmastership," the teachers' varying ability to handle the multiple strands of interaction that occur in the classroom. "Continuity" is another concept that, if included in the teacher's repertoire of skills, can aid teaching effectiveness. Other components of the art of teaching are "sequential smoothness," relations within lessons and in interaction between lessons; "pacing," the ratio of amount of activity to time; and "teaching-in-motion," moving around versus sitting at a desk.

Shaping through successive approximation is a phenomenon illustrated generally by the organization that exists in today's schools, that is the graded educational program from kindergarten through high school and even beyond. In the classroom these steps are scaled down. The concept involves teacher-belief in gradual change, teacher-patience, and teacher-rationality. We see other concepts that are less centered on learning theory but are valid as concepts of teacher-behavior. "Autonomy and aloofness," "skirmishing," "banter," "getting-off-the-hook," and even the "ferocious tiger" role describe elements of teacher-behavior and possible outcomes.

Finally, we suggest that the phrase "individualizing instruction" has been used too often as a method of teaching contrasted with a textbook-oriented class. Much of what went on in Mr. Geoffrey's classroom suggests that in "textbook teaching" one can find many aspects of programmed learning. Related to this we found what seemed to us a high degree of personalized instruction, which has consequences for classroom control, individuality in children's self-conception, and academic achievement of pupils.

CHAPTER FIVE

THE FLOW OF
THE SEMESTER

Big City has a beautiful fall season. Indian summer, those deliciously warm, mild days after the first frost, provides for the esthete as well as the sensualist an interlude between the humidity of summer and the slush and snow of winter. The urban teacher misses most of this, for he is confined to the building from early morning to late afternoon. The brick and metal of the factories, warehouses, and tenements, and the noise and exhaust of buses and trucks in the early morning, in the noon hour, and after school, shield him also from the pastoral quality of other people's Indian summer. Usually the teacher finds satisfaction in the stabilization of his group into a working unit. Expectations have been clarified, roles have been settled, and movement toward generally accepted goals is well begun. Downtown this is true also, even if to a lesser degree. At the Washington School these days end abruptly, for on Friday, September 27, the school shudders with the consequences of a room being closed because of falling enrollment.

In addition to the high drama of this one major event, we sketch briefly in this chapter the flow of the semester, a glimpse at the narrative of the rest of the year.

A ROOM CLOSES AT THE WASHINGTON SCHOOL

The Faculty

When a room closes, a faculty member leaves. As we watched the events take place, several forces seemed at work: (1) seniority—the ever-present tenure of those who by some stroke of fate arrived earlier than others converts this event into righteousness; (2) sex—Mr. Gennep, a relatively recent arrival, will not be displaced, for Mr. Willower wants to keep male teachers in the building; (3) informal social rank—Miss Roberts, a new teacher, has been well received for doing a very good job. She is enthusiastic, tries hard, and supports the procedures of the dominant clique. Miss Simeon, who is not liked, who has had brief tenure, and who is alleged to have less competence, is the "people's candidate" for removal. The resolution comes when one of the middle-grade teachers agrees to a transfer to the east side of the city, which is closer to her home.

The observer's notes on Friday morning carry references to considerable discussion about the transfer problem. Crises make people more articulate, at least to their close friends.

> Norton and Eagle went over the list of kids that Geoffrey gets from Gennep. Eagle full of pithy descriptions "That's a Jones." (In a prior conversation she had told me about this family. All of them were in continuous trouble; when asked "Why," they would reply, "I'm a Jones.") She went on, "That's a dull one. This one will try. This one will try *you.* This one has got half a brain. This one never comes," and so on. (9/27)

The notes contain several statements Gennep made about the children. The first was early in the semester, September 13, before any serious discussion of the room-closing occurred.

> **8:00** Mr. Gennep comes in for coffee. There is a brief discussion of the difficulties in teaching a group such as Mr. Geoffrey's. I commented on yesterday's map incident. Gennep, in turn, related the difficulties he was having with arithmetic fundamentals, for example, 3-column addition. Gennep feels he has a tough (hard-to-teach) group this year. He talked about program schedules. Gennep is curious as to when they are due. He apparently tries to follow a schedule pretty closely.   (9/13)

Later, early on the Monday morning following the change, the notes read:

> Gennep comes in. Geoffrey and he talk about the kids who have come up. In regard to language, Gennep had been working on parts of a sentence (to p. 21). In regard to arithmetic, "Good luck" is his comment.

In reading, only three of twenty-two read at the sixth-grade level.
This precludes certain work in geography. "I've been working on a
list of terms, 'longitude,' 'latitude,' and so on. They can't read the books.
It takes too much time." Gennep has three pairs of siblings; Geoffrey
has three sisters now and one pair of brothers (Billy and Harry). Geoffrey
comments that Binder shouldn't have any gripe about Edwin and Allison. (There's been conflict between Binder and Geoffrey over this.)
(9/30)

Miss Norton related other troublesome events on that Friday morning of
the change. One of her fifteen-year-old boys bit another boy on the arm.
"His shirt was wet, and teeth marks were on his arm." She suspected that
there would be trouble some night in the city park. She spoke also about an
earlier difficult class she had had: forty children, twenty-one suspendees,
and her first time with a sixth-grade group. She "broke this group," mainly
by getting kids suspended.

Interpretatively, a comment seems warranted: even though the major
energy and resources of the teachers will be turned now toward the shift
in classes, minor problems and frustrations keep occurring and must be
handled. While psychologists have long had basic knowledge of frustration,
the concept has seldom been integrated at length into discussions of teaching.
In effect, we argue that the urban teacher's job contains a continuous series
of problems that block him from attaining his goal of teaching the children.
Each of these adds its increment of the disagreeable tension of frustration.
Occasionally a major problem, the shift in classes, occurs and causes a
major reallocation of resources. As the total resources available for creative
problem-solving become exhausted, the teacher seems first to try to stereo-
type his reactions to other problems, thereby making resources available.
He may also lower his level of aspirations and take his chance with guilt,
the discrepancy between what he does and what he feels he ought to do.
This guilt, in turn, is a barrier to another goal, maintaining self-respect, and
further complicates the situation. When these alternatives exhaust themselves,
the teacher often responds emotionally—with hostility, perhaps, or with
more general disorganization and distress.

In short, a teacher such as Geoffrey, who had produced a workable
equilibrium with his children, perceived this shift in classes as a major
frustration. All the efforts to stabilize the group must be started again.
Further complications exist, for Geoffrey will have a younger group than
he has had before, and he will have a split-level group that in itself presents
some additional problems.

The Children

The New Pupils Initially the new class is composed of thirty-five
children. Geoffrey has kept twelve of his original group and acquired one
new seventh grader, Henry H. He has twenty-two new sixth graders. Fig-

Thelma	Pete	Walter G.	Evelyn	Agnes	Betty
Patty Jo	Rose	Grace	Marian	Josephine	Esther
Eileen	Molly	Walt B.	Joe K.	Albert	Leona
Kent	Susan	Timmy Jones	Norman	Virgil	(Henry L.)
Sandy	Billy	Sydney	Marshall	Harry	
Elma	Peggy	Leonard	Alan	Joe G.	
Henry H.					

Figure 5.1   Seating chart after the closing of the room.(9/30)

ure 5.1 contains the names of the pupils who composed the class on Monday morning, the first school day after the Friday shift in classes.

The Seventh-grade Group   The seventh-grade children who remain are Thelma, Patty, Eileen, Kent, Sandy, Elma, Pete, Rose, Molly, Susan, Billy, and Peggy.

They include Sandy's clique, two especially difficult children (Pete and Elma), and three exceedingly dull pupils (Billy, Peggy, and Rose). Included also are sisters, Rose and Patty, who will be joined by a younger and more highly-achieving third member of the family, Evelyn. Except for Sandy, who interacts to a large extent with Geoffrey, most of the class spokesmen and virtually all of the "scholars" will be gone from the original seventh-grade group. On the first afternoon several of the clique of girls visit with the observer and he notes:

> Sevens feel like old hands in the room. They do not like the new group of kids. The boys are "creepy." Molly misses Sam's good humor. Other boys were "cute." Rose wanted to go to Binder's room because her sisters are both now in Geoffrey's room.   (9/27)

A few minutes later the observer presented in the field notes his more general reaction:

> In reflecting upon my brief conversation with the girls, the sentiment structure and belief system that existed in the class became clearer. The humor, the friendly adolescent nudges and tête-à-tête, the chiding back and forth between Geoffrey and the focal members—Sam, Sandy, Oliver, and others—leave one with a real sense of sadness. In retrospect, Geoffrey's ferocious tiger role seems much more a role and less real personal severity (in which he never was very high).   (9/27)

The Aggregate: Initial Perceptions   The social structure of Geoffrey's new room had a subdivision that we came to call "the aggregate." It was not a subgroup or clique for there seemed to be no stability of interaction, leadership structure, common sentiments, or norms. It was instead a collection of individual pupils. In the observer's eyes the pupils were clustered because of the severe problems they posed for the teacher and because of the mental ill-health components that seemed to be present. The aggregate included Alan, Joe K., Norman, Timmy, Leonard, and Marshall. Almost all of the other boys were directly or indirectly influenced by them on one occasion or another. These included sixth graders Joe G., Harry, and Walt G. as well as Pete from the seventh-grade group.

Our notes on the opening morning indicated that several were engaged early in "nonsense."

11:32 Geoffrey explains seating. Someone (a mother?) comes with a question. Geoffrey goes out into the hall. Most of the sixth graders sit quietly. Timmy and Leonard do not. They are horseplaying already. Seventh graders chat a bit. Pete talks with Walt G. Leonard looks over at me after pulling Timmy's hair. (LMS—I'm struck with the small size, grubby appearance, and need for haircuts).

11:37 The boys start into motion. They are considerably more squirmy than the girls. (Earlier, Norton had commented about the young kids, "You would just about get their attention, and they would knock off a stack of books.") (9/27)

Leonard skipped school the first afternoon. Harry alternated between poking Joe G. with his fist and with a ruler. Regarding Marshall and Alan, the observer noted:

Back two kids in middle row of new children are daring, squirrelly kids. They carry on with "nonsense" while Geoffrey is in the room—when his glance is turned. (9/27)

Geoffrey's Initial Gambit

The classes were traded after recess. Geoffrey's group left with smiles and jokes by Sam and Oliver. The new group came in quietly. To the observer they looked more "motley," although he had some feeling that perhaps he had grown accustomed to the others. Geoffrey proceeded with discussions of rules, acknowledgment of reputations, and stern looks indicating what he expected and that he would tolerate no nonsense. The field notes, as we have indicated, contained some revealing observations on children basically unknown until this point who would figure prominently in the semester's story.

Grooving the Children We commented at length, in our earlier description, about the concern for establishing teacher control. One mechanism for this is what we have called "grooving the children," the accumulation of simple directions and compliance. The observation arose again during the first afternoon with the new group of children.

1:57 Geoffrey keeps up his steady flow of orders. "It's all right to talk, but talk quietly." (LMS—In all sorts of minor ways, he creates the direction of flow of commands. All are simple, easy-to-follow requests (demands). It's almost as if he were cutting a groove. Concomitantly, it's almost possible to see a change occurring. Even though the pupils talk and chitchat back and forth, as soon as he comes over and raises a question or begins an order, the group swings around and attends to him. The shapelessness of the group alters. They subgroup out for talking, poking, and Indian wrestling (abortively), but when Geoffrey comes by, a look brings them around.) (9/27)

On Monday, September 30, at least eight children were absent or tardy. Geoffrey systematically began to pursue the reasons and to indicate that absenteeism was inappropriate and would not be condoned. He quizzed Evelyn concerning the whereabouts of her two sisters and then eased off gently when she became embarrassed. He then sent messengers to find siblings and cousins who might know the reasons for children's absences.

Tells the sixth graders that since most of the monitor assignments are made he'll use them as messengers. He suggests that they might like this, and they agree. Sends one child to Miss Binder's room for the brother of Joe K., who is absent from Geoffrey's room. (LMS—Once again as I should have predicted, Geoffrey is on top of it. William James would be proud, for not one turn of the ball of string will be unwound. Once again this ripples across the classroom.) As Geoffrey comes back in the room, a messenger, one of the sixth-grade girls, is still waiting for her message. Geoffrey has a vague look, smiles, tells her that occasionally she'll have to remind him. Again smiles gently and sweetly to her. This kindly, fatherly role comes through beautifully. Has Thelma and Molly out for relabeling pens. They groan, and he groans back in mock sympathy. As old hands and compatriots—from before the change—they go at it again. (9/30)

The Possibility of a Self-fulfilling Prophecy One of the major questions that remains with us concerns the weight of the children's internal problems in contrast to the weight residing in a self-fulfilling prophecy (Merton, 1957). We have described briefly the "aggregate" of children who from the first hour were observed to be "squirrelly, restless children." We have commented also on Geoffrey's initial attempts at "grooving the children" and setting up classroom control. At this point we need to mention also a difference between the second and the first groups that the observer detected. Geoffrey had been primed by Gennep and by Eagle, with her pithy remarks, as well as by his own acquaintance with the children. The contrast to which we would point is that he identified some individual children and warned them verbally or through glances as he talked with the group. For instance, the notes contain the following:

10:57 Begins identifying them by name. Often last name. Gives a knowing look to several—including Timmy and Harry. Paces about as a "silent tiger" while waiting for additional pupil desks. Teases his seventh-grade girls for chirping like mosquitoes. Asks Thelma if she would like the noise happening behind her at an Elvis Presley-Sandra Dee movie. New boys sit quietly and watch.

Geoffrey continues directions on seating. He is quiet, does not smile, directs attention to all the pupils. Indicates that he'll change the desks later to get appropriate size. Looks for absentees. Comments that some of the pupils he knows and some he does not. He gives Elma a blistering glance for jabbering; this one radiates across the room. Calls roll. Smiles at girls he knows and smiles knowingly at the boys. Gives Leonard an "I'm ready to do battle" look. This is ferocious. (9/27)

Later he comments, "You are responsible to me and I am responsible to you: Hallways: *Joe K.* (by his last name). Playground: *Timmy.* I may be impatient about things—especially nonsense." (9/27)

And just before lunch, Geoffrey shuffles the seating about in order to put some of the larger boys in the back and the smaller girls in front. As he moves Leonard, he comments, "I can already see that this isn't a combination to be desired."

There were differences in the children and differences in Geoffrey's approach. The second month "went differently" from the first month. Considerably more conflict existed; the lively repartee was not the dominant tenor of the class as it had been. The causal relationships are not clear.

CLASSROOM SOCIAL STRUCTURE
AND SOCIAL PROCESS THROUGH THE FALL

Earlier in the report we presented an extended description of several days of school. While it is somewhat repetitious to do this again, it seems important to introduce the new group of children who came after, as we called it then, the "October Revolution." The days are not atypical. The notes capture the flavor of the conflict that existed and Geoffrey's attempt to reach a workable equilibrium. In addition, the notes provide further illustrative material for the more abstract analysis and interpretation we have been making.

Two Days of Class

The Seriousness of Conflict: An Early Day An equilibrium was not reached easily. The days were difficult, frustrating, and close to open warfare at times. The notes from part of the morning of October 8 are included to clarify the difficult and troubled times in the school and in Geoffrey's class.

Before school, as we walked into the building, Mr. Osten, the custodian, commented, "All our problems are solved now." He pointed to the news article on the possible election of a Negro Board president and laughed heartily. His attitude seemed much more of a big joke than of hostility. Saw Mr. Miller.[1] I quizzed him on how the afternoon went.

He said, "Very well. I beat them." Jokingly, I said, "With both fists?" As he clarified the events, they fell heavily into immediate verbal commands, issuing of orders from himself, and strict and rigid holding everyone in seats. As he commented, "They called me crabapple behind my back. But it went very well. They were quiet. We got some work done." (LMS—He's learning the role as it is played here.) I asked him, "Is there a general principle lurking in there somewhere?" He replied, "On one afternoon it was successful." (LMS—Raises for me some question of the immediacy of the reinforcement, the intensity of reinforcement, and the number of instances to make such apprenticeship learning a general principle.)

Geoffrey gave me a note he had received from Louise J., a former student (See Figure 5.2). He recalled an incident in which she had stepped into a violent quarrel between her father and mother. The father was seriously beating the mother. The parents made up, but the father would not speak to her for several weeks. Geoffrey, in the course of classroom banter, had commented that he would have to send a note to her father. (He didn't know of the quarrel at that time.) She broke down completely. In his words, she "shed water more than Old Faithful."

8:05 Geoffrey went down to supply room.

8:10 Mr. Gennep came in for a few minutes. I commented positively about the French pastry. He replied that it could be bought at the Rivera Bakery. In brief conversation we raised a number of points. (1) There are occasional "good" classes. Apparently, this means more stable homes, economically a little better off, more achievement-orientation and ability. (2) Yesterday was a very restless day in his room also. He "blew up" at one girl for mirrors, bobby pins, and hair combing. He had warned her a week before. I raised the question of whether it was "mock anger." The distinction, and we didn't have time to pursue it, seems to be "only once since I've been here have I really gotten mad . . . They can tell when you're bluffing." Apparently, the in-between ground is taking the kid out in the hall for a lecture. (LMS—To me this is bureaucratic rather than personal anger. The behavior is dysfunctional for the system. It's mock anger in terms of your personal feelings, real in terms of group maintenance.) (3) Talked of suspension differences between schools. Apparently, the school in which he apprenticed, the Roosevelt, was much easier on the kids. They would have four or five temporary suspensions and the kids would still get back in class when the parents came. This is similar to comment that had been made about that school by a colleague who taught there for a year or two. Gennep has a strong feeling of wanting to be rid of these kids. "They shouldn't have been born. The parents haven't instilled any standards."[2] (4) Gennep comments some about

---

[1] Mr. Miller is an apprentice from City Teacher's College. He spent two weeks at each grade level over the course of his semester's work. His story makes an interesting account of the socialization of new personnel into the system. A more extended analysis of this unique practice occurs in another investigation (Connor and Smith, 1967).

[2] These remarks indicate the degree of the problem, for Gennep is a gentle man. Most children like him, and several of the girls in the sixth cried when they left his room.

```
Dear Mr. Geoffrey,

Hi, I thought I'd write a note and say
hello.  I've had a terrible lot of home-
work to do here lately. I don't like the
school I'm going to now.  In June, at
lunch, I'm coming to Washington to get
you to sign my autograph book.

Well bye, Mr. Geoffrey, and thanks for
one of the best years of my life!

                    Sincerely,
                    Louise Jones
```

Figure 5.2   Letter from a former pupil.

class that he had before (the sixth). I asked him if there were any boys in the group he could like or warm up to. The only one he mentioned was Sydney. As he looked at the seating chart, he responded positively to several of the girls. Commented that they seemed "preoccupied." I thought this was apt and said so to Gennep. (5) He commented about use of humor which he's found successful.

8:35 Kids file in.

8:45 Timmy and Leonard are late. Geoffrey blows up loudly from hall. Stabs forefinger at Leonard.[3] Won't accept excuse that he was late because of homework. "You do it the night before." Kids in class can hear it.

[3] Leonard had been a continuous problem since the switch in classes. Geoffrey had repeatedly warned him.

Some (Harry and Virgil) tickled over it. Others (seventh graders) apprehensive. Geoffrey comes in, looks exasperated. "You make up time triple. 30 minutes at noon. You think you're going to walk in this room late, you're wrong. . . . You don't run this school, and you're not going to run it." (Most of this directed more toward Leonard.) "Take your time at recess, 15 minutes at recess and 15 minutes at noon." Leonard looks angry. Geoffrey takes attendance. Asks for notes excusing absences.

8:49 Groups go out and enter for reading. Leonard and Timmy exchange grins. Leonard borrows a pencil, then leaves. One of the other kids finds Molly's pocketbook; yesterday there had been big "to do" over its being lost. Geoffrey has paper monitor pass out small lined paper. (LMS—As he calms down, this has been the angriest I've seen Geoffrey. The mock quality I've detected before was not apparent. If the kids were issuing challenges he was going to meet them head on. There seems to be no question as to the ground he is on and the alternatives open to him. The Simon decision-making model seems to fit beautifully here. It fits also decision-making about lessons.)

8:59 Geoffrey finishes chores, getting workbooks in and distributed. He talks to Eagle. Then he brings a note over to me. "The 'good' teacher never loses his temper. Education 101." I smile in reply.

9:02 Starts them on workbook exercise.

9:07 Geoffrey still is restless. He paces around, into the hall and back. He checks around the room as kids do assignment and helps Billy.

9:08 Geoffrey goes out and returns two more times. He clears up paper work and waits for kids to work the brief assignment. Then he paces with book in hand. Children all very quiet even after finishing up.

9:10 Quietly and patiently the children work through the phonics exercise. Geoffrey checks around-the-room recitation. Even Pete is expected to and does have work. When Geoffrey reaches Timmy, he finds Timmy on wrong page. He walks over, checks his paper, orients the child, and has him work the problem. (LMS—Difficult for me to tell whether he's resisting, stupid or both. Probably both.[4] As I look at Timmy, I'm reminded of Gennep's comment, "preoccupied," in his description of the pupils. They are so far off in their own worlds that they seem not to be resisting consciously or in any unified manner. In regard to the latter, they don't even make a group. Occasional horseplay and dyadic interaction but no general purposes or goals. I am somewhat reminded of the group at City Hospital in the inpatient ward.[5])

9:17 Geoffrey gives them time to work page 2.

9:23 He asks for someone to go to the board. At least half the children volunteer (10 to 12 out of 20 or 22). Sends one child to board for each row of initial consonant problems. Where there is disagreement, they enter into gentle discussion over disagreements.

9:27 Workbooks are collected (*High Roads*). Geoffrey instructs monitors on collection in future.

9:28 The students from Room 12 leave. (LMS—Much time is spent in getting to and from rooms. Also, time is spent in getting materials. This raises some doubts on values. However, Pete's working is major good sign. Also, all pupils, even Billy, are doing something they have a chance at when

---

[4] Later we were to have data that Timmy has a serious hearing problem along with his ability, attention, and behavior problems.

[5] This is a children's psychiatric ward in a local hospital.

the teachers exchange students in order to group them homogeneously.)

9:29 Geoffrey continues recording attendance (he keeps a note sheet per day). He asks for notes from parents, naming each child and mornings or afternoons he missed. Harry had been "to the country." In his case it was a small town 40 miles away. (LMS—Ease and acceptability of this excuse suggests that both parents and pupils see a day in the country as no harm to child and believe that it won't hurt to miss a little of school.)

9:32 Geoffrey has history with sevens while sixes check their maps. After a moment with a first-floor teacher he says, "If I don't see you people working, I'll give another assignment."

9:35 Leonard, hiding behind his book, eats a chocolate candy bar. All others are coloring, drawing, or copying maps. (It's not hard to see why Leonard is becoming lardy. He will be a big, overweight man someday.)

9:38 Leonard and Pete slide wadded foil candy wrappers and pencil stub up and down the aisle. Geoffrey is involved in intimate informal discussion of history lesson with the sevens and ignores this behavior. Timmy observes and enjoys this vicariously. Billy watches also. He backs his chair into the path on occasion. Geoffrey continues discussion of Puritans.

9:42 Leonard is up and down from his chair at least ten times as he misses a pass. Two or three times he's totally out of chair and uses his hand in a shuffleboard style.

9:43 No one but Timmy is affected by this, and he only mildly. He keeps his pencil in hand.

9:44 to 9:46 There are about five passes. Geoffrey discusses religious toleration.

9:47 They are pitching—mostly softball style—the foil. Billy, who is talking, catches a mild "I don't want to compete" from Geoffrey.[6]

9:48 All the other sixes are still working. Walt G. is now disturbed. Mostly he is an onlooker. (LMS—Leonard's behavior has a quality of neurotic stupidity, an obsessive-compulsive type play. It seems as if he wants to get in trouble.)

9:49 Leonard crawls around on all fours looking for objects. Geoffrey finishes lesson with sevens and comes over to sixes. He pulls down a map of Africa. Pete and Leonard continue to sail wad of foil. Geoffrey totally ignores. (My reaction is that Leonard is cutting his throat.)

9:52 "Look to page 249 and map exercises." Geoffrey starts identification of bodies of water around Africa. Geoffrey raises question about boundaries of Indian and Atlantic oceans. Next they move to rivers of Africa. Josephine identifies and Esther writes.

9:55 "Leonard, take your books and put them on my desk and go downstairs." Geoffrey stares him down. "Put them anywhere. Now go down and sit on the bench at the principal's office." Sends Eileen with message to clerk and principal that he has sent Leonard down and that he, Geoffrey, will be down shortly.

9:57 He sends Pete to hall. He continues geography lesson with hardly a hitch. Esther finishes writing rivers and then he has her write on the oceans. He indicates how to finish drawing the maps: color, label (in pencil), content.

---

[6]This is Geoffrey's comment regarding competition against noise level while he teaches.

10:02 He asks Walt G. if he was involved. Walt says yes. (Although this was minimal.) Walt is sent to the hall.

10:03 Geoffrey goes out into the hall for discussion. Walt is sent back in. (LMS—I have odd emotional reaction: felt bad when Walt went out, relieved over his "acquittal.") Geoffrey returns.

10:04 Geoffrey helps Esther finish list. He asks what else goes on map. Cats for cataracts; "Don't draw kitty-cats." Asks, "What are rapids?" Harry says, "Fast water." "What about transportation?" Virgil fumbles on electricity, and Harry says "Tears up boats." "Going to pass out pens and new maps. Too messy, can't write in crayon. Do it over. Include all of these." He reads the list and indicates that ocean should be colored light, soft blue. He looks for a bad example. There is discussion, and they decide not to color water in. "It's blue already." The assignment remains the same. They are to redo map. Indicates which map should serve as guide.

10:11 "I'm going down to the office after recess. Is there anyone who needs to go down with me?[7] After recess you come up and get to work. Everyone have something to do?" Asks for volunteers. *Every* child volunteers. Paper-picking-up detail. Geoffrey passes out pens. (LMS—Really need strategy data on the Leonard episode. What was Geoffrey thinking through all of this? When did he make up his mind to "go all the way" with Leonard? What are the complications with Pete? What consequences with Timmy S.? What is the "example-setting" phenomenon? What is the impact on adult social system now that issue is out of the classroom.)

During recess, Geoffrey comments that he became aware of the disturbance about five minutes before. (LMS—This is slower awareness than I thought he had or a misestimate of time on his part.) He will ask for temporary suspension.[8] Parent must be in within three days or it is permanent. Doesn't know what to do about Pete since he has only two months. (Apparently, he doesn't want to use his credits.)[9] Cautions Norton about taking Leonard. She hasn't had problems with him in reading.

The Later Equilibrium The morning is not very atypical, although there is less overt conflict between the children and the teacher and the teaching goes better than usual. The notes are from the morning of October 21.[10]

At breakfast,[11] Alton commented about his concern for and his inability to sleep because of his bunch of kids, fourth graders, who came during the "October Revolution."[12] They have been giving him fits regarding

[7]A common practice at the Washington School was to take one or more of the uncontrolled children when one was to be out of class for an extended period of time.

[8]Leonard was given a temporary suspension. He returned to class after his mother came for a conference, and later they moved from the Washington School area.

[9]This is a reference to Hollander's (1957) concept of idiosyncracy credits. Pete turns sixteen in December and presumably will drop out of school on his own volition.

[10]These notes were written shortly after the conversation occurred and before school began.

[11]The observer frequently arrived early at Italo's.

[12]This is an early name we gave to the shift in classes; presumably cued by Homans' (1950) account of the Electrical Equipment Company.

discipline—they won't listen, they don't do their work, and so on. The achievement levels are so low that they don't fit his instructional "maps" either. All of this has boxed him in tightly. (Geoffrey says that Alton even has trouble with good groups.)

8:37 Kids come in quietly. Joe K. and Joe G. come over to my desk. Geoffrey talks briefly about attendance and absences. He comments on Evelyn's new hairdo. He asks Thelma about her lack of glasses and quizzes her about what she does or does not see. There is some banter, and he has her change places with Rose N. Most everyone has a dull, sleepy look this morning.

8:45 The reading groups go out and in. Peggy passes out paper. Geoffrey reviews words for syllabication: cardboard, happen, Kodak, poodle. Joe K. volunteers for all and goes up on poodle. Gets it right, but for wrong reason. Geoffrey enters into corrective discussion. (LMS—How can Joe be nurtured along?)[13] A list of ten words is put on board. Pupils solve these individually at their seats.

9:02 Geoffrey has them bring papers to him when they have finished.

9:05 Henry H. arrives. His brother came in about 5 minutes before. Norman had arrived about 10 minutes before.

9:06 Geoffrey calls on individuals one at a time to work problems on board. Kids are very quiet. Most attend to the board. Pace is very easy. No pressure. Most handle words okay. There are a few difficult ones. Geoffrey corrects but does so in relaxed way, asking, "What do you think?" "What's wrong with it?"

9:18 Geoffrey offers general principle: Syllabication helps us read words we know in our speaking. Geoffrey presents the word "unmanliness." Asks Joe K. about word. He's stuck. Has Harry analyze it into syllables, then has Joe K. pronounce it. He comes very close. Then enters into "manly" to get "like a man" and "un" as "not." Through most of this, Harry is the most help. He knows root and prefix as conceptual labels. (LMS—The trick here, in part, is using the able kids to start discussions and to help on rough and difficult points. As the others are able to respond on easier points, you call on them. If the lesson has "appropriate difficulty level," you have got to tax the average student and gradually extend him to be differentiated and shaped. The responses of able kids serve as prompts to the less able; they start the processes and permit reinforcement. This is pertinent to group structure, its development and its use.)

Geoffrey extends his lesson around "man" to include "mankind," "gentleman," "policeman," "fireman," and "mailman." (LMS—This is elaborated beautifully: Prompts are effective, generalization clear, examples pertinent, and there is humor, for example, when someone suggests postman to someone else's mailman, Geoffrey gives him a big smile. Time runs out and prevents analysis of postman.)

9:30 Reading groups change. Geoffrey checks around. He wakes new boy, Henry L., who is very drowsy.[14]

9:35 The sevens have history. The sixes study. Absent are Pete, Eileen, and Timmy S.[15] Leonard eats candy behind his book. (LMS—Low energy? No

[13] Joe K. is a continuous problem. Today is a good day, and the observer speculates on the care and nurture of good days.

[14] Henry L. consistently spent his days with his head on his desk. The stupor he was in made it difficult for the observer to judge whether he slept or just rested.

[15] The several absences and several tardy pupils are consistent events.

breakfast? Need for more rest? Candy as anxiety reducer? As he rustles paper, masochistic need for punishment? Simple diversion?)[16]

9:38 Leonard is on second piece. I noticed earlier that Marshall has a haircut. Like Sam, he was really shaggy. Looks like a different boy. Geoffrey develops history lesson, a review on trade routes.

9:41 Third piece of candy goes in. They are Brach's Neapolitan Coconut Caramels. Leonard chews away with chin on geography book. No work so far.

9:43 Joe K. comes over to the observer's desk. So does Joe G. Leonard is on fourth piece. Joe K. initiates conversation with Joe G. He tries to entice him into a drawing competition. The observer comments, "No talking, or you can't sit here."

9:46 Leonard is on fifth piece. Geoffrey is working on monopoly concept. Monopoly in trade is related to game of monopoly. Most have played this. (LMS—Concrete experience or lack of general intelligence? Best negative case so far.)[17] Joe G. has been influenced by Leonard and has taken out some bubble gum. He draws into the contagion Joe K., who is drawing a ship.

9:48 Leonard is on sixth piece.[18] (LMS—The evidence of fatigue and general physical malaise is very evident this morning: Henry L., if not asleep, is very close; Alan M. is hardly conscious; and Leonard is now resting.)

9:52 Albert H. is resting. Harry is holding his head up with hand. While most of sixes are quiet, few are working (about one-third). Others sit, rest, draw, or color. Josephine counts arithmetic combinations on fingers. Betty copies arithmetic problems. No answers as far as I can tell. (LMS— In tracing effects of home environment on school behavior, the rejection-abandonment scheme suggests that lack of supervision results in too little sleep and inadequate meals and that these deficiencies cause fatigue in school, low frustration tolerance, and inability to attack vigorously any type of task—especially one that at best is uninteresting and at worst is openly disliked.)

9:59 Geoffrey comes over to the sixes for geography. He notes pages and reading assignment. "Think Egypt. What pictures come to mind?" (LMS— Note the phrasing of this.)[19] Calls on Harry. (LMS—Note social structure.) They then enter into discussion of recent television movie, *Land of the Pharoahs*. Most of kids are with this part of discussion. Geoffrey discusses pyramids, size of stones, slavery, sleds. "Pyramids still there?" Asks regarding picture page 276. Asks if they've been to the Municipal Art Museum. About half have. Quiz about the mummy. Agnes talks of mummy on third floor of central library. Leona (when did she arrive?) comments about a coffin in her church. Geoffrey moves back into discussion of text: "Two cities and the Suez Canal." Raises Tyrone Power movie re-garding Suez. Comments on lack of historical and geographical accuracy of movies. Raises problem of difficulty in digging canal, such as Suez,

---

[16]Note the attempt to develop alternative hypotheses that could be continually reassessed.

[17]This illustrates the continuing concern for alternative hypotheses. Even when Geof-frey "teaches well," that is, in accord with concept attainment literature, progress is slow and difficult.

[18]Quantification is sometimes most revealing: six caramels in thirteen minutes.

[19]The phrasing of this has reference to Geoffrey's attempt to evoke concrete pictorial images rather than verbal-semantic ones.

in desert. Asks Grace why a canal. Tries to coax ideas out of group. Alan suggests transportation. Marshall notes connection between Mediterranean and Red Sea. Harry and Alan see the point, others don't immediately.

10:13 Calls on Joe G. and gets involved in gum-chewing problem. Mild threat regarding sentence writing. Has him get rid of it. Joe K. throws his away also. Continues with Suez and other canals. Harry suggests Panama. Calls on Marian to find it on world map. She's lost (Geoffrey does this with humor). Calls Sydney up to help. He finds it. He asks about similarities and differences. Joe K. suggests length. Geoffrey asks where they can find it. Pushes toward index in geography and pages 201–204. Meanwhile, Leona has joined the head-down resting group. Others have heads up, but Henry L. resting head on perpendicular of book. Geoffrey makes quick assignment, for lesson is incomplete because time has run out.

10:18 Bell. It is recess. One of the physical education teachers comes up to see Alton regarding Flora, Susan's sister, and problems with her in gym. The usual group meets: Alton, Holt, Norton, and—briefly—Gennep. Alton makes a pointed comment to me alone about seeing the consultant sometime yesterday (must have been a chance meeting) and about having "enough from Norton." He enters into brief discussion with Geoffrey regarding everyone's fatigue.

10:37 Leonard moves Joe G. over to "where he belongs." He was rough in a gentle but intimidating way. Thelma comes over. Talks about her glasses.[20]

10:40 Geoffrey enters in and comments, "Take out language books." He sends Esther, Virgil, Sydney and Josephine to board regarding outline. Geoffrey checks around on homework. Most of the kids have theirs done. Only negative comment that I've heard is regarding Joe G. "Where were you Friday? You're supposed to have it done!" (LMS—Noticeable difference in social conflict today.)

10:47 Leonard walks up to Geoffrey's desk for a pencil. Joe G. moves his desk back. Leonard returns, "Teacher told me to move this way. You dig, Mac. Listen, fella!" Leonard makes an issue. Joe K. suppports Joe G. by putting feet on desk as Leonard tries to move him. Geoffrey calls out to Joe G. to move back. (LMS—The volatility of the class, the rapid rise to naked aggression in the children, is amazing to watch. It's in the voice, the menacing facial expression, and the physical closeness of the way they stand. From an illustration such as this, it is easy to see how the racial issue might easily be invoked by the use of discriminatory differences, epithets, and stereotypes common in the community.[21] It wasn't.)

10:53 Geoffrey goes through and checks outline. Assigns page 64. Talks briefly about it. He stretches and yawns. Moves to "other part of language." Has pupils turn desks toward front. There is a bit of confusion. He banters briefly with Susan, "I sometimes become confused." He checks homework. Concurrently, sends kids to board to demonstrate answers on sentences by underlining adverbs and indicating referents. He sits toward front and has kids work sentences.

11:01 During this exercise, Alan bothers Josephine, teases by pulling at books, then pinches her lightly as she protects books. She bats him on arm and shoulder. Geoffrey interrupts this by calling on Alan. Joe K. is doing tomorrow's outlining homework. When Geoffrey looks for volunteer for

[20] The glasses have been broken, and she cannot afford to replace them.
[21] Joe G. is a Negro boy who came with the sixth graders.

the answer to number 7, Joe K.'s hand goes up. He doesn't miss a stroke on his outlining. Joe K. gets called on for number 8. He has volunteered. He picks up his paper and goes up to the board. He errs. Geoffrey asks If it is correct. Joe K. goes back and changes his answer. He is still in error. Geoffrey tells Joe K. to watch. Billy goes up to correct. He gets it. Geoffrey corrects language papers while this is going on. Kids moving up and back.

11:10 A note is sent in from Mr. Inman regarding the write-up suspension of Melvin in Room 12. He wants a brief note from Norton and Geoffrey because they "know him better."

11:12 Geoffrey starts in on "waking up."[22] He has a ruler and snaps it on the desk. He advises everyone to keep eyes open. He teases Leonard. "You can't see if someone hits you." Leonard in best masochistic self starts letting his head droop.

11:13 Geoffrey comes around and quietly tells Alan to go into hall. He had continued to bother Josephine. She earned some of it, though. For last sentence, Geoffrey asks, "Who can I pick on?" Finally selects, in good humor, Susan. There is banter regarding quitting while ahead. Geoffrey is still behaving in relaxed, informal way.

11:18 The sentences are finished. Geoffrey begins introduction to conjunctions and interjections. Sends Joe K. to his seat. "You can't see from there." Joe K. goes readily. He's almost finished his geography. Elma erases board. Geoffrey is full of humorous prompts regarding conjunctions. He gets Billy involved on comment about "Billy *and* Harry . . ." (who are brothers). Pulls in good humor: Conjunction—a word that is used to connect words, groups of words, or whole sentences. "There are three conjunctions that if you miss, I'll grab you by the top of head, whirl you around, and throw you out the window." In humor he rails at Billy. There is banter. You are *never, ever* supposed to miss "and," "or," "but." Someone says "a," and Geoffrey says, "This is the last time you'll be excused." Adds "for" and "nor" to list.

11:25 Now he asks for sentences giving examples. Calls on Susan and teases her about her low voice. Asks for "or" sentence from Billy. There is more banter. He can't give a sentence. Neither can Grace or Evelyn.

11:27 A girl, one of Geoffrey's former students, comes in. He converses briefly. Then he shifts his recitation by having Josephine, a volunteer, come to the board and write an "or" sentence. She puts, "You or her may come with me." He indicates "her" should be "she" but makes no issue. He looks in English book for assignment but changes tactics and suggests fifteen sentences: five "and," five "but," and five "or."

Sandy goes to write the assignment on the board. She moves Henry L. away. Leonard makes a suggestion. She tells him to "shut up." She, in combined fashion, ignores him and treats him like nothing: a don't-bother-me-boy attitude. She comes back to complete assignment. Leonard continues to give her a bad time. She couldn't be bothered less. Geoffrey had corrected Leonard a moment ago for marking assignment board.

11:36 Geoffrey finally sends visitor along. He goes back to work with sevens on scoring arithmetic papers. Geoffrey is at his desk. (LMS—It seems that an occasional check on assignments—for example, on Mondays,—would be helpful to get group going and prevent later incompleteness

---

[22] He is responding to the sleepy, groggy look of the class members.

and frustration. There is a fine line between "close supervision and abandonment.") Joe K. and Leonard are both restive

11:40 Almost all are working. Geoffrey breaks up Grace and Walt B., who are bothering one another. He handles this with slightly embarrassing humor about boys attracting girls and girls attracting boys. Other kids get a kick out of this. (LMS—Geoffrey's humor and velvet-glove approach are beautiful. How this is processed over time is another major theme.)

11:43 Leonard to observer, "Can I borrow your eraser? Gee, thanks." (LMS—He's so much the little boy in many aspects.)

11:45 Leonard comes by for help on his outline. He has the topic and first subtopic. We go over other subtopics, and I try to give him the idea before he goes on to the details. This gets at the process of outlining rather than emphasizing the product so heavily. In discussion he asks about capitalization of outline words.

11:52 Leonard goes back to his desk to finish. He works along at it. Geoffrey finishes grading arithmetic papers. He finishes note regarding suspendee. Informs Walt B. about audiovisual box. (Error results in no films this week.)[23]

11:58 Kids get ready for lunch. Bell rings. Geoffrey says no one up until after gym at 2:00 P.M. There is some banter regarding this. Leonard asks me if I'll be here this afternoon. Told him probably not. Inquire, "Any special reason?" He says no in slightly uneasy way.[24]

The Lessons

Our nearly verbatim accounts of two separate days have emphasized the moment-to-moment realities of the classroom. An overview of the lessons that Geoffrey taught will make concrete the activities which were continued throughout the semester. Geoffrey's plan book, a calendar with space for noting days, periods, and lessons, provides a framework into which more detailed observations can be inserted. In broad strokes the plan book allots time for lessons.

8:30–9:30	Reading
9:30 10:15	History for seventh graders
	Geography for sixth graders
10:30–11:15	Language
11:15–12:00	Open
1:00–2:00	Gym on Monday and Wednesday
	Choir for some on Thursday
2:00–2:30	Spelling
2:30–3:30	Arithmetic

The late morning period usually involved the conclusion of the language

[23] Washington School has procedures requiring each teacher to place orders in Gennep's mailbox for regular receipt of films.

[24] The contrast in Leonard's behavior between these brief moments and his more general difficulties is striking.

arts lesson, time for study, and a period to pick up lessons missed because of other events.

The plan book also contains three major entries and in abbreviated form "C," "R," and "A," followed by numbers of pages, problems, or topics. These suggest the major dimensions of the approach to the lessons. "R" refers to reading in class and to the specific pages involved. "A" refers to the problems or pages assigned for the next day, and "C" refers to the work that has been corrected. The assign-study-recite tradition dominates the approach to teaching.

The Joplin Plan Reading Group On October 1, Geoffrey and Norton implemented their daily reading groups in which they traded pupils and received additional help from Eagle, the remedial reading teacher, who took the most able pupils for special help. The notes reflect the organizational meeting with the pupils.

9:00 Geoffrey makes a seating chart for reading. (LMS—Administratively there is a lot of time spent on these shifts.) He indicates this is where they are to sit in reading. "No exceptions." He talks about materials and schedules.

Monday—*Skylines*
Tuesday—Workbook
Wednesday—Review
Thursday—*Reading for Meaning*
Friday—Literature book.

9:04 Geoffrey sends Peggy and Elma out in hall to "get all their talking finished for the day." He finishes schedule. He indicates they are here because they are 2 to 3 years behind and are only about fourth-grade level. "If you can't read at grade level you have trouble in language, geography, and other lessons. I don't expect you to blossom overnight. I do want you to try.[25] Most of you will be graded on how you improve. I want a silent working group. Come in expecting to work. You shouldn't be tired this early. None of you will be beaten, whipped, tortured, boiled in oil, so long as you work. Some of you will be working by yourself. This isn't punishment. It's to help you." He raises questions about outside reading: *Henry Higgins, The 500 Hats of Bartholomew Cubbins, This Boy Cody,* and others.

9:10 Talks about reading some of the books together. He raises question regarding having read fifth- but not fourth-grade books. (LMS—This low group is full of the dregs of the sixth and seventh grades. It is close to a special class in ability and comparable to a class of potential dropouts. My guess is that hardly one will finish eighth grade, much less high school: low intelligence, low achievement, history of problem behavior.)

9:17 Peggy and Elma return. Geoffrey picks monitors. (10/1)

Language Arts Initially, Geoffrey decided to group the entire class for language arts. When this began on October 1, it required the dozen seventh graders to work in the sixth-grade textbooks. The discussion began

---

[25] Once again, the reader will note our reference to "trying" which recurs throughout.

shortly before recess and the lesson continued afterward. The notes reflect this problem and the multiple strands of activity in the classroom.

10:13 There is some argument with sevens over doing sixth-grade language. Geoffrey lays Sandy out because she has no sixth-grade language levels tests done and yet complains because she isn't allowed to work in the seventh-grade book.

10:17 Recess. Geoffrey commented about a new boy, Henry H. Geoffrey is angry that he got him rather than Miss Binder, who has an intact class. He talked briefly to the boy. "Did the police bring you?" "No, they told me I had a choice of here or 'State'" (the reformatory). Geoffrey: "That wasn't a very hard decision, was it?" "No."

10:40 A brief explanation is asked regarding sixth-grade language books. (LMS—Considerable anxiety over being put back. Their lives are bound by frustration, by failure, and by a world that leaves them powerless.)

Geoffrey begins discussion (p. 15) "Understanding Sentences." He follows text. He reads with expression, enthusiasm, and incitement to learning. He raises questions and pulls votes—yes or no—and responses to specific items. Equilibrium here. Introduces practice exercise. Shows how on board. Does item No. 1. Paper passed out by monitor. Monitors (Peggy and Elma) are not enthusiastic or very competent. They are similar to coffee monitors (Sandy, Eileen, and Thelma).

10:51 All children are working. Even Pete has pencil and paper. (LMS—As Geoffrey commented before school and as Friday's notes show, the sevens are now "the responsible ones." They seem so grown up now, whereas they were the young ones in the prior grouping.) New boy, Henry H., sits and stares at book. As far as I can tell, he has not done any writing. This boy looks like another "sit and be quiet and I won't bother you either." He looks like a fifteen-year-old who's ready to quit. Billy and Timmy are aware of his blank paper. Sydney goes to board with number 2. Geoffrey is checking around the room. Notes that new boy has blank paper. Says nothing and goes on. Josephine to board for number 3. She writes, "It isn't a sentence." Geoffrey asks why not. "It ain't got no verb." Number 4: Evelyn goes to board. Timmy goes to board on number 5. Geoffrey continues to pick volunteers. Billy errs on subject of number 6. Susan volunteers for number 7. Geoffrey continues checking around class. Number 8: Joe K. (LMS—Almost all of the kids are responding quite enthusiastically.) Number 9: Sandy saunters up to board in full casualness. Geoffrey engages in banter with and over her. Number 10 answered correctly by Rose.

11:08 Geoffrey assigns exercises *A* and *B* on page 18. Harry and Leonard give Peggy, who is decked out in wool sweater and skirt, the once-over. (LMS—As we got into language lesson, there was a real difference in difficulty level of the sentences being analyzed. This difference suggests the need for careful analysis of texts for principles of sequential learning. Note similarities to programming. The teaching manuals should also be analyzed for the principles of learning latent within them.)

While assignments are being done, Geoffrey passes out dictionaries. Begins to get books out for new boy and has him write his name on each. (LMS—Note the kind of demand that he makes: The children possess materials, and Geoffrey indicates that they have responsibility for them. He has not made other demands yet.) Leonard begins "courting" Peggy. They talk rather than work.

Spelling   Spelling was a vehicle with multiple opportunities. While many analyses suggest that spelling often is a rote activity in the classroom, in Geoffrey's class the interconnections with such variables as individualization, warmth, and concept development appeared during an early lesson with the new group of children.

10:42   "All right, you've had three weeks of spelling. How did Mr. Gennep teach it? Sevens, you have spelling as normally. Sixes, every Friday you'll have a test. On Monday you'll have definitions; Tuesday, sentences; Wednesday, section *B*; Thursday, section *D*." He picks up on unit 4, page 10: short and long vowel sounds. Starts in by reading material from teacher's manual. (LMS—Has not prepared for this?) He raises question about children's names. He asks Walt G. his name and where he's from— Geoffrey has no records yet—and tells him to pronounce a word. The boy does. Evelyn answers questions regarding number of vowels and long and short sounds. Geoffrey raises "mope" as illustration. Talks about meaning. Gives illustration of moping around house. And with a smile he comments about moping in class last Friday (several of the girls had been crying because they had left Mr. Gennep). (LMS—This kind of warmth puts the girls "in his pocket." They react very warmly in return.) Geoffrey continues to ask for names and raises aspects of spelling and sounds. (LMS—This identification has multiple aspects for warmth, for control, pinpointing responsibility, and so on.) The initial interaction is mostly with the girls. The boys come in occasionally, but they aren't as able, as interested, or as desirous of pleasing Geoffrey. He returns to the assignment and enters into discussion of "hem." Several confuse this with "hymn." He has one girl look it up after one of the boys has spelled it. He goes back to setting up his procedures on spelling. "Count back five sheets—ten pages—in your composition book."   (9/30)

The rhythm was identical to the description appearing in Chapter Two. On Fridays, Geoffrey would test the words of the week and introduce the new unit. On Monday's, definitions were due, and on Tuesdays the use of the words in sentences was due. Wednesdays, the "Learning Your Words" and "Word Study" sections were due, and on Thursdays the sections "Using Your Words" and "More Word Study" were due and usually checked. The text materials programmed the substantive content to be learned. Geoffrey facilitated learning these materials with his humor and knack for individualizing through continuity comments. The reader will have inferred correctly that the classroom was bathed in language study. The parallels in reading, language, and spelling exercises, overlapping and reinforcing content, provide intensive stimulation in literacy training.

Social Studies   The tactics and strategy in social studies lessons are observed in a brief period on the first school day after the state teachers' convention and the Veterans Day holiday. Geoffrey has finished a brief 15 minute lesson with the seventh graders and begins a geography lesson with the sixth graders.

9:49   He comes over to sixes for geography. "Where are we? . . . Page 296 . . . Central Africa . . . To remind ourselves, look at map on page 287. . . . We're way behind the other room and must catch up. We have to see movies with them. There will be some long reading assignments." He has Betty come up and trace the Congo River. Corrects her and clarifies. Has Agnes begin reading. Has Evelyn read. (LMS—No attempt to explore recent conflicts over Katanga and the substates in the former Belgian Congo.)

9:56   Eileen and Peggy tend to coffee pot. All the kids follow along in reading. Geoffrey has them find towns on Banana, Matadi, and Léopoldville. (Alan and Henry L. are asleep.)

9:58   Josephine begins reading. She has trouble reading the number "320,000." (LMS—She's one of the better students. Is this a problem of building meaningful ideas on fragmented base?)

10:02 Joe K. volunteers and begins reading. He, too, has reading trouble—with "stucco" and "thatched" and with simple "with-which" errors. (LMS—Suggests considerable inability to grasp much of the content.) Geoffrey stops at end of paragraph and has kids check "stucco" in dictionary. He asks about "thatched roof."

10:06 He reads on. Asks about missionaries. Grace hits it closely. He extends and suggests their own churches might have them. Raises questions about comparabilities of schools. Pauses on "Electricity is generated in a hydroelectric powerhouse on a small tributary of the Congo." Asks meaning of "hydroelectric" and "tributary." Leona responds and so does Marshall. Asks about foreigners and illustrates with the examples of a Japanese lady who visited last week and if one of the pupils in the class were going on a job to Léopoldville. Teases Agnes about swimming in Congo and being eaten by crocodiles. He reads on. Points up pictures.

Reading includes a vivid passage on army ants. Geoffrey does quite a dramatic job on this. Kids follow attentively. Makes assignment of next few pages and three items in question.

10:15 Bell. (11/12)

The materials are difficult for the children and cause considerable frustration in independent work. The split class demands a considerable amount of independent study. The textbook dominates the sequence of information and ideas. Geoffrey does considerable incidental teaching of concepts—"stucco," "hydroelectric," and so on. The pupils are not hyperactive this particular morning, although after recess they are difficult to settle down. Alan and Henry L. withdraw into resting or napping. To move the class along faster, Geoffrey carries a major portion of the oral reading.

Teacher-Pupil Relationships

Schoolwide Control: The Continuing Battle   On Thursdays, Geoffrey usually had yard duty—the supervision of the children before school, at recess, and during the lunch hour. Usually the observer would accompany him and "legitimately" wander about the playground. On October 3, we were with the older boys, grades four through eight. The notes were recorded shortly after 10:30 when we returned to class. They illustrate mostly the school-wide discipline problems which erupt from time to time and with which the teachers continually struggle. Methodologically they indicate also the gradual accumulation of varied but relevant data.

> At recess the older boys were quite volatile. There were a number of episodes of "horsing around" up to the point of really hurting one of the kids in each episode. Miss Brown was somewhat reluctant to break this up. For the first time I stepped in as one boy was about to cry. . . . Fight at end of line coming in. Edwin, Sam, and other older boys break it up and bring the kids to Geoffrey, one Negro and one white. The latter is a known troublemaker. Geoffrey lectures both.

> Mr. Inman comes upstairs with an eighth-grade girl who is in some trouble. Holt stands and watches. May be part of Allison's problem. She was in a fight downstairs and walked out on Mr. Inman. On the playground her brother, Edwin, reported to Geoffrey that his grandfather had called the police the other night because Allison was fighting in neighborhood with an eighth-grade girl. Apparently there is no love lost among members of the family, even though grandparents live downstairs and Allison and Edwin live upstairs.

> Miss Binder yells down stairwell at pupils. Geoffrey asks, "Are they mine?" Binder says no. On playground Miss Carr, after breaking up fight with a troublesome child, grabs him hard by the hair so he will look her in the eye while she talks to him. (LMS—As the days go by, I see evidence of *every* teacher, at one time or another, with greater or lesser frequency, contributing to hold some kind of line against the volatile, explosive behavior of the kids.)

> Geoffrey also had picked up information on Joe G. and his transfer hopes. He lives in the Housing Project but was booted out of Jefferson School. He hopes to get back in. As I watch him here, he is in foreign territory, with no friends, and is the scapegoat of aggressive kids such as Harry and some others whose names I don't know. Henry H. has some law and court problems. Geoffrey thinks it was a wrong time and place and a wrong item in his pocket.

> At recess I had noticed a pocket knife. These are forbidden in school. If Geoffrey had seen it, he would have taken it away. They don't get returned.   (10/3)

On "Trying"   Within the classroom the indispensable factor in bridging the gap between middle-class values and behavior and lower-class values and behavior seemed to lie in the concept of "trying." The issue arose in the following fashion shortly after the change in classes:

8:58   Geoffrey begins the search for siblings of absent children. In at least one instance he runs into a half sister (I think) who lives elsewhere in the neighborhood and knows nothing of the whereabouts of the absent boy. This morning also there's a flavor of warmth, approval, and gentleness as kids respond "appropriately." He responds in kind. This is to new children and to the original members of the class, for example,

Sandy, who is willing to "try" to put time schedule on board. And one of the new girls who will "try" to find a sibling on the second floor. (LMS—Perhaps the key concept is around the word "try." This may be the key to the noncorresponding problem; the locus of causality—to use Tom Johnson's phrase—is within the pupil.[26] It is achievable status rather than ascribed. It has nothing to do with money, with ill-fitting clothes, with intelligence. It is also momentary in the best sense—more achievable immediately than academic achievement. If you try, there is no punishment even if your accomplishment is low, or if what you produce is negligible. On these mistakes and failures, except perhaps for reiterated aspects such as addend, minuend episodes in notes, the teacher gives in regularly—or even easily—without losing face.) (9/30)

Many of the kinds of pupil behavior, such as grooming, achievement, personal-social behavior, about which the teacher and pupil know there is disagreement, are ignored by the teacher if the pupil is perceived as willing to try.

Those on "The Contract" A major element in the social structure of the classroom after the exchange of pupils in October was what we came to call "the contract." Several pupils established a relationship with Geoffrey typified by the expression, "If you don't bother me, I won't bother you."[27] After long weeks of conflict, as we have indicated, Pete reached this point. In retrospect we might call it a reasonable solution to a difficult situation. Two new boys, Henry H. and Henry L., achieved the same status, although much more quickly. As we have quoted earlier, Geoffrey's notes on October 1 relate that Henry H. chose the Washington School instead of the state reformatory.

In addition, Henry H. once said to a classmate's probe regarding his work habits, "If you'd failed seventh grade as many times as I had you wouldn't do anything either." The notes indicate also he was arrested in late October because of an incident involving "stripping down" a car. Geoffrey was not clear whether he was asked or "cornered" into it. In his February summary notes, Geoffrey reflected upon Henry H.:

> *Henry H:* A waste of average talent. Could function satisfactorily in an average job. Can function well intellectually at sixth- and in some areas seventh-grade level. A chronic truant in the past, his appearances at school were enforced by the order of the court. Perhaps he can grow up and conduct the secondhand store or a similar enterprise with some capability and shrewdness, and occasionally with pure crookedness. He behaved himself somewhat well in the classroom, except that he bugged Susan and others around him whenever he could do so quietly. Not doing any work, he must have found the days long, and this entertainment was not too serious a violation.

[26] See Jackson's (1960) concept of noncorresponding normative structure and Johnson's recently (1966) published paper on teacher perception of causality.

[27] The contract, a belief system which exists in the classroom, and the complementary roles played by the pupil and the teacher, indicate the interdependencies of the elements in the system.

The critical cues that Geoffrey seemed to respond to were (1) the boy's past reputation in the school; (2) the truancy record; and (3) the immediate reason for his being in the school—the prison alternative.

Henry L. was a bit different from Pete and Henry H. He came to Geoffrey in a "trade" for Norman. Norman, a bitter, hostile, upset child, was demoted to Norton's fifth-grade room for several reasons: he was neither able nor willing to do the class work and he was a constant source of difficulty in classroom control. Geoffrey hoped to impress upon the other members of the class that there was potency in his warnings. In return for Norman, Geoffrey received Henry L. from Miss Norton. Henry, a tall, thin boy, had been a difficult adolescent for her.

In an effort to clarify Geoffrey's decision-making, the observer asked him to respond to the question: "What are the similarities and differences between Pete and Henry L., on the one hand, and Timmy and Joe K., on the other, which lead you to behave differently?" Early in January, Geoffrey wrote a reply into his notes:

> When Pete and Henry came to me, they came to me as dead losses. That is, they had a history of doing absolutely nothing in the classroom, and in Henry's case being truant and doing nothing including no nonsense. In the case of Pete, he came to school regularly, did nothing except nonsense. Thus the only deal I would make with these two is that I knew they were going to be there until age sixteen or suspended. If so, I had no objection to their sitting there in perfect silence and creating no nonsense. They would be asked to do nothing, would be given automatic U's, would receive no promotions. This would be in line with the informal understandings of Rooms 11, 13, and 14 on grading and promotion policy.
>
> I cannot do this with Timmy and Joe K. They are both younger and have two or three more years in the school ahead of them. Pete had only a matter of months, Henry less than a year. This is the basic reason why I attempt to get them doing something. I would hate to think that I was the one that resigned them to finishing out their careers like Pete and Henry, although I have no doubt that nothing else would have been any good with Pete and Henry. I do not have the test scores of these children here before me, although as I remember, Henry can function close to a normal level, while Pete, of course, can do nothing. In the case of the two sixth graders, they are both below the mean, but they are really not so far below that they cannot achieve some success in their school work. Both of these students have occasional flickers of decent intellectual functioning, especially Joe. In addition, they both have some energy, again especially in the case of Joe, which has to be channeled in some direction before it finds its outlet in mayhem. Thus I feel a greater responsibility to the two younger students, and I also feel there is a little bit more there to work with. I can think of no other considerations than these. Some may be added at another time. (1/3)

The complexities of "the contract" arose during a recess coffee break. The observer recorded the issues this way:

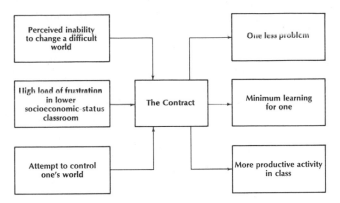

Figure 5.3   Aspects of "the contract" in teacher-pupil relationships.

Holt asked Geoffrey about his new group, and he replied, "Timmy, Joe K., and Alan." All these kids are known from their hall behavior, playground behavior, and siblings. Sympathetic grins are given. (LMS—Raises the question of a kid's reputation and the ability of a teacher to alter the child's behavior. When they receive treatment, should they also go to another school? This is a tough one, for they also go with a reputation. For instance, Alton commented about receiving today a kid with a list of six suspensions. This comes on top of another pupil he got last Friday who also had six suspensions. The latter, I think, has given Norton trouble on the playground—two fights in one day. She labels him "No good" and makes a comment about running him out of school. She used different words. I think the phrase was "get rid of."

Situations of this type are related to (1) the mental health of teachers and lessening their own load of frustration; (2) their attempt to shape the pupils' world; (3) continued strain of high interaction; (4) conflicting demands from institutional supervisors and from recalcitrant subordinates; (5) accumulated frustration of "being patient," and (6) ability to change pupils who are twelve-to-fifteen years old as opposed to working with them in a truce-type equilibrium.   (9/30)

We have schematized these hypotheses in Figure 5.3.

The Ever-present "Nonsense"   One of Geoffrey's favorite words was "nonsense." This term included the variety of minor nonacademic activity and interaction engaged in by the pupils.

In spite of my somewhat Pollyannish views, which have arisen from time to time, and in spite of the fact that in many ways the school has settled down into a workable and comfortable equilibrium, there are many specifics to the contrary, at least as the specifics apply to Mr. Geoffrey. He scarcely gets one kid pretty well in the line and working before another one pops up. In the last couple of days, Joe K. and Joe G. have been involved in one kind of incident or another. These include fighting, between Joe G. and Virgil; smoking, both Joe G. and Joe K.;

and sticking each other with pins and pencils, which involved both Joe G. and Joe K. The nonsense seems like an unceasing flow. All this occurs in spite of the fact that both boys were on temporary suspensions just a week or so ago, and both boys had parents or guardians come into the school for conferences then. (12/10)

Contagion's Broader Implications   While considerable investigation (Lippitt and others, 1952; Davis, 1965) has occurred concerning contagion or indirect influence, the additive effects upon the group and upon individual children have not been carefully analyzed in the classroom setting. Children with marginal academic ability and interest, who might be able to maintain themselves in a classroom of more motivated pupils, find themselves seduced into a never-ending spiral of alienation from the school's general purposes and goals. In December the observer noted:

> Yesterday there was a long, beautiful example of Timmy's mounting tension and the ever-present manifestations of it. He and Grace spent the last half-hour of school yesterday in fifteen different kinds of nonsense. In the midst of all this, Alan remains a pretty seriously disturbed boy also. The negative effects of these children on a boy such as Walt G., who has enough trouble maintaining himself, is also a most interesting picture. In a stable classroom he might well have maintained himself and gone along. As I see him and reflect upon the changes that are occurring, he looks as if he is in for ever-increasing difficulty and trouble. Similarly, Grace would make another illustration of a child who under favorable circumstances would adjust pretty well, but in this particular group she is continually getting into difficulty with one or another of the children. If it is not Timmy, it's Alan; if it's not Alan, it's somebody else.

> Geoffrey on occasion has commented, "I just don't have enough good kids to separate these others." This seems to me to be as explicit a statement of the proximity principle as anyone could find. (12/10)

Accumulating Fatigue and Frustration   Most occupations exact their toll in frustration and fatigue. Teaching in an urban school is no exception to this general phenomenon. As the semester continued, some of the specific contributions were captured in the notes. In retrospect we would argue for the importance of the interwoven threads, for example, the difficulty of the materials related to the need for independent work that has been precipitated by the split classes.

> In talking briefly about the work, and in no sense in an interview situation, Geoffrey commented how the history and the geography were getting him down. The materials are extremely difficult for the children. Geoffrey has to divide his time from one group to the next, and the children have to work independently a fair amount of the time. They are just not equipped to handle this kind of work as the field notes all indicate. He talked about the difficulty of the questions in the history

book for the seventh graders and the fact that on an earlier occasion he and another teacher had written other questions to go with the materials. These questions tend to be much more specific and much simpler than the really tough and interesting complex questions in the textbook.

In these subjects, too, Geoffrey still has a problem of getting the homework in. Somehow being able to analyze that problem should be a tremendous contribution. In regard to this, Geoffrey made a comment the other day, which he has made before, that the real problem in teaching these children is not discipline and aggressiveness but their extreme "apathy"—which may not be the exact word for it from my point of view. Without strong home support the kids just do not do the things that one might hope for. This also is a very interesting aspect of the general problem of Homans in which he states the principle— the leader will not give orders that will not be obeyed. Geoffrey gets caught up in this everytime. What are the constraints not to give orders in this area? Is it better to eliminate homework altogether? (11/21)

Three weeks later a more general summary of this same broad area was noted.

Another major position that should be taken in the write-up analysis of the materials concerns the general problem of "the difficulty, or the stresses and strains, of being an elementary school teacher in an urban slum." I don't think that anyone has ever really teased apart these frustrations which exist in such numbers and with such intensity in an elementary school classroom. The phenomena that I have in mind include the following items. First, Miss Holt's remarks about "the need for conversation with adults and being with children all day." Second, my own feeling of being "cooped up" in the room and in the building day in and day out, and especially when the weather is as pleasant and beautiful as it has been this fall. A third item would be one that Geoffrey mentions from time to time: boredom. This refers to the tremendous pall that comes over one teaching relatively the same content of fractions, history, or social studies from year to year. Fourth, another point concerns the almost complete inability to make progress in the academic areas and the difficulties that one has when there are no results even after hard teaching. I think this was well focused in Geoffrey's behavior yesterday when he gave a brief and simple test on fractions and found a large number of children who could handle very little of the material even though he had spent practically all day Friday trying to convey, with the best techniques available, the meaning and conceptual frame of reference for fractions. A fifth and related phenomenon is the apathy of the children toward any kind of outside work, be it homework or volunteer activity. This usually extends to the parents and with the whole neighborhood culture. "And nobody cares" seems to express the tenor of community feeling. A sixth item of frustration would be the never-ending battle, discussed in the above paragraph, with "kookie," maladjusted, acting-out, aggressive discipline problems. In Geoffrey's class this still has not ended. From what I can gather this is a pattern in other classes as well. These frustrations are the realities of this world and no amount of wishful thinking, it seems to me at this time, will eliminate them to any great degree. (12/10)

ISSUES IN THE IMPINGING ENVIRONMENT

The broader environment, the school, the families, and the community, had a continuing impact on Geoffrey and his classroom. These influences were multiple and of major and minor importance. We have singled out several sets of events that were highly significant during the semester, but we do not analyze and elaborate upon them in great detail.

Report Cards: An Introductory Illustration

The institutional demands, their complexity, their inappropriateness for a slum school, the faculty interpretations, and the individual teacher decisions are caught in the notes summarizing an early morning discussion.

Before school Geoffrey and Norton and Gennep were all in the room. Usually Gennep came in later. One of the initial topics of conversation was the fact that the teachers have not received the report cards that they will need to fill out this fall for the ten-week period. This is going to create some difficulties, because next week is a short week, with a teachers' meeting on Thursday and Friday and Veterans Day holiday on the following Monday. The problem of making out report cards for students of this sort is quite an interesting and complicated process. There are a number of written and unwritten rules about how a teacher must behave. These are complicated by the special kinds of kids here at the Washington School. For example, a teacher is not supposed to give a "C" in reading unless the child reads at grade level. Almost none of the children in these classes reads at grade level. Second, in a number of the areas, particularly art and music, science and health, there is very little teaching going on. This seems partly because of lack of time, partly because of lack of skill on the part of the teachers, and partly because of lack of interest in the areas. One teacher commented that she would give an "F" or "UNSATISFACTORY" to all the kids in science because they can't read the material since they are not up to grade level in reading. She, however, has had only one lesson in science from what she reports. Another commented that he will give grades of "C" to all those who are taking choir. Those who don't take choir will receive no grade in music. I don't know how he handles this problem with the principal or with the students' parents. There are some variations among the teachers in this grading procedure for Geoffrey tends to reserve his "F's" for the pupils that he intends to fail while another seems to give these pretty much to almost everyone at her discretion. At this point I do not know how the others do their grading. This suggests another subtheme of the total report. There are points of crisis when the classroom system formally becomes interdependent with the outside systems. These outside systems include the school policy and the overt implementation of school policy, such as sending report cards, and the parental system or community system. The report cards are a good illustration of this contact. At such points in time and with such groups, the actual functioning of the classroom becomes to some extent—a limited extent but greater than usual—apparent to the rest of the world. Some kind of masking or deception must occur, at least to some degree. (10/28)

The early observations and speculations received further specification and clarity in November when the eventful day occurred.

Passing out report cards, even when considerable teacher-pupil discussion and warning have occurred, remains a trauma for an elementary school child. The episode went like this at the Washington School on November 13.

3:01 Alan returns. Geoffrey has Agnes dust the table. He has boards erased. Gets ready to pass out report cards.

3:03 "Don't have envelopes . . . treat with care . . . back tomorrow . . . signed by parent. . . . Need clean hands (to pass them out). . . . Hardest thing to find." Selects Grace. Kids look cards over carefully. Most are pretty solemn. Explains absences Wednesday afternoon prior to teachers' meeting count for Thursday and Friday. Alan had asked. There is some joking by Timmy.

3:09 Geoffrey leaves the room. There is comparing back and forth. Walt G. brings his over to me: "Mom said I'd get a spanking if I brought one "U" home." He has a string.

3:11 Geoffrey returns. "If you're unhappy about report card, You, Y-O-U, try to do something about it. Be here, behave, and do your work. If you have any questions on your report cards, come up to me now and ask." Esther, Leona, Joe G. go up. "Tests, assignments, and so on." Timmy and Alan trade. Marshall comes over to Albert. Walt shops around to several. The clique trades information. Geoffrey explains to Joe G., "Whenever you're ready, you can do something about the "U's"." Kids all generally excited and anxious about home consequences. Geoffrey lets this go.

3:18 He rings a bell and calls them to attention. "Can't do anything regarding the past. . . . the slate is clean. That is, except for book reports. . . . Know three rules: Behave, be here, and do your best work. Mr. Doobee. The new work period began yesterday morning. I see some already haven't got work in . . . . Alan, don't monkey with that. Put you there because you said it would help." He explains why there is no grade in writing and science. "Haven't gotten to them yet. . . . so many back things we've had to catch up on." Grace asks regarding art. "Did you miss the lesson? Remember I'll be happy to talk with your parents. Will be happy to see them Tuesday. But I don't want any parent in who hasn't been told the whole story. . . . I am starting a new grade book for next ten weeks. I tore out the old one and filed it away. Only about five of you didn't have at least one "U." . . . Up to you. . . . Asked yesterday about passing. One boy said he didn't care. . . . all others said they care. Come back tomorrow. . . . most of you have been working well last two days. . . . can tell parents you are starting to shape up. Get going now. . . . Any questions. . . . Up to you. Will be here 7:30 to 8:15 next Tuesday."

3:27 Bells. Girls get their coats and line up. A few girls, Agnes, Betty and Esther seem near tears.

Open House

Public Schools interact with the community through parent-teacher associations and evenings such as an "open house." The observer caught much of the impact through comments from the faculty, from announcements at a faculty meeting, and in participating in the evening.

> The faculty meeting was a little bit disorganized because Mr. Inman had to wait for the wandering ones to get in.[28] Several points of interest are appropriate. First, in talking about the teachers' participation in the coming open house for Tuesday, he, the principal, indicated that he understood how none of them liked to come down to the neighborhood at night, and he didn't either, and that he had arranged for police protection for the evening. The matter-of-fact way in which he expressed this struck me once again with the great differences between the Washington School and other schools in the community. The entire image that one has is so different for this school. Second, he commented that he did not think there would be a large crowd, although he did want all the teachers there to talk with the parents who did come and that he wanted them to indicate that the parents were welcome to come. In the course of describing the crowd, he commented that the Patrons Association had five or six people in attendance at the last meeting. Third, he mentioned that the Patrons Association was going to take care of the Christmas gift to each child, which he thought would be a candy bar and a piece of fruit. They were not going to have a Christmas party at the Community Center. (7 A.M. 11/19)

The field notes continue in the early evening, the night of the open house.

> It is raining slightly on a cold, damp, uncomfortable evening. I am on my way down to the Washington School for the annual fall open house. I have been told to expect very few people, especially if the weather is bad. The weather is bad. The parents who come are often the people who need not come, in terms of the difficulties and the problems with the children. I have been told also that the parents will walk around with a bewildered look, not knowing what they are supposed to do. I was warned that the people will respond in a rather fearful manner for they are with others who they feel are from a higher social class than they. Geoffrey had asked the children how many of the parents were coming. Only five or six raised their hands. With bad weather he estimates that only one or two will show up. He had said that he was not going to decorate his room or go out of his way to "pretty up the place at all." Those are not his words, they are mine, but they carry the full flavor of what he was saying. Miss Norton raised at one point this morning, either before school or during recess coffee, that the first floor had gone out of their way to do some of these things. Once again, the notion of keeping the group equivalent so that there are no unfavorable comparisons among the teachers on the second floor comes

---

[28] Someone had pulled the fire alarm lever at 3:25, five minutes before school was out, and the building had been cleared.

through pretty clearly. Geoffrey did put off having the kids count their books, the assignment that came through the official channel the other day, until this afternoon so that they could clean up their desks at the same time. This cleanup involves removing old waste paper and old assignment sheets and generally tidying up. It will be interesting to see whether he behaves the way he has said he would. On occasion the teachers' talk is different from the actual results that are accomplished and exhibited.

The basic learning experience that I am interested in at the moment is developing a clear perception or image of what the PTA is like in an urban slum school. As a learning problem, this is very interesting. It seems comparable to the experiences that a student teacher has when he is "learning how to be a teacher." Part of the learning seems to be in overcoming general anxiety, which is a function of not having a clear, specific referent for talking about this particular phenomenon. I do not doubt that the expectations given me by the teachers are correct. But somehow, I am not convinced that I know what open house really is. I am not sure that after I experience it I will be able to describe it conceptually any better than I have in the above paragraph. Certainly I should be better able to put some specific illustrations into the statement. This, it seems to me, is a most interesting commentary on the whole program of teacher training. I will have to develop this at more length later. (6:45 P.M. 11/19)

The notes continue on the morning after the open house:

It is difficult to know where to begin in summarizing the open house last night. There are a number of impressions that should be recorded. First, the crowd was not large although it seemed larger than it was because many of the families brought their children with them. Often this involved one woman with five kids trailing about through the building. I quizzed the teachers on the number of visitors. It seemed that they ranged from about two to seven, maybe one with eight, per room. They average about three, maybe four at the most, parents per room. Of the three "transportee" rooms only one set of parents came and they were in Mr. Quast's room. In Geoffrey's room the only kids that I saw were Thelma, Marian, and Peggy. There were probably disproportionately more children in the primary and lower grades than in the upper grades. As I looked at the parents and the children, my general feeling was that the socioeconomic continuum was distributed but there was a proponderance of the higher social strata (for this group) parents. The older girls who were around, both in Geoffrey's room and in some of the others, were dressed in their finest outfits. There were several pairs of highheels, and so forth.

There were two groups of three or four adolescent boys roaming about the building. We met one of these groups as we walked in. Geoffrey knew several of them from earlier years and they were quite flip, yet friendly toward him. They fit the general notion of "a fun-loving group of adolescents." They buzzed around the building talking to him; they went over into Miss Holt's room; they talked to Miss Binder among the others. There were several families of local Negro children in the building also. I spent a good deal of my time talking with the two custodians and also with the coach. We teased and joked about a range of things from the New York City custodians who make $50,000 per year, to local school conditions, to gambling and betting. This conversation ought to be extended in much more detail. There was a policeman in the building who stood in the inside hall by the door talking most of the evening to Mr. Inman and the PTA president. Almost all of the teachers were there; in fact, I cannot think of any who were not. (11/20)

After visiting in the classrooms, the total group of children, parents, and teachers gathered in the kindergarten to see a film strip and hear a recording describing the costs of public education and the need for passing tax levies in support of public schools. All in all it was a very quiet evening.

The Racial Conflict

Part of the "flow of the semester" lies in the building-wide events which provided a context for the classroom. The Washington School participated in the "bussing" solution for the overcrowded Negro areas in the Eastern ghetto of Big City. While this is a long and complex story in its own right, we need to mention briefly the background narrative as it has implications on Geoffrey and his classroom. The critical elements are these: three classes of eighth-grade Negro pupils and their teachers attended the Washington School. They arrived approximately at 8:45 and were maintained as intact classrooms. Their teachers rode the buses with them. Geoffrey's children shared a common gym period and a common playground during recess and lunch periods. The contact among the teachers was minimal. During the course of the semester several incidents of fighting occurred. Rumors spread of riots, parents were in the school, and children were taken home. Older brothers and sisters, and presumably unrelated outsiders, cruised the neighborhood in cars. Police were in and out of the building.

The consequences for Geoffrey's classroom were multiple: (1) as an informal leader of the staff he was drawn out of the classroom for extended periods of time to help solve the problems. (2) The children he had in class were quite excitable generally and during the periods of racial unrest they were practically uncontrollable in the classroom; in the vernacular they were "all jazzed up." (3) Specific children drew automatic suspensions because they were involved in fighting and leaving school without permission. (4) The several local Negroes were drawn into choosing sides, that is, identifying as a Washington School pupil or as a Negro. When the latter choice was made by Elma it precipitated more uncontrolled behavior in the classroom, and made it even more difficult for Geoffrey who, because of her reputation as a behavior problem, had been handling her with kid gloves since September.[29] The situation complicated itself as Elma began

---

[29] The reader will recall Miss Holt's comment about Elma's temper tantrums in prior years and the Mother's question of the child's legitimacy.

accusing Geoffrey of discriminating against her because she was a Negro. (5) From the beginning of the semester, the afternoon recesses had been eliminated to minimize the probabilities of incidents. (6) The physical education schedules were shuffled to maximize integration. The teachers reacted to this with some hostility. Finally, these problems prevented Geoffrey and Norton from asking Mr. Inman to allow them to trade classes in areas other than reading. They realized Mr. Inman did not especially like the trading practice and they were reluctant to approach him while he was engrossed in so many other difficult issues.

Cold Weather: Indoor Recess and The Heating Problem

With the arrival of cold weather, we had our initial experience with "indoor recess."

> Indoor recess means waiting until 10:30 in the morning and then lining up the kids and walking down to the restroom with them. In Geoffrey's case he took the boys from Miss Norton's room also, and she took his girls and down they went. He stopped by at Room 10 on the way up to have a coke and to rest for a moment. As he explained to the children in a very brief comment, "It is something that the teachers hate worse than the pupils do." The part that amazed me was the children's extreme docility in responding to this change in procedures. My feeling was that I wanted my coffee more than they wanted their recess. It hardly broke the routine of the morning in which Geoffrey pushed very hard once again in language and in arithmetic. (11/21)

Later, such recesses exacted their toll, for the children had little break from a setting of control, of physical inactivity, and of difficult lessons. Mechanisms like indoor recess suggest the ways in which environmental variables such as the weather have impact upon the classroom social system.

During December, Big City had an unseasonable stretch of cold weather. As the temperature went below freezing outside, the interior of the building never climbed above 70° on some days. The staff was never sure whether the fault lay in the aged furnaces, the laziness or physical handicaps of the custodians, or the custodians "getting even" for earlier slights. Nonetheless it was cold in the classrooms. The children wore their wraps during class periods; on several days the teachers taught in their overshoes in an effort to keep warm. The observer shivered with his hands in his pockets and with his feet searching for the rays of the pale winter sun coming through the window. The consequences included the "loss of a week," as the teachers described it. Little academic work was performed; absences were quite high; children were sick and not feeling well. The conflict between teachers and custodians increased. Considerable discussions occurred concerning whether today was better or worse than yesterday, what could be done, and so forth. The frustrations accumulated.

Out of School Activities

The classroom, for all of its brick and concrete, downtown directives, textbooks, and faculty control never really escapes the community in which it resides.

> Geoffrey related that Marshall had commented that Henry H. and a boy from City High, a last year's eighth-grade graduate, had been involved in a deal to wreck a car for the insurance. Henry just couldn't see wrecking a "perfectly good" car, so after driving it around they proceeded to take the engine out and then persuaded Sam, Marshall, and brother Albert to push it down the street and off a bank under the bridge at Dry Creek. Apparently all were picked up and the latter three released. Henry is still out of school. He's been on probation and may now be in serious trouble. (LMS—The impact of community forces in the lives of these kids is tremendous.) (10/29)

Holidays

Calendars embody rituals of several kinds. We have noted that Geoffrey's classroom had a daily and weekly recurring mode. His plan book, when laid open, possessed a weekly outline. The weeks of the last half of the semester were decimated by holidays. Halloween, even for upper elementary pupils, is an occasion, as we have indicated elsewhere in our report. Preparations consume time and energy; the party itself took most of Thursday afternoon, October 31. The following week, Thursday and Friday, November 7 and 8, the annual State Teachers Convention was held in Big City and school was recessed. The contiguous Monday, November 11, was Veterans Day and a school holiday. The last two days of the week of November 25 were Thanksgiving Day holidays. Three good weeks followed, although Christmas was in the air. A party on Monday afternoon, December 23, was followed by two weeks of Christmas recess. January consisted of a three-week lame-duck closing of the first semester. Two days of this were the tag ends of one week, Thursday and Friday, January 2 and 3. The last week was interrupted by a count of library books and text books, and no school on Friday afternoon of January 24, the last day of the semester.

The switching of classes at the end of September now has a negative context. The loss of that month, and the destruction of early October because of beginning again with a new group, struck out the best time during the fall, for November and December always have many scheduled interruptions.

Mobility of the Children

As we have indicated, the closing of the classroom had a dramatic impact on Geoffrey's class. It removed many of the more able and stimulating members and brought in a group of younger children with whom

Geoffrey felt less comfortable for they were more difficult to relate to. Besides the age factor, it brought in the "aggregate" (as we called them), a number of seriously disturbed and maladjusted children. However, in addition to this mobility, the flow of the semester brought many other changes. For instance, Sandy returned to Kentucky; her mother wanted to have her baby "at home." Molly moved. After appropriate tears on each departure the clique began to reconstitute itself around Eileen, Patty, and Thelma. Pete left. Billy's family moved and he finally switched schools, although long after his brother Harry had gone.

Two new boys, Matt and Allen arrived. They were able students, especially Matt, and soon, along with Kent, they developed as a self-motivated team who facilitated not only their own instruction but that of the girls' clique as well.

In the sixth-grade group, Norman had been demoted, and Leonard moved from the district. Harry's departure via a suspension was imminent; however, his family's move permitted a transfer. The arrivals included Henry L., who came early in the trade for Norman; Elizabeth, a tall, pale, very attractive but sad girl whom Geoffrey systematically tried to bring out with TLC, tender loving care; Shannon, a girl who came very late in the semester, who wore very pretty, homemade dresses, and who, like Ruth, another new sixth grader, just began to be a part of the group. Ted, while new to Geoffrey, was returning to the school he had attended before and was known to several of the boys. A new Ben and a new Betty arrived just as the semester ended.

At the close of the semester, the observer asked Geoffrey to comment on his tactics of orienting the new children into the activities of the group; he responded in his notes as follows:

> I make no fuss over a new child. When he comes to the room, he is assigned a desk with the group into which he has been placed, given his books, and let alone. I tell the child normally that I will not demand that he complete all the assignments the first few days. Rather I allow him this time to get gradually into the swing of things. In many cases I do pick spelling as a way of getting him started working. Since most of the kids understand the mechanics of doing the assignments, I can assign another child to the new one. The other child can explain what I want to the new one. This also gives the new child at least one kid he can talk to who will answer questions for him. In the greater portion of the time the kid is not new to the system, and in many cases is not even new to the school. When the child is not new to the school he seems to have no difficulty picking up a friend or two for company. A kid who has come from another public school in the system will also not find things too different from before. In the cases of children from another system, especially those who have never been in our system, I watch these a little more closely to see that they gradually work themselves into things. In most cases I find that other students take care of the new ones. In some cases, such as that of Elizabeth, when I see that the child is not as happy as she should be, I make an extra effort to set her at ease.

I must admit that I have never done any serious thinking about what I should do when a new child comes into the room. However, it seems to me that this is what my particular group of teachers does, and who am I to change this? After a few days, if the child is doing his assignments and things as he should, no special attack is necessary by me. If the child is not doing what he or she should be doing, then I start making a special effort to make the child understand what I want. Perhaps you might say my orienting of them is simply exposure to me in the classroom and to the kids around him. Some might say that if I want to get them off on the right track I should just sit down with them myself and tell them right away what I want. On the other hand, after they get used to things they are going to do what they want anyway, so what value is this? Again, I have never thought that seriously about a better way of doing it. Besides, I can get to know the kid better by watching him in the classroom than by talking with him myself. (2/15)

TEACHER DECISION-MAKING: A FURTHER ILLUSTRATION

Geoffrey's Dilemma

The second group, the sixth graders, were a more difficult group. Our notes record Gennep's earlier frustration in moving them toward academic goals. Our accounts of two days indicate Geoffrey's difficulties, also. Within our decision-making model Geoffrey faced a further difficult problem, which was a three-alternative dilemma. The dilemma centers around "demand level," the amount and kind of activity that Geoffrey thought the children should produce before he would approve or disapprove. This conception of Geoffrey's was implemented in his behavior in class: he told the children what he wanted, he showed them, he approved those who achieved it, he probed those who did not, and later he warned, threatened, and exercised a variety of verbal and social punishments at his command.

As time continued and a number of children had not responded, the question arose whether to maintain the demand level or lower it. On October 9 Geoffrey commented on the difficulties with his sixth graders and speculated on several alternatives for resolving the problems. The resolutions concerned curriculum materials:

I must make radical shift here. Curriculum enters in. These kids aren't getting anything out of this. All this nonsense must stop. Choir is held at a miserable time. What steps are there to take: Pitch language books for most part? Pitch arithmetic books to great extent? (10/9)

We have diagrammed the alternatives and consequences in Figure 5.4. To maintain the demands seemed to imply that the children would learn more. Past experience had told him that pupils like these will achieve

Dilemma	Alternatives	Consequences

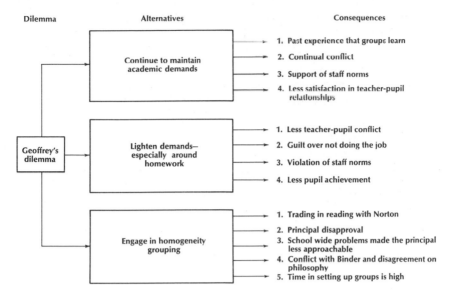

Figure 5.4 Geoffrey's dilemma.

under pressure. The basis for this seemed to be his several years of experience in which he had ridden a group or two quite hard. A positive outcome occurred at the cost of continued conflict with the children and considerably less satisfaction to himself in teacher-pupil relationships. The staff, especially the small group with which he was a member, would support this alternative; they had little sympathy for teachers who did not try, who coasted or who "dogged" it. The consequences of lowered demand level reflected the other end of the several continua mentioned above: less teacher-pupil conflict, guilt over not doing the job, the social disapproval from violation of a particular staff norm, and less academic attainment of the pupils.

As we have indicated, Geoffrey did move out of the regular textbooks. In reading he traded with Miss Norton. Miss Eagle, the remedial reading teacher, brought additional resources to bear. In arithmetic and language arts he obtained sets of exercises on "fundamentals," whole numbers and word analysis skills. However, October was still a most difficult month. Geoffrey commented in his notes on October 28.

> The sixth grade group continues to show an unhealthy attitude toward assignments. Only three of the group had completed the exercises for today, while another three have legitimate excuses for not doing so. The seventh grade group is much better about assignments than the sixth graders. In the seventh-grade group Henry, Peggy, and Pete do very little work, with only Peggy, of the three, attempting to get something down on paper in order to do any of the reading. In the sixth grade group, however, the situation is almost reversed, with less than

half-a-dozen regularly doing the assignments. Thus far I see no way of motivating them to get their work done. I will have to see what the report cards bring in the direction of pupil improvement or parental pressure. I do believe, however, that, as is generally true in this school, the latter will not help me in any way to get these pupils to do their work. The norms of this floor, at least at this end of it, include the belief that teachers give work and expect the pupils to finish it. (10/28)

The Proposal for Reorganization

After a month with the split-level classes, Mr. Geoffrey and Miss Norton began discussions of trading pupils for more homogeneous grouping. On October 30 the observer recorded at length various aspects of their deliberations. The notes reflect the thinking related to their decision-making, the kinds of problems they anticipated, and how they planned to circumvent them:

The major item which I need to talk about is the coming early November revolution.[30] Norton and Geoffrey have been extremely dissatisfied with their split-level classrooms. Up until yesterday, they have just talked and moaned about the difficulties they had with their groups. Yesterday morning before school they entered into serious negotiations about the problem and the possible resolutions. They talked briefly of the ungraded classroom in some Big City elementary schools, which for some reason Mr. Inman does not like. This plan gathers together deviant children grouped according to one criterion or another, pulls them out of the regular classes and attempts to teach them "at their level." Big City also handles this problem at the fourth-grade level by having what they call "Rooms of 20" in which twenty children are given intensive help, in reading especially, to enable them to take on the work of the middle grades. Usually these are children with low-average ability who have the potential to accomplish much more than they have so far demonstrated. At its worst, this is just a mechanism for failing a kid easily. At its best, it does provide chances for individualized instruction and attention. Geoffrey and Norton are working toward this kind of solution in a semi-departmentalized fashion. The basic goal is to have all the kids at the same level of text or outside materials and instruction in order to teach the whole group as a single entity. There are several aspects of this: one is the conservation of teacher energy, which may well be the main reason that these two teachers are entering into the discussions. A second is the fact that the regular work is too difficult for a great majority of their children. When this is true in a textbook, traditional-type school, it plays hell with the whole instructional program.

The way the thinking developed between Geoffrey and Norton was another beautiful example of the decision-making model. Certain conditions were accepted as unmodifiable. For instance, as Miss Norton said, "The gym periods have already been shuffled too much; we can't

[30]The observer saw the October shift in classes and the intended trading of pupils as major alterations in the system.

touch those." This knocked out one morning period and one afternoon period when both have formal gym periods. Another accepted condition, which cut out several alternatives, was Geoffrey's very strong preference for what he calls straight-line freedom across the week. This means having Monday, Tuesday, Wednesday, Thursday, and Friday all clear at the same period—for instance at 2:00 in the afternoon so that he could run arithmetic or a language arts program right through the week at that hour. Geoffrey doesn't want to be switching classes at one time on one day and another time another day. He likes his program to be consistent and stable. Another given was that the arithmetic and the language arts needed work every day. These points were discussed during the early morning. A point not made on this occasion—but which has been made on other occasions—was that Geoffrey and Norton were essentially in agreement as to how classes should be managed and how teaching should be carried out. Both of them have considerable trouble with Miss Binder's point of view and consequently very little is done with her, so she sits as an undigested irritant in the general functioning of this part of the second floor. As Geoffrey has said on a couple of occasions and said again yesterday, "If only she weren't there we could work things out very neatly in this end of the building."

Another item up for discussion was Miss Norton's question "Do we switch by pupils or do we switch by achievement levels?" The major reasoning seemed to go this way: One, it's easier if the same kids move all the time. Two, Mr. Inman would probably be less disturbed if only a few were affected. Three, no marked irregularities or uneven profiles (LMS—That's my word) occur in the various achievement areas. (LMS—That may have been a rationalization in saying that the one way is a better way, and what we really want to do anyway.)

Another aspect of the problem concerning the splitting of the kids: Miss Norton volunteered to take the "kooks" and work with them on essentially upper primary materials. She said "I know you don't like teaching that easy stuff and it doesn't matter that much to me." Geoffrey then expressed a willingness to take the larger number of pupils, since she had the more difficult bunch. Between the two of them they have approximately 70 students, which will make a 30-40 split, with Norton getting the smaller bunch and Geoffrey getting the larger bunch. The ease with which all of this was planned struck me as indicating extremely strong motivation underlying the whole enterprise. Both teachers were willing to make many concessions. Geoffrey's motivation is his general unhappiness with the quantity and quality of work done by the children. I can also perceive his repeated frustration with the split groups. He soon must face a judgment day in arithmetic. He has been using some supplementary materials that are about to run out. In a sense he has been biding his time and now he has got to go to work and move into more difficult materials. There is no easy resolution of this problem within his class. In the same way his language arts program has been mainly an attempt to hold the line. In the language arts they have had some easy materials in parts of speech and sentences, which fit the levels program, and which are again outside the general run of the text. He spent a good bit of time on the outlining material from a workbook. These lessons have been most difficult and yet, in terms of response from some of the pupils, seemingly quite productive. Geoffrey is bored stiff with this material and any kind of a change will be a change for the better. Miss Norton's motives are not clear at this point. Presumably she is caught by the same pressures, for she has often reported her pupils' test scores, which should put them in special class (I.Q.'s below 75) rather than in the regular fifth and sixth grade. What these changes will do to grading and to promotion is very unclear. If I understand the discussion so far, the two teachers give a tremendous number of P's and U's anyway, so in that sense it wouldn't make a whole lot of difference.

To the best of my knowledge all of this is being carried out unbeknownst to Mr. Inman. Yesterday morning when Miss Holt came up the stairs after being out on yard duty, she looked at Geoffrey and Norton and commented "What's being plotted now?" Geoffrey and Norton traded grins and proceeded to tell her, "A little departmentalization." Miss Holt gave her characteristic "Oh" type response and then made a slight dig or two.

Another point that I should have mentioned earlier is the reading program. As both of them commented, "We can't upset Miss Eagle's program again." Also, Miss Norton in her fifth-grade group has one girl who is brighter than the rest and is a willing as well as a reasonably achieving student. Norton raised the possibility of giving the student to Mr. Gennep. This would be for the child's benefit since she is seemingly profiting very little from being with the bunch that Miss Norton has. Later at recess this was raised briefly with Gennep who immediately grinned and talked about "trading one of his students for one of hers." She replied that wasn't quite what she had in mind.   (10/30)

In Actuality

Trading was being implemented already in reading, where Geoffrey took the lowest achievers, based on test scores and teacher judgment, Norton took a larger middle-level group, and Eagle, the remedial teacher, took a smaller group of the most able children. An aspect of this alternative not only involved a shift in demand-level regarding homework but also a changed perspective on appropriateness of curriculum. For instance, Geoffrey legitimately moved into simpler workbooks and later into even simpler exercise sheets. These pupils were defined as the least able, below grade level, and most unlikely to finish elementary school, much less high school. Consequently a different standard was held for them and activities proceeded with minimal homework, lowered demand and less frustration. The interaction was freer, less conflicting, and more enjoyable. Without question, in the observer's eyes the affective learning, attitudes toward school, were positive; the academic learning remains open to question.

Additional trading did not occur. The major reason was Mr. Inman's general dislike for the procedure and the hesitancy on the part of Geoffrey or Norton to approach him. The racial strife was so serious it occupied much of Inman's time and attention. The staff never found a time that was "right"; the outside problems remained throughout.

SUMMARY

Briefly, this is the way Indian Summer moves into Winter in an urban slum school. Lives of pupils and teachers play themselves out with both major and minor problems and satisfactions—and with considerable tragedy. We have pinpointed only parts of two days. However, they are not atypical. The change in classes after the first month produced major consequences. The split-level class in the best of circumstances is an extremely awkward organizational strategy. In a slum classroom, tied to traditional textbook teaching, it is a major frustration to all. As we have tried to specify, the story is larger and more complicated than this alone.

The closing of the room affected the faculty and the children in a variety of ways. It affected the former mainly because the year's work, in a sense, had to be started all over again. It affected the students in that they found themselves in different groups and in many cases different rooms. They, too, had to begin over again.

The new pupils presented Mr. Geoffrey with more difficult, and, as he saw it, a greater number of problems than he had before. The sixth graders were an aggregate of severe problems of mental health. Geoffrey's attempts to "groove the children," shape them to a manageable group, seemed to have less success than they had had with the class at the start of the year. We described the seriousness of the conflict and indicated that the "later equilibrium," a phrase which might denote an improved situation, suggested that while lessons were being presented and more time was being devoted to purely instructional matters, the conflict was not really solved. The lessons themselves highlight some of the difficulties to be found in the same class—difficulties which existed in the September group but which are much more serious in October's children.

The problem of pupil control is schoolwide and is a continuing battle. In the conflict between children and faculty, however, the tension was re-duced if the teacher perceived the child to be trying or if an implicit truce was established between the two. The latter case we have identified as "the contract." However, what we have termed the ever-present "nonsense," the problem of contagion, and the accumulation of fatigue and frustration militated against resolution of the conflict between child and teacher.

In addition to the problems indicated above, other broader environ-mental problems affected the classroom. Report cards illustrate that district-wide institutional demands may be inappropriate for some schools, especially the slum school. The "open house" indicates to some degree the lack of interest parents had in the school. Racial conflict pushed educational efforts aside. Often even the weather seemed involved in conspiring against instruction. Out-of-school activities, holidays, and the mobility of the children affected the instructional program adversely. It is in this October context that Geoffrey and Norton looked for ways to work with some effectiveness and less frustration. However, what they proposed doing in their two classrooms was lost in the problems of the school and the community.

CHAPTER SIX

ACTIVITIES

THE STRUCTURE OF THE DISCIPLINES

Geoffrey's Schema

Earlier in the report we described in some detail Mr. Geoffrey's introduction of the class into the instructional areas. At this point we want to begin to work the concrete material into our developing conceptual framework as we look at the "3 R's" more analytically. Perhaps the easiest way is to cite Mr. Geoffrey's response to the general probe: What special joys, limitations, difficulties and "whatever" exist in teaching reading, language arts, arithmetic, history, and geography? From this we can then move analytically and synthetically.

Let's lump reading and language arts together, as reading falls in there, and state that this is the most difficult area to teach effectively. The

complexity of language arts is such that it is difficult to break the subject matter into parts and teach special skills. For example, in grammar,
one cannot teach all the parts of speech at once, and yet it is a little
ridiculous to ask a student to pick a noun out of ten words in a sentence
when he has no idea what the other nine words are. In reading, one can
teach syllabication, at least teach the mechanics of it, and yet of what
value is it if the reader comes to a word and just simply will not try to
divide it into syllables. There are no special joys in teaching reading
and language arts. The limitations and difficulties are legion. Textbooks
do not help. The bad habits of speech have become so firmly entrenched
over the years that hammering and hammering perhaps may bring about
the correct response in the classroom, but this will be lost the moment
one leaves the school. As for reading, it is quite important that these
students learn how to read, and even a lot of them can recognize this.
However, what does it really matter whether they know a noun from a
pronoun as long as they can make themselves understood? I think of
the special reading group that I had in the morning. I can look at children like Lorene, Wendy, and Kevin,[1] and believe wholeheartedly that
they will never read anything in a magazine, newspaper, or book for
the rest of their lives, unless it be something to do with ads, funnies,
or perhaps the sports page. It would be most fascinating to see these
students 10 years after they have left school and test them again on their
reading ability to see if it has improved or deteriorated.

In language arts, one makes a composition assignment. Some of the
compositions come in so garbled and twisted that corrections cannot
even be made. There is not enough right in the first place to point out
what is wrong. What does one do with these students? No, there are
no joys in teaching language arts.

Arithmetic is a great joy, when compared to teaching language arts.
At least arithmetic cannot be bastardized. 2 plus 2 equals 4 in our school,
at the corner of Green Boulevard and York, or in Appalachia. We all
use the same numbers and the same processes. We all start out with the
simple and proceed to the difficult. When one teaches addition, he need
not be worried about what to do with subtraction, multiplication,
division, or how to shove those out of the students' sight until he is
ready for them. 2 plus 2 is 4 and no other complexities need enter in at
that point. This, of course, cannot be done in the language arts. Thus
in arithmetic you have a more orderly structure, which can be arranged
in an hierarchy of difficulty, one which some evaluation of student's
progress is possible. It is difficult to judge in language which is better,
a student who knows what a noun is but not a pronoun, or a student
who knows what a verb is but not an adverb. In fact, it is difficult to
imagine the student really knowing what a noun is if he doesn't know
what a pronoun is, and vice versa.

In arithmetic, however, addition as a process can stand by itself and
that is that. It is easy to abstract for instruction, the presentation of examples presents no problems, and always we can return to more simple
strata of questioning if the student cannot achieve at the point where

---

[1] These are children from Norton's room whom Geoffrey taught as part of the homogeneous grouping through trading of pupils. They are extremely dull and probably should be
in special classes for the retarded.

we are. The limitations and difficulties are those mainly prescribed by time and how much these students have been taught before. Of course, there are other limitations of general intelligence. However, I believe that the effects of environment and culture, will have much, much less emphasis upon arithmetic than on the study of language arts.

Let us lump history and geography together as social studies. The difficulty here is that the textbooks are at too high a reading level for most of the students in the grades. In addition, in this school these subjects are farther removed from the interests or experiences of the students than they would be in other socioeconomic groups. I feel that middle-class homes really provide many opportunities for reference to history and geography, while the lower-class homes have little use for the subjects. Middle-class parents are closer to an understanding of the political and economic factors in our life, and their children are more exposed to these concepts. It seems that there is little in the lower-class home to link the student with our heritage in history, or our relationship to the world geographically and economically. In teaching these subjects, I feel that although there is no resistance to them in the home, there is nothing positive in relation to them either. One can teach arithmetic, because it is used. One has difficulty in reading and language arts because these skills are unimportant in the homes. History and geography, however, seem to have no relevance at all. They may seem dull to a great many students, and indeed, the way they are presented, I can well understand this. But there is nothing either particularly for or against their place in the curriculum. I feel a great deal of frustration in teaching them because I cannot make the concepts real to my students.

As we see the pupils' behavior in relation to the curricular areas we can maintain our consistency of language by speaking of activities—transactions of the group with the physical environment. Also, we can see Mr. Geoffrey's initial categories of activities that follow basic public school distinctions —language arts, which include reading, grammar, and composition. Arithmetic is well differentiated from the others. Geography and history are social studies. As he talks about teaching these categories of activities a latent set of activity-dimensions arises. These include:

1. The ease into which the whole can be broken into teachable parts.
2. The probability that the children will engage in the activity elsewhere out of class.
3. The continuum of development from immature (amateur) to mature (professional) performance.
4. The commonality of usage in all parts of the culture.
5. A readily visable hierarchy of difficulty.
6. The degree to which ancillary skills (reading) are demanded.
7. The degree to which one's day-to-day experience is relevant.

This analysis suggests that the activity concept has several potentially fruitful subdimensions. As an illustration we see the need for research testing the relationships between activities varying in number of teachable parts and (1) frustration experienced by teachers and pupils, (2) learning by pupils,

(3) interaction of teachers and pupils and the myriad of other group and individual variables we have isolated. Within the context of our decision-making model, we can speculate on the invention of ways in which other curricularly defined areas (science, art, health, and language arts itself) can be analyzed into less interdependent or more teachable parts. If relationships between this kind of "part-whole" phenomenon and frustration and learning are verified then the teacher has within his conceptual armamentarium a very strong tool.

The probability of the activity occurring elsewhere in the environment leads also into aspects of the "What should the schools teach?" problem. This discussion we will hold for another section.

Mr. Geoffrey's point about the "garbled and twisted" compositions that defy correction suggests that considerable research effort is required in the "natural" course of development of skills as well as their development in special school environments. If our analysis is well taken, there are implications that teacher training for upper elementary grades should include something of the nature of primitive or primary skills and techniques for working with children who are still at that stage of maturity, although at a higher age level.

The readily visable hierarchy of difficulty as Mr. Geoffrey uses it suggests an interlocking with teacher interventions. Is there clarity in the options open for questions—that is, a line of retreat when the pupil cannot handle the material?

The degree to which day-to-day experience is relevant suggests the wisdom of a "meaningfulness" concept. If history and geography suffer from this condition of low meaningfulness, and if conceptual learning is highly dependent on this, then one is faced with the proverbial difficult situation. Hypothetically, however, several alternatives are available. First, a good bit of the history dealt with the origins of European cities, the developing reasons for colonists emigrating, and the problems of the colonial period in America. Each of these issues has parallels in contemporary America and each has parallels in the Washington School as a community within a community in flux. To raise the ubiquitous problems of authority, civil rights, interpersonal relationships, and so forth would have violated the norms of the faculty, would have opened many issues to questions, and would have instigated potentially a self examination that might have well become a Pandora's box.[2]

The Stated Schedule

In our discussion of the early structure in Chapter Three we indicated the demands set forth by the organization and the program that resulted from this. After the closing of a room Geoffrey's activity-structure was altered.

[2]See the discussion of this in Chapter Eight.

Schedules

	M	T	W	T	F
8:30-9:30			Reading		
9:30-10:15			History and Geography		
10:15-10:30			Recess		
10:30-11:15			Language		
11:15-12:00	Science	Music	Science	Music	Spelling test
1:00-2:00	Gym	Art	Gym	Art	Health
2:00-2:30			Spelling and Writing		
2:30-3:30			Arithmetic		

Figure 6.1 The schedule of activities on October 1.

The schedule, which was posted on the board for the pupils' benefit, is reproduced in Figure 6.1. We have also indicated that there were only occasional science, art, music, and health lessons. The problems of reading, spelling, arithmetic, and language were the key ones attacked.

Another way of defining schedule is to speak of the relation of activities to time. In terms of our earlier discussions of classroom processes, the schedule can be stated and diagrammed as have our earlier analyses. (See Figure 6.2) Presumably daily schedules may vary in such dimensions as clarity, flexibility, interest, and also difficulty.

Reading ⟶ Social Studies ⟶ Recess ⟶ Language ⟶ Study ⟶ Lunch ⟶ Gym ⟶ Spelling ⟶ Arithmetic

T_1　　　T_2　　　T_3　　　T_4　　　T_5　　　T_6　　　T_7　　　T_8　　　T_9

Figure 6.2 The daily schedule as a relationship of activities to time.

THE DAILY LESSON AS AN ACTIVITY

Introductory Example

Instruction is a special word in the language of the Big City teachers at the Washington School. It refers to the teacher's presentation of a daily lesson from the textbook. The key concepts are: teacher presentation rather than pupil direction or control, the daily lesson which accents the short time span and a perceptible unit of activity distinguishable from that which went before and that which will come later, and the textbook which frames or programs the longer sequences. These, as we indicated earlier, show variation from the spelling lesson, which has a recurring weekly rhythm besides the daily units of work, to the social studies lesson we present below:

2.20 "All right, take out your history books, please. Page 254. What continent are we reading about—Elma? What? First country?" He urges Davey to read loud and clear. Davey reads several paragraphs and then Edwin reads. He stumbles on "decline" and "ruin." Geoffrey quizzes regarding archeologists—Allison, Billy, Helen, and Dick. Davey reads but Geoffrey raises soft voice. "I hope the rest of you can find the glossary in the back of the book." They read on: Jimmie, Allison (she has serious trouble —security, punctilious, and so forth). Geoffrey quizzes regarding security.

Billy reads. He also has considerable difficulty. (LMS—He could not follow content on his own in this material.) Edwin reads haltingly; Sarah, beautifully. Eileen has trouble on "caravan" but generally is not bad. Sandy reads quite well. Geoffrey reads for a turn.

The subject is African gifts to civilization. Allison reads on. She does much better here, although there is some loss of meaning (thorns and thrones). Allison finishes section. "Sandy, where is arithmetic assignment? We need a history assignment, also. . . ." Sandy: "When due?" "Tomorrow, always tomorrow unless I tell you otherwise." (LMS—During all of this, the pupils have quieted down. Restlessness is gone; quite attentive; almost all are following carefully and with interest. Assigns self-tester, pp. 260–261.)

2:55 Messenger comes in (key's lost). Geoffrey sends Thelma for Sam and Oliver (who have been working on a sign). There is banter on "Can I" versus "May I" pin up sign?

3:00 Billy raises second question for me: Ethiopians? Geoffrey is busy; he is with several other pupils. He raises procedural questions about filling in blanks on self-tester. People are working on varied assignments. Geoffrey moves about the room checking and helping. Billy collects chalk and erasers. Geoffrey brings Pete to desk to do some reading.

The lesson began with a new section in the text. The teacher and pupils engaged in reading, in questions and answers to clarify information and concepts, and in a study period involving a homework assignment. Other illustrations scattered throughout the monograph document this recurring unit of activity. If a pupil were asked, "What did you do in school today at 2:30?" he would respond, "We had a geography lesson."

Analytically, the lesson is a subpart of activity. It involves a specific teaching purpose or objective and it can be analyzed also as a process over time. Our analysis suggests that the phases or episodes involve initially an opening or entry, which includes a simple question or two, sometimes an abrupt "turn to page 254," as in our example, and sometimes an out-of-text illustration, as we will cite shortly. The body of the lesson carries the weight of the means toward the teacher's goals. In Geoffrey's class this usually involved "covering" several pages in the text. Sometimes reading the materials was the focus, sometimes reciting answers to homework questions occurred and often an easy dialogue of questions and answers to clarify concepts or emphasize information, was the mode of operation. The lesson closed occasionally with a summary but usually with an assignment of text questions. In many instances an epilogue occurred in the form of a study period or homework. Figure 6.3 presents in simple fashion the usual sequence of lessons.

The Opening or Entry:	The Body:	The Closing:	Epilogue:
Directive	Reading	Summarizing	Study period
Common experience	Questioning	Assigning text questions	Homework
	Reciting		
T_1	T_2	T_3	T_4

Figure 6.3   A process conception of the lesson.

Variations in Openings

Common Experience   Although textbooks constituted the major core of the classroom activity, on occasion Geoffrey appealed to movie and TV watching and this provided the common focus for entering a new unit.

> Geoffrey raises topic of Central Africa (p. 287). He talks about jungle movies, Tarzan, Sheena, and so on. (LMS—Geoffrey builds upon movies and TV very extensively. This is an interesting well of experience.) Esther says she saw one last night. Joe K. suggests Jungle Jim, Johnny Weismueller and Safari. Leona suggests "Curse of Dracula." "What's that got to do with Africa?" "Maybe Dracula's been there." Geoffrey asks who hasn't been to the zoo. Only one, Elizabeth, the new girl, has not been. He asks sixes about difficulty in the lesson. Too much reading? Too little time? He asks about earlier geography lessons. Evelyn complains about too much work, too many question sheets, many questions from book. Geoffrey asks about reading—by oneself or out loud. He moves to generalization of doing it the same as last year. "Read carefully pages 287-291 and answer questions 1, 2, and 5." He asks Betty if she needs anything. "I'm usually nice to people the first week. After that I change." Assigns Josephine to help Betty.   (10/28)

Presumably, such a gambit or entry early in a new section of work provokes concrete images relevant to the information and concepts to be developed by the text, permits orienting questions to be raised and heightens motivation for the task. For the group the initial discussion clarifies the pupils' beliefs about the teacher's focus, insofar as he is a source of influence, and the discussion crystallizes group goals and relevant activities to reach the goals. As the illustration indicates, inappropriate images such as "Curse of Dracula" also are raised, and presumably clarified, and more general procedural problems, earlier geography lessons, also interfere.

The Body of the Lesson

A Textbook Is a Textbook, Is a Textbook?   The textbook controlled the content and sequence dimensions of the body of the daily lesson. In earlier examples (see Chapter Two especially) the spelling text presented lists of words and a variety of extending experiences. Week after week the

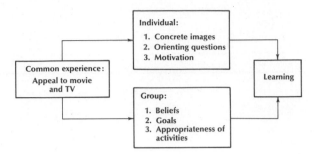

Figure 6.4 Impact of a lesson opening with appeals to common experience.

children were involved with these materials. Similarly, we have cited considerable detail from the language arts and arithmetic books. However, we were struck on a number of occasions with an important difference among texts. It reminded us of Merton's (1957) conception of functional inequivalents. There are times when describing the lesson as "textbook" teaching is too simple. During the course of the semester two social studies texts were used. As the observer listened to the lessons, he was struck by the differences in the questions asked by the text authors. In one, the questions were:

1. Why did some European countries seek a westward route to the East? Why did Columbus think he could reach the East by sailing westward? Why did he fail?
2. Why was Columbus' voyage important?

In contrast, the questions of the other text were of this order:

1. The Ethiopians were successful (*traders*).
2. The Ethiopians have been (*learning*) from early times.
3. A ruler of the Ethiopians was the (*Queen of Sheba*).

For the moment, we don't wish to enter into a discussion of which questions are better. The point we would make is that the latter accents the recall of fairly specific facts, category one in the *Taxonomy of Educational Objectives* (Bloom, and others 1957), and the former accents analysis and evaluation skills. Even though both are illustrations of a common approach, textbook learning, they don't function in the same manner. This raises a critical complexity in the analysis of classroom activities.

Contextual Discussions Much of Geoffrey's time was spent in homework recitations in which the major questions were factual. Occasionally he entertained what seemed to the observer to be brief and abortive contextual discussions:

3:03 There is no assignment for Monday. He reads a few pages of *Rise of Nations*. He picks up synonyms: country, state, kingdom.
3:04 He has Allison begin reading. Has France picked out by Dick. Raises question as to why so much time is spent on people of Europe. Thelma, Molly, can't answer. Sam has some trouble, too. Out of Dick's answer he begins to pick up historical origins of United States. (IMS—These discussions seem open to question in terms of their development and usefulness.)

At this point the interrelationships of pupil ability with the dimensions of activities, for example, contextual discussions in the body of the lesson, occur. Strictly from the point of view of the structure of knowledge in seventh-grade social studies, there seems to be no question about the necessity of this kind of question as it leads into the origins and development of the United States as a unique political entity. Perhaps the fault lies in the observer's too quick interpretation regarding "their development and usefulness." Apparently, he was responding to the failure of the first three pupils, the partial response of the fourth, and the degree to which the system can tolerate that kind of strain hour after hour or day after day. In terms of our decision-making model, the question of alternatives is the immediate next step. Here, we refer to Geoffrey's consternation as he described the problems of relevance to pupil backgrounds and the difficulty in moving to a simpler level in such subjects as language arts and social studies.

Closing the Lesson Geoffrey's most characteristic way of closing a lesson was a move toward giving an assignment—usually for the next day. Two dimensions, preciseness and emphasis, are worthy of discussion.

The notes contain innumerable references on the care and detail Geoffrey gave to making assignments, for instance, "This was done with usual care," (10/3). Typically, he would finish a lesson in the text, indicate the problems in language or arithmetic to be done for the next day, have the assignment monitor write the new assignment in its proper place on the board, work at least one of the items with the total group, take any pupil questions, and check about the room to see that everyone was on the right track. Frequently, too, he would give the children a few minutes immediately so that they might read farther into the assignment and find difficulties. This is diagramed in Figure 6.5.

Assignments are given as directives; pupil compliance sometimes occurs. When it does not, the teacher is faced with an interesting choice. Geoffrey had multiple vehicles for handling this problem. On occasion he ignored, reprimanded, or sent children to the hall. On October 29, he engaged in an analysis of the problem.

9:37 He tells Sandy to make 100 7's. She had put illegible 7's in arithmetic

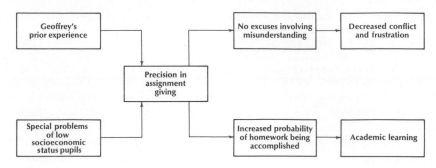

Figure 6.5 Aspects of Geoffrey's assignment-giving.

problems. This is done with humor again: "One complaint is too many." Geoffrey begins geography with 6's. Sandy numbers 1–10 vertically on board and starts in. Geoffrey asks Alan to find Kenya on map. He doesn't have assignment. Geoffrey decides to check assignments and gets his book. He starts in to find out who hasn't and why. At least four-fifths have not. Reasons: forgot, baby-sat, wasn't here, lost it, didn't understand, sick. The yes's are Walt, Sidney, Esther, Evelyn (one-half done), Josephine (one-half). Geoffrey enters into a "What do you propose to do about this?" He sits at front in stern, questioning fashion. "I guess my alternative is to call your parents. . . . Maybe you'll have to go to Miss Norton and have geography while others sit." Sends to the hall the pupils who have finished. They check papers with each other. In the meantime, he tells Elizabeth she's responsible beginning tomorrow.

9:43 He has Grace start in on first item. She was the child who didn't understand. (LMS—This is good face-saving procedure.) He pushes her to try. (The item No. 1, p. 291, is a beautiful, thought-provoking item. It is difficult, though.) Most children are fairly well involved in the lesson. Grace has trouble reading, finding continent on wall map, and finding the country within the continent. She seems very dull as well as unprepared. Geoffrey has Walt B. find it. Then Evelyn goes to find New York. He takes guesses on the way to go. "Now is this so hard?"

9:56 He talks about today's and tomorrow's assignment, if they are to get back and stay in geography class. "What gripes me is that I gave you plenty of time." He spells that out. Geoffrey goes out with the other sixes. (LMS—The tremendous apathy and indifference is striking. Is this response a function of the traditional text approach or the total environment? Would a dramatic change from what they need to what would be fun ultimately lead to trivia and no systematic cognitive development? The returns now seem so little for the effort.) (10/29)

Epilogue: The Problem of Homework   The psychological literature does not give a clear definition of problem. Usually, the implication exists that problems have a novel or obstacle character and that no simple or direct behavior exists in the repertory of the person confronting the situation. In these terms, homework qualifies as a problem to the teacher. From our conceptual point of view, homework qualifies initially and simply as a "kind of activity" and aids us in moving toward a taxonomy of this concept. Also homework is treated as a critical part of the daily lesson, and it must be integrated with this discussion.

As a problem, it possesses linkages with most aspects of the system we have been developing. The story started early in the semester, and began without the observer being aware of its significance at those early moments. On Tuesday morning, September 10, the field notes contained several interpretive statements sandwiched between other more substantive comments:

> Geoffrey finishes questions 12–15. He corrects Rose by putting in periods and capital letters. "Any questions? They were very well done. Pass them forward. If you have more than one sheet be sure your name is on both. . . . Starting tomorrow I will record everything in the Little Black Book. It is not a telephone book. Every single assignment and test goes in this book. If you are in doubt about your assignment ask me and you can check. I hope there will be no blank spaces. Most of you have a good idea of run-on sentences, better than fragments. Skip page 9. . . ." Reads material and raises declarative, interrogative, imperative, exclamatory. (9/10)

Only a few minutes later, the notes record another series of episodes:

> "I'll give you an easy assignment for tomorrow." He reads directions and looks for volunteers to write No. 1 on the board. "There are the same volunteers all the time. Eileen, you come up and volunteer." She does; writes declarative. Forgets the period. Geoffrey asks what's missing and sends her back.
> **10:02** Paper monitor passes out the paper. Edwin and Billy go out on errands. Molly is asked to fill coffee pot. "You may have the 10 minutes before recess to work on your assignment. Don't rush through."
> **10:04** "Sandy. What's that board down there?" She moves on to put up assignment for language. Helps her to get it all and get it correct. She's pouty and heel-dragging.
> **10:06** All are working—except Pete. Elma "borrows" some help from Sarah. Allison asks Helen regarding No. 4. Lonny "borrows" from Davey. Sam checks No. 12 with Oliver. Geoffrey asks Molly if she wants to get out of that job—coffee monitor.

The activity of homework blends into the system in at least several ways: Geoffrey has an initial example so that the children know how to carry out the assignment; the monitorial system facilitates having materials (paper); time is provided to begin the activity; details on due time and precise nature of the assignment are recorded publicly; and provision is made or tolerated for children to give and receive aid from each other. Figure 6.6 contains some of these implications.

Summary: Traditional Teaching by Another Name

Early in November the observer's other interests cued several relevant thoughts concerning the Washington School. While the notes are cast partially in terms of the methodological implications, the attempt to analyze the dimensions of activities is the point we wish to emphasize.

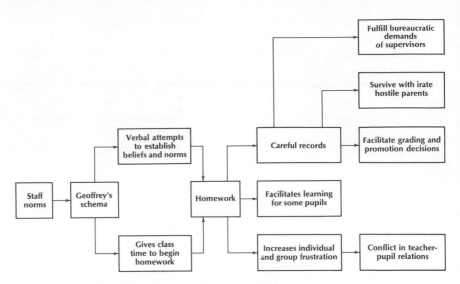

Figure 6.6 Ramifications of homework as an activity.

In terms of the conceptual development of the problem, it is important to note that this weekend I read the Phillips and Haring (1962) book, *Educating Emotionally Disturbed Children.* Their point of view is essentially this: they offer a strong criticism of the psychoanalytic, nondirective, and permissive approaches to educating emotionally disturbed children. They include such individuals as Bettelheim, Redl, Slavson, Axline, and so forth. The central construct in their approach is what they call structure. Structure involves several only partially related phenomena. They talk about it as based upon a learning-theory approach, yet there is very little theory present. Their immediate predecessors are Strauss and Lehtinen and also Cruickshank. In many regards they sound like they are offering a program of the typical traditional form. Lessons are brief, organized, and in some kind of sequential order. The kids are able to do them, are helped in doing them, and are controlled in both their social behavior and intellectual behavior. In effect, the teacher rules the room. The variations from a traditional scheme involve isolation booths for kids who get beyond control, which is similar to Geoffry's putting the kids out in the hall. There is variation in the difficulty level in the curriculum, which would make it different from some forms of traditional teaching.

They ran a two-year experiment, which suggests that this structured classroom is better than two kinds of controls: (1) a more permissive special class, (2) leaving the children in the regular classroom. It is important to have this on the record for a number of the ideas which have been looming up in the reports are quite similar to the kinds of things that are suggested here by Phillips and Haring. Insofar as many of these were arrived at independently, then it gives added weight to the thoughts that have been suggested. Insofar as they are noninde-pendent, there is this possible additional shaping of the observations to see what one wants to see. (11/4)

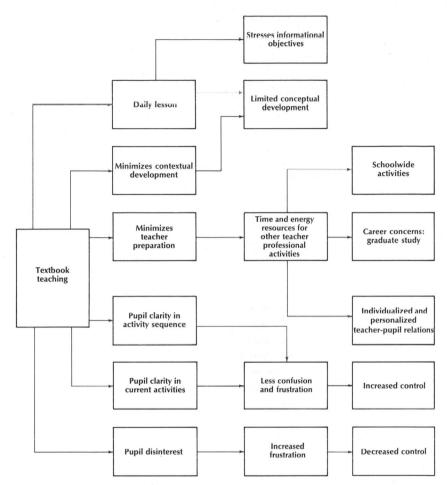

Figure 6.7 Impact of textbook teaching on aspects of classroom and school social structure and processes.

Thus it seems possible to describe textbook teaching and its corollary, the daily lesson, by good as well as bad names. Phillips and Haring (1962) seem to be saying for emotionally disturbed children what the Washington School staff is saying for children from a slum community. Structure in their sense might well be comparable to such concepts as clarity and preciseness that we have used. Our analysis of Geoffrey's class, however, suggests several additional implications. The field notes early in the semester contain our first perception of these implications. Later, in the middle of the afternoon after long arithmetic and history lessons, Geoffrey makes an announcement or two and the observer makes an interpretation or two:

2:27 "I have a couple of items. Some of you have been wanting art. We'll need some newspapers. If you have some lying around, bring them from home." Then scurrying around for paper, pencil sharpening, assignments, and so forth. Everyone busy. Book reporting. Geoffrey shakes his head "no" over Billy's report, while keeping eyes on class.[3] (LMS—(1) Art seems to be held as a privilege in contrast to other subjects that are a duty. (2) Textbook teaching eases the preparation by the teacher: there is no problem organizing, no problem bringing in materials, preparing exercises, and so on. There's a clarity of sequence for pupils. Also, and probably very important, there is a firm focus on where one is at all times.) (9/10)

Our more formal statement of hypotheses lies in the model presented as Figure 6.7. The problems in the development of broad integrative concepts are accented. The conflicting predictions regarding confusion and frustration seem quite important. In Geoffrey's classroom, the lack of interest in the textbook was countered, especially with the seventh graders, by his skill in interpersonal relations, for example, personalized interaction. As we have indicated, the sixth graders, and especially "the aggregate" were considerably less responsive to this approach. Finally, the impact of the textbook-guided daily lesson on the teacher's preparation, time, and energy seemed to us to be important. In a situation that is so demanding and fatiguing, any savings is a tremendously reinforcing contingency.[4] We hypothesize that this relates to career concerns such as graduate study and school-wide activities that "gain the attention of superiors"[5] as well as energy to play the classroom game.

ACTIVITY DIMENSIONS AND THE FLOW OF TEACHING

Deciding what shall be taught lies at the heart of curriculum theory. In practice at the Washington School the textbooks to a large extent determine the teacher's decisions in this aspect of his work. We have alluded to faculty norms that determined other aspects of the program. These problems and others flow in and out of a consideration of activities, the things pupils do.

Innovative Activities

In late October, a brief before-school conversation generated the following account in the field notes:

In chatting, I was groaning about the "new math." This introduced a few minutes discussion regarding base 5's and so forth. This is one of

[3]This is another excellent example of our concept "awareness" which we raised in Chapter Four.

[4]Our experience suggests that the typical college instructor who meets two to four courses (six to twelve hours) and the typical layman does not appreciate this dimension of urban elementary school teaching.

[5]See the "GASing" concept elaborated by Griffiths, and others (1963), in their discussion of teacher mobility in a large public school system.

the few times that anything of this sort has occurred here. As a group, the second-floor clique does not talk about such issues. Neither Gennep, Norton, nor Geoffrey was thoroughly aware of the position.   (10/21)

As we reflect upon this, it strikes us that the teacher in a lower socioeconomic status school is out of the mainstream of current educational innovation (which may be good or bad). It raises problems of teacher in-service training, and it suggests why some people are content to remain teaching here and why others, after being here for some time, are unable to move. Perhaps most significant of all are hypotheses suggesting that low activity innovativeness dampens teacher enthusiasm and excitement about teaching and this, in turn, spreads to pupil motivation as well.

Unimportant Subjects as Activities

It is possible also to dimensionalize activities in terms of the importance to the teacher. As activities are so categorized then certain consequences seem to follow. Earlier examples of these consequences surrounding art were presented. The slight emphasis on science was illustrated late in the afternoon early in September.

3:01   "Please stop working and take out your science books." He gives them a choice of units in science. They must skip machines and electricity because they lack equipment. He asks for suggestions. (LMS—Geoffrey does little to develop possibilities. Perhaps his day has been as long and as tiring as I feel it has.)

Rocks and soils get the most votes, so they begin there. "Rocks and soils are not so bad because we can get a few movies. We won't start today—probably next week." This is met with mild cheers. "We will have health lessons every few weeks, but most of these will be from films. We have books in the back but we won't use them."[6]

3:05   People go back to finishing lessons and Geoffrey returns to getting things organized at his desk—probably for next day. (LMS—The science and health episodes, the text orientation, the long labor this A.M. on simple language art skills, the minimal homework all suggest the cumulative deficit in substantive knowledge that these kids will be facing in high school competition and later in college if any get that far. The contrast in time and variety of experiences of a suburban seventh-grader is astounding.)   (9/11)

Selective Emphasis

An additional conception, which seems very important in teaching culturally deprived children, we have called selective emphasis. The point arose early in a discussion with Mr. Alton.

Alton related some of the difficulties he was having in setting up a bulletin board for current events. He had been trying for three days to

---

[6] Later Geoffrey commented that the health books were "sexless"—totally uninteresting.

get the kids to bring him articles from newspapers on relevant social studies topics. Apparently this had born little fruit and he was quite discouraged and had decided to stop. (LMS—I would add a point concerning the three-day interval. The major concept is time. The more I see of these kids, the more I have the feeling that one has to select an activity in terms of its importance and then keep emphasizing it day after day and week after week. If this hypothesis is correct, then Alton has erred in one of two ways, either by taking on a not-so-important topic or episode to develop, or by quitting too soon. At this moment, I think the error is the latter.) (9/11)

While selective emphasis might seem to be a mode of rephrasing reduced demands, our intent is to accent the need to set clear priorities and to hold tenaciously to them. If our analysis has been correct, Geoffrey did this in establishing classroom control and in accenting the *3R's*. In our present illustration Alton had attempted (and Geoffrey indicated he had tried this several years ago also) to introduce additional aspects to the program. Apparently the costs were very high. One must be willing to pay these. To make this kind of decision one needs a clear statement of priorities and a clear indication of what one may lose.

Appropriateness

Later in the semester, the observer hypothesized about another element of activities—appropriateness. This occurred in a language arts period:

11:34 Geoffrey is back to the lesson on adjectives. There is recitation up and down rows and criss-cross about the room. Many children have not done assignments. This makes the recitation slow, awkward, and difficult to follow. (LMS—Once again I am struck with the inappropriate curriculum content. I don't know what would be better, but the returns seem so minimal for the effort being expended. It might be better in a total-substance curriculum, with reading focused on the reception of information and with writing to tell about things. Only occasionally, and then usually in context, would one introduce grammar.)

11:45 Geoffrey stops in his presentation of new lesson to wait for Joe K. who has been yawning and studying the ceiling above and behind himself. (LMS—This is another good illustration of their lack of contact.) Geoffrey finishes phrase-modifier lesson and asks Walt S., Grace, Evelyn, and Marian to write sentences. (The sentences are all hopelessly beyond their depth.)

The concept appropriateness refers to the combination of the materials and their impact on the child. In this instance minimal, observable correct responses occur.

Drama in Teaching and Inappropriateness of Activity

Geoffrey's teaching often contained a dramatic quality. By this we mean it often was vivid, unusual, or striking. We described this in part in the discussion of the "ferocious tiger role." However, in the observer's judgment this dimension of teacher behavior often seemed overridden by the inappropriateness dimension of the activity, the content of the material from the text. Geoffrey is coping with his new group of children and has combined both the seventh graders with the sixth graders for this lesson.

10:55 Language lesson begins. All children are grouped together.

11:05 Geoffrey checks around the room for homework. He gives Joe K. a look and a comment for doing his assignment immediately before the lesson.

He begins a review of sentences, verbs, subjects. He discusses the two kinds of verbs—action and being. This is another kind of problem. It is nice when they are simple: for example, he slams book closed, hits Walt on head (lightly), and so forth. He raises the helping verb problem and builds discussion out of reading on page 21.

11:12 Leonard and Norman come in. Alan has his feet under the desk of the kid in front of him and raises and lowers him. (LMS—As Geoffrey raises the sentences in the book, I'm struck again by how inappropriate these exercises seem to be. I would like to try a year of language having kids spend time writing and shaping this behavior rather than getting them aware of these "book sentences" and the naming of parts of speech.)

They continue exercises on "helping verbs." Geoffrey passes out paper so they can write helping verb in the sentence, "We have been playing every day." He checks around individually and tells of "boiling all of them in oil." Geoffrey becomes theatrical in "How find verb?" and "Need a little action." (LMS—My fatigue and fascination make it hard to record this.)

11:26 On to sentence 3. "If I don't scream at you . . . What is this thing? (Throws away a piece of paper.) Look at that again! Where is it? You'd better put that there. Why do you wait until I get here to look about? All right, much, much, much better. A couple of you weren't with me. . . . All right—sentence 4." Thelma asks, "Is that right?" He says, "Better be." Gets to Evelyn. "Describe a means of torture, the rack. I'd have you 10 feet tall. Think! Think! Think!" Shrugs shoulders at Billy. Goes on. "Sh-h-h! No. No. Too much, and you've got a word wrong. People use the help you've got. Look at top of page. Grace, Grace, Grace! Think! Oh, oh, oh! Do you want me to take your language books? Use it. Use it."

11:32 Makes assignment p. 22 Nos. 1–10; p. 23 Nos. 1–16. This done with usual care. Kids move out to chores, monitors, lunch duty, and so forth. Geoffrey stops and asks "Who is excused from tomorrow's assignment?" "No one!" (10/3)

In a very real sense the stimulation in the dramatic and theatrical quality of the teaching is overridden by the inappropriateness dimension of the activity itself.

Difficulty Level

As Mr. Geoffrey taught a language arts lesson, identifying verbs, the impact of pupil background and lesson content ties down the important activity dimension—difficulty level:

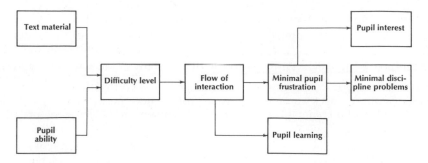

Figure 6.8 Hypotheses relating to difficulty level of activity.

9:29 Geoffrey begins exercise on page 17, "Find the verbs." He begins with No. 1 and works down through calling on nonvolunteers. He accents the "has been cut" as total phrase. He asks for subjects also. As girls (especially) get stuck he keeps raising questions and probes. Teases Susan who will not speak out loudly . . . No. 7. "She's making it of patches of old orange and blue clothes." "Stop and think." Deals quickly and neatly with "She's making it . . ." Ben answers "is making." "Where's is?" In "She's . . . ," Helen picks up contraction. On next item, even Elma is with it. (LMS—What a difference there is when they have basic idea and approach.) (9/12)

In trying to conceptualize these events, we produced Figure 6.8.

However, there were days when the difficulty level of the material was greater and the consequences were different. Late one fall afternoon, shortly after a world series game in which the children and Geoffrey had watched Koufax set a strike-out record, an arithmetic lesson began.

2:30 Sevens begin fractions. Some of this has gone on in prior days. Geoffrey re-introduces concepts: proper fractions, improper fractions, mixed numbers; numerator, denominator. He states the rules. Has them check their notebooks. Takes up problems 9 and 10, page 33. While this goes on, the sixes work on spelling and other assignments. Leonard spends time with a gossamer speed pod. It is ludicrous to watch. He's the biggest boy in class—more oafish physically than Billy—yet he tenderly cuddles and floats the cottony seed. He sees me watching, smiles sheepishly, and quits.

2:40 All the sixes working. The sevens are working on changing three-fourths into twelfths. Geoffrey has tremendous difficulties getting Billy to see point of multiplying to get higher terms and dividing to get lower terms. He finally draws a diagram on board. He makes assignment (p. 35). The group has serious difficulty in recalling previous 2 years of work on fractions. Eileen is charged with taking Billy outside and helping explain arithmetic to him.

2:45 Geoffrey begins arithmetic lesson with sixes. He starts ferocious tiger role on six different answers to 2 × 9.65. He goes on. There is beautiful acting in mock indignation at wrong answers. He seeks logical estimates, asks some to make a stand for others to defend, and so forth, all the while pushing for how to make out "bills". Raises concepts of estimating and checking. (LMS—He presents a neat problem showing that 3 × 12.85 must be between 36 and 39.)

3:06 He goes on to next problem and has different kids fill in lines of Billing.

3:10 All sevens (except Pete) working. The sixes are restless during this long putting of materials on board. Geoffrey keeps close eye, with a comment or two, on Norman and Joe K. This drags on and on. Many have incorrectly tallled their materials—only final columns. They finally get the sum. Geoffrey comments: "Children, I'm disappointed in your addition." Assigns page 7 No. 1, and page 15 No. 1.

3:22 Chores begin and everyone organizes for going home.

3:25 Geoffrey has boys go outside, wait in line. "I want to talk to the girls. I'm not happy to see you before the end of gym period. I am still not clear as to why you have not been behaving as you should be. If you are ever sent to me for nonlegitimate reason, I'll have a nice long gym assignment. No knuckle popping, Evelyn." "I wasn't only one." "Don't ever say that to me. Whom are you responsible for? Who is most important to you?"

He brings the boys back in.

"One other item. All be fully honest with me the first time a question is raised."

3:30 They line up. (10/3)

In a brief fifty minutes, sandwiched between the ball game and the recurring discipline problems in the girls physical education program, Geoffrey has tried to teach a short arithmetic lesson to his two grade levels. The seventh graders had had considerable work in fractions the prior 2 years yet retained considerable confusion. The sixth graders have similar difficulties with multiplication of whole numbers. Into this lesson also he tries to have the children step back from the problem and estimate answers. While the notes do not indicate the children's reactions to this kind of reflection on arithmetic problems, in general they possessed little flexibility. Lack of basic skills in understanding the fundamentals and the text's applied setting of "billing" seemed to pose insurmountable problems.

The observer's interpretation of other books and easier levels suggests one mode of handling the difficulty level problem. The recent innovations in computer-assisted instruction presumably would be in this vein also. Geoffrey's own resolution was a move to the utilization of "yellow practice sheets," materials he borrowed from another teacher. These problems accented simpler work in the fundamentals. They comprised the program for most of October, after which he returned to the text materials.

Fractured Quality of Activities

In American education generally, and as we have indicated throughout our discussion of Geoffrey's classroom, textbook teaching is widely practiced yet strongly controversial. In effect, what happened in Geoffrey's class, what manifest antecedents are visible, and what latent antecedents and consequences might be envisioned are the questions we ask. An early interpretation in the notes serves to illustrate the discussion:

2:09 Introduces section of *Restless Vikings*. Geoffrey begins reading. He has Billy find Norway, Sweden, and Denmark on map. Billy has trouble but finally succeeds. Geoffrey reads on and raises question about "climate and humidity." He finishes paragraph and has Sam begin reading. Geoffrey picks up next paragraph. Edwin reads. (LMS—Sections are so small that it seems impossible to build up integrated concepts about any aspect of history or geography.)   (9/10)

Later we return to other problems of concept development; here our concern lies in the fractured quality of the activities and the limitations these seem to pose for building broad viable views of the world.

Interrupted Activity

As we keep indicating, activities have many dimensions. If we were creative enough, perhaps the dimensions would be infinite. An important one of these is the degree to which an activity is interrupted or uninterrupted. One of our clearest illustrations occurred in this way: Geoffrey has broken into a study period with an announcement of an insurance form:

Goes through the insurance form carefully.
2:41 Messenger comes in (P.E. 9:30–10:15 Monday and Wednesday). Second messenger comes in before first is out. Third messenger in before second is out.
2:43 Back to insurance.

Messengers from the office or from other teachers are just a single manifestation of the general concept—interrupted activity. We have tried to sketch some of the implications in Figure 6.9. The complex interdependencies within the dimensions of teacher behavior, and this aspect of activities suggest the complications that face the researcher pursuing verificational strategies as well as the classroom teacher working with a group of youngsters.

BEYOND THE 3R'S: OTHER DIMENSIONS OF ACTIVITIES

While the daily lesson and the *3R*'s dominated the curriculum of Geoffrey's classroom, other aspects of activities arose. Many of our comments involve terminological or semantic issues, for in Education good things sometimes are not considered good things unless they have the correct label appended. It seems important to begin such an analysis. The remainder of our comments focus on events that were only fleetingly present in the classroom but which seemed to have broader implications.

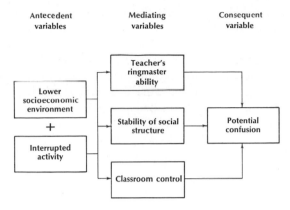

Figure 6.9 An analysis of the interrupted activity dimension in relation to other aspects of social structure.

Concept Attainment

An additional category of activities engaged in by the children might be called concept attainment. While Geoffrey varied his approach and emphasis, the usual format for teaching concepts is reflected in the notes of an early language arts lesson:

> Page 10. Kinds of Sentences. He reads material and discusses declarative, interrogative, imperative, and exclamatory. On the "Please Raise the Window" illustration, Oliver clowns a bit. Illustrations by Geoffrey are *all* from the book. He has them close books and try to associate the names of kinds with defining aspect. Goes around the room; no one can answer. Sarah responds. Three boys say "She looked in the book." "Which kind do I use the most?" asks Geoffrey. Several respond with humor about interrogative, exclamatory, and imperative. Has them close books and starts around again. He illustrates interrogative with policeman interrogating. "If I make a statement and declare something, what kind of statement?" Gives other illustrations. Returns to book and defines all four again. (LMS—Good illustration for developing concepts. See learning theories for analyses.) He moves to section on punctuating sentences. (9/10)

As we have indicated, the procedures for concept attainment are in accord with the deductive-inductive position, use of examples, statement of rule or definition, and involvement of the pupil. While we don't have measures of results for such a specific illustration, we were impressed throughout the semester with the limited learning that occurred and was retained. In thinking about this, the key issue to which we always returned concerned the appropriateness of this curriculum for these children. The concern for the theory or language system of language arts (and naming kinds of sentences which is part of that theory) reflects a sophistication that should be required only at a much later point in the life of the student as a writer. A sophisticated communicator will know that interrogative or exclamatory statements are required in certain contexts, that they subtly change the meaning and implication of a situation, that they require different punctuation, and that some authors make greater or lesser use of them. To talk intelligently at a sophisticated level about writing requires these distinctions. If one is working with bright children and with children who have strongly developed life styles of deferred gratification then this kind of program might be appropriate and workable. But to engage in this work with the youngsters at Washington School seems to err seriously. The vast majority seem to have neither the ability nor the concrete experience for making such subtle discriminations.

Intellectual Skill Training

On October 3, Miss Eagle is ill and the reading groups are canceled. Consequently, Geoffrey begins the day with spelling. Also on his mind are the prior day's concern with the girls' physical education teacher, who had sent the children back to the room because of discipline problems, and a list of boys who had left Rhody's Confectionary and been tardy while he, Geoffrey, was on morning yard duty. At 9:30 he begins geography with the sixth graders. In such a context it is difficult to imagine that the lesson centers on critical analysis in reading and raises questions about appropriateness of activities and concept learning.

9:30 Moves to the sixes. "All right, let's go." (Life goes on in the sevens.)

9:32 "What is a glen? . . . Glacier? Hold it. Someone in that group (sevens) is too noisy." Goes on. Then he stops and looks over at Sandy and Molly who are talking. Molly turns and Geoffrey says, "My patience is about exhausted." He goes on picking up aspects of content—firths, estuaries, and lochs. After some facts and some concepts, he queries regarding bold face type and the kind of outline. "All right, the first is 'A close look at Scotland.' What do you think it will tell you? Next bold face is, 'The Great Glaciers Scour Scotland.' What do you think this will tell you?" Pulls answers from several. "You've been told there are three sections of Scotland. Now what should this tell you?" This leads into highlands, lowlands, big cities (in lowlands), borderlands. Geoffrey goes back to outline. "You've got to get into the habit of looking at the bold face type to help you see what's going to be talked about." He next picks up questions (p. 41). "What are main regions?" He asks where you would look. He picks up several answers. He cues them that "Most of their geography lessons will be organized this way." He picks up other questions and asks where they would be found. Summarizes: "read lesson before questions, get used to using bold face type, think about answers." (LMS—The development of this

lesson is one of the first such strategy tuitions that Geoffrey has engaged in. He makes assignment of nine questions on page 41.)
9:50 Goes over to 7's.

As the example stresses, concept attainment continues in geography as well as in our earlier illustration from language arts, and continues as the reader will note throughout the monograph. The significant additional generalization centers on the possibility of analyzing across subjects for such a dimension as emphasis on intellectual skills. Within the context of a traditional textbook geography lesson the pupils are being introduced to an important strategy of thinking.

Reading as Analytical Thinking

Critical thinking and intellectual skills are omnibus terms and provoke considerable confusion as objectives. As we have indicated, several times over, the Washington School focused most heavily on the *3 R*'s as objectives. Geoffrey's pupils have had difficulty in deriving meaning from history and geography reading. On October 4, he commented:

> "Open books, *Skylines,* to page 255." He raises fact that they have been turned loose in history and geography. "The results have not been too good. Have they, Sandy? Eileen? Page 255 starts 'Studying a Paragraph.' The text talks about outlines." (10/4)

He shifts the instructional program here for what will be a long series of lessons on the important intellectual skill of analysis, the breakdown of a communication into its constituent parts with an awareness of the relationship among the elements. Teaching the lesson involves asking for the main or topic sentence, obtaining several answers from pupils, and reaching general agreement. As they move from topic to subtopic to details, Geoffrey prompts by elaborating the example in the text and makes such statements as "Find details on why education was narrow." He provides them with a classical solution of an outline:

    I.
        A.
            1.
            2.
        B.
            1.
            2.

The lesson continues with a "homey" illustration of his own: going to an Elvis Presley movie and being quizzed about it by one's mother. A second paragraph from the text, a statement about Benjamin Franklin and his inventions, is assigned for analysis. They have about 10 to 15 minutes for this.[7]

Then:

9:44   He has group stop and they begin a group discussion. What is first thing they do, Virgil? What is the topic sentence, Molly? Agreement? He calls on Eileen, Thelma, Kent, Evelyn. He takes up some of the less adequate topic sentences and raises questions about them. He has Thelma write hers on the board. Geoffrey checks around class and comments individually. They continue to fill outline. He asks questions. Has "first stove" suggested, then "lightning rod." Asks where the stove and the lightning rod go. He corrects Billy's error (B rather than A 1.) Ties in "details" as a concept. He keeps probing for answers.   (10/4)

On the board is the first part of the outline:

I.   Benjamin Franklin's Inventions
    A.   The first stove
       1. Heats better than fireplace
       2. Burns less wood
    B.   Lightning rod
       1.
       2.
       3.
       4.
       5.

In short, learning a difficult intellectual skill, analysis, has been operationalized into a lesson on outlining. The principal tactics involve the use of a text illustration, the presentation of teacher prompts, and the class "working through" an example. After this the model form was illustrated with a "homey" example and then each pupil tried to implement the model with a further problem. Geoffrey then entertained a mixed group and individual discussion and recitation to add further clarification. The ultimate hope was that these exercises would transfer and be utilizable in a variety of academic and daily affairs. Our later observations suggest that such intellectual accretions are slow indeed.

The role of skill training, using other formats, approaches, and media, and perhaps most basically, using other labels was open to some question in the faculty social system. One morning late in October, Geoffrey had on his desk an audiovisual catalogue. Miss Norton and the observer were conversing as usual. The conversation triggered the following notes:

---

[7] In order that the reader continue to maintain a clear image of the total class, we need to indicate that in the meantime Geoffrey tends to Norman and Joe. K. who have been sent to the hall for chewing wax and inattention and the observer notes that Pete and Henry H., the "on contract" boys, sit, and Geoffrey ignores them completely.

In looking over the audio-visual supplement, Norton commented about the series of film strips on thinking skills. They are slated for grades 6–9; her reaction was that they were inapplicable for "our kids." She was not going to investigate further. I commented about the resemblance to outlining. She saw the point. (LMS—Couple of important reactions: (1) her personal belief "they're not appropriate for our kids" screens out many possible innovations and productive leads, (2) her belief is supported by the peer group norm. I keep returning to the very difficult problem of which reality is real—is it the kids, the teachers' norms, or some blend of these? How much is alterable, or how much is not, is the key question. This is one of the basic premises or givens in the decision-making process. As you agree or disagree with this, you predetermine a tremendous range of behavior and decisions and you close out another large section of possibilities. (3) Another important principle comes back again—varied experience and concrete emotional and perceptual experience. You need this fund of basic Stimulus-Response connections if you are ultimately to attach symbols (concepts, labeling and so forth) to classes of experiences. (Part of this arises from watching a suburban child's trouble with the language of the new math. She can't feel or evoke images concretely regarding the stuff.) (4) This relates to Wientge's[8] problem: make the abstract concrete and then the individual can follow it. Thinking skills require this. Film strips on aspects of thinking should present some lessons in another format; the outlining problem. (5) This raises questions also about facilitation in classroom control through demand qualities of the activities.)   (10/21)

Openness of Activity and Creativity

Seldom did Geoffrey's class accent creativity as an objective. The problems of literacy were too overwhelming. Occasionally, however, the seeds were sown through his own sense of humor and the naïveté of the pupils. One day, with the low group in reading, the vocabulary development lesson went this way:

8:53 Geoffrey begins lesson with reading groups. Puts "man" on board and looks for all the combinations that can be made: mankind, mailman, policeman, fireman, milkman, fisherman, unmanly, manly. (LMS—Possibilities in enhancing creativity can be expanded.) Geoffrey raises hell in banter fashion with Billy for reading a magazine in class. "Billy, I'm pleased that you are reading, I'd be the last to discourage you . . . but . . ."
8:58 He goes on with "manhood," and so forth. He then has each child write his own list using "boy" as a root word. This is difficult for these children. He urges, banterwise, ten. Kids have two to six, only three or four have more than five. He then allows them to use their dictionaries.
9:03 The pace here is easy, Geoffrey is not pushing hard—nothing beyond an "Oh, dear" or two. The kids are quiet, working, and seem interested.
9:05 He has Patty go to board to write and has other kids volunteer items.

[8] At that time an unfinished doctoral dissertation; now see Wientge, 1965, and Traylor, 1966.

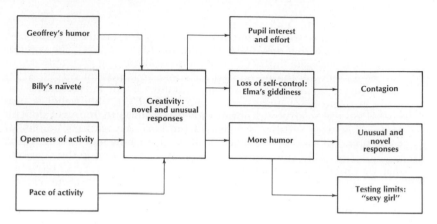

Figure 6.10 Aspects of open activity and creativity in language arts.

Boy Scouts, paperboy, boyhood, boyish, boyfriend, cowboy, tomboy. Billy suggests boysenberry.

9:07 (Janitor enters to put wood cover over broken window.) Everyone gets a kick out of Billy who defends use of boysenberry and reads dictionary statement. Farmboy. Someone suggests boycott. Geoffrey says, "Hold on. We've got to get something straight. Is this something that a boy sleeps on?" He explains core necessity of boy. They go on with playboy, sheepboy, babyboy, lumberboy. All is done in good humor. (LMS—He finally stops them ostensibly from getting silly, but perhaps also because his repertory of objectives doesn't accent creativity.)

9:13 He starts in on "girl". "Work this at your seats." (LMS—The possible contagion and loss of general control are evident in that Elma has the giggles; so do Sandy, Billy, and Timmy S.)

9:17 Geoffrey sends Elma to board to call on people and write down their answers. She's slightly embarrassed about calling on people at first but Elma soon finds this is fun and calls on them by pointing. There is much humor as they call out particulars. Joe K. suggests "tomgirl." This brings down the house. They list some more. Billy suggests "sexy girl" and Elma with big chuckle writes it on the board. Geoffrey finally says "Enough of that nonsense" and has Elma erase it—along with rest.

9:22 Geoffrey sends Marian to board to write:
dough-
doubt-
down-
Marian has trouble spelling—"doudt." One of kids corrects her. Geoffrey has them go ahead. Tells Timmy to turn around. Explains meaning of "doubt" to Billy. Tells Joe K. and Lee to close dictionaries. They work.

9:26 "If you're stuck, you may now open your dictionaries."

Geoffrey's humor, the growing levity of the morning, the openness of the task, and Billy's naïveté concerning "boysenberries" provided novelty in language arts. The complexities arose from Elma's giddiness and the contagion to others. The demands that this places on teacher skill in interaction are apparent, also.

The 30 minutes seem full of implications for additional analyses. With Billy, the use of humor instead of stern verbal reprimand seems contingent on Billy's general geniality and cooperativeness. Potentially relevant also is the time (the beginning of a lesson) and the behavior (reading) reflecting a more general goal. The limited ability of the children shows in several ways—brief lists of words, Marian's misspelling of doubt, and so forth. Multiple objectives are being met—vocabulary development and use of dictionary as a functional tool. The pace of the activity seems appropriate. Geoffrey's behavior in selecting Elma, a source of contagion, for the board-writing job seems artful in interrupting a sequence he did not want, yet maintaining Elma's momentary status. Finally, morality and the limits of sex in the elementary school are clarified. For a summary see Figure 6.10.

Affective Goals as Curricular Activities

Many bases exist for the selection of curricular experiences. Our description has indicated that the major decisions occurred in the selection of the textbooks and in the faculty norms regarding the important things to teach. Because of the apathy and motivational problems we noted experiences that might fit the category "joy of knowing." The notes contain few of these in contrast to the innumerable references to banter, joking, and joy in the children's relationship with Mr. Geoffrey as a person full of humor who is interested in them.

In a spelling exercise dealing with compound words, a few words have been put on the board and a few are done orally in a recitation that moves up and down the aisles. The notes read:

> Picks up on occasional alternatives—welfare and farewell. This brought out a glimmer of an epistemic smile from Kent. One of the first pleasures of knowing that has occurred. (9/10)

Later in the morning of September 10, Geoffrey begins a poetry lesson.[9] The episode develops this way: Sam and Irma are excused because they are repeating the grade and have heard the poem, "The Son." Geoffrey reads the poem to them and asks them to write down what the woman is talking about. He walks about the class making his usual individual comments as he checks papers: "That's part of it," "Almost," "Lost?," "That's right," and so forth. The notes contain next:

11:41 Reads again and interlocks explanation with questions and discussion. Sandy sees the light, "Oh." "What happened?" Geoffrey asks and she replies, "He died." (LMS—Second illustration of surprise and joy at seeing the point.)

11:42 Second poem regarding snow. "What kind of person is that? Write it down." Geoffrey checks around. "Where did you get that idea?" Davey:

[9]This was one of the very few poetry lessons taught during the semester.

"Lazy." Dick: "Dull." Jimmie: "Small." Dick: "Smart." "You just told me a minute ago 'dull' . . . which side do you want to be on? Do you think she's the kind who . . . finds gold in Alaska, gives a speech, leads a group to museum? Member of a group? Do nothing? Do things on her own? Or others tell her?" Edwin asks, "What is it?" "No exactly right answer," says Geoffrey.

There is an announcement about Level Five books in Gennep's room. He picks another poem.

"What's happening?" Davey: "Don't know." "Listen again." Reads first two verses and quizzes. Asks what finally happens. Peggy: "Got killed." "Where or how?" "Sea fishing and boats crashed." (LMS—This is the best example of inferential thinking so far.)[10]

What are poems about—love, death, girls.
11:52 "Richard Corey."
"What's poem trying to tell you?" "Rich but not happy . . . wanted to be like others . . . not be greedy . . . so rich, others don't like him."

A number of possibilities are raised in discussion. Some far-fetched . . . Geoffrey doesn't let this go too far.
11:55 "I guess that's all for today. I just wanted to have you hear these." (LMS—At this point he is apologetic about the poetry. This is an interesting point for most kids listen along, respond eagerly to hypothetical questions and guesses. There are no reservations regarding "sissy stuff.") (9/10)

As a final illustration, a long half-hour lesson on Roman numerals was followed by a briefer "mental arithmetic" session. Geoffrey had followed the text discussion; he presented the basic rules, for example, a letter placed after one of higher value increases the number, XII; he worked problems on the board; he had pupils work problems at their seats; he moved about the room checking and commenting; he entered into banter along the way with Oliver and Sam; and he had volunteers put answers on the board. The notes conclude:

This whole exercise has been approached in gamelike fashion. Most of the children have responded with enthusiasm. All (except Pete) have worked at it. (9/10)

Beyond the joy of knowing, it's difficult to know which variables are carrying the major burden: lesson difficulty, which is low enough that most of the children can do it, lesson clarity about principles, importance of principles, the variety within the lesson, the individual or personalized teacher-pupil interaction (banter and humor on the one hand and individual checking and correcting on the other), or the high degree of pupil activity. These are indicated in Figure 6.11.

---

[10] As we've indicated, minimal amounts of this kind of open-ended thinking occurred.

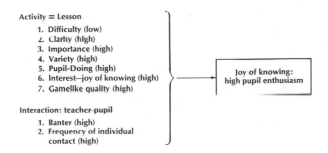

Figure 6.11 An attempt to analyze the activity concept in relation to pupil enthusiasm.

Halloween Parties as Curriculum?

On Friday morning, November 1, the following notes were dictated as the observer drove down to the Washington School. The interplay among foreshadowed problems, close observation of the memorabilia of an on-going situation, the general faith in putting order in the data, and the press to conceptualize loom large. We continue to question "What should the slum school teach?":

> A number of odds and ends to clear up. The more I think about yesterday's Halloween party, the more convinced I become of its importance and necessity in the lives of these children. It is difficult to know (1) whether this is a typical phenomenon of preadolescent and early adolescent timidity and embarrassment, or (2) whether it is a phenomenon of culturally deprived children, or (3) of generally maladjusted children. My guess is that it's partly all three. Billy's hiding behind the desk so he wouldn't get called upon to dance is particularly an adolescent, or early adolescent phenomenon. Leonard's inability to pass out the extra milk without clubbing somebody with the metal case containing the cartons, and his wolflike slashing away at Henry L. with his teeth on his arm as Henry tried to get an extra carton, looks more like the needs of a seriously disturbed kid. Joe G's reservations about entering into any active participation seemed partly a function of his personality and partly a racial problem. (Generally, not locally.) As I watch them trying to limbo to the music of the Limbo Rock, I feel that many of the boys found some means to relate themselves to the enterprise at large. In the preparation for the party there was more task-oriented behavior on the part of kids such as Alan and Walt G. as they made the paper chains, and among some of the girls, for instance, Leona and Marian, and of the boys who were hanging things, Leonard and Joe K, and so on.
>
> Another interesting aspect concerns the fact that a good number of the seventh grade girls were absent. These girls were part of the clique in the dominating group. This gave some of the sixes an opportunity to become more responsible and to engage in a variety of tasks. It is a

difficult problem to make distinctions between having parties for their own sake or for legitimate educational objectives. That could be a very difficult one to think through carefully. (It's reminiscent of the old Warner, Havighurst and Loeb paper on "Who Shall Be Educated?") For some reason I am totally amazed that I had not thought about that monograph. As far as I know it has not been quoted anywhere in the recent literature on the culturally deprived, yet it may contain a beautiful integration with past literature. That would really be high comedy if it became a major thesis. It would place considerable emphasis on how fads come and go, and the fact that now it is out of vogue and no one has quoted it and everyone is thinking "tough intellectual thoughts." Another very interesting aspect is that I arrived at the problem without any conscious awareness of the possibility of the Havighurst statement. Now, as I look at my data, and as I watch the children behave in situations such as this one, it becomes a very real and potent interpretation. In this sense, it's an independently-arrived-at interpretation and should carry more validity than if I had just been reading it. If this is true, then it opens up a further possibility that the prescriptions that came out of the depression era literature may be applicable to the big city now. I am excited about this gem as I have been about the decision-making gem. This will bring focus to the whole issue of cultural deprivation and provide authority to carry the arguments.

My guess is that one of the reasons the "Who Shall Be Educated" point of view dropped out of vogue was the tremendous increase in general affluence in our society and the growth of modern suburbia in the post World War II years, which presented a whole new array of problems to American education. Only now as people go back to the central-city issues do the earlier observations become pertinent once again. As I recall, in some of this literature they raised the problems of ethnic groups in great detail, even though the racial issue was not as heavily accented. The issue here is not teaching children middle-class values in behavior, but accenting some of the broader and basic cultural traditions at the core of our society. In this sense, Halloween is a nice superficial example. More important is an issue such as resolving conflicts through judicial processes. It's amazing how this interpretation began with making sense of the Halloween party. It suggests the need for a wide and varied background of the participant observer. It accents the importance of saying to oneself, "What's really going on here," or "How can I make the most sense of what's happening." Or, "What is the pattern here," or "How can I fit the pattern into the materials." The implication is that there is a connective structuring process going on all the time. In this sense the "data don't speak to you." They have to be shaped and molded and pushed and pulled about. (11/1)

SUMMARY

In speaking about the structure of the disciplines, Geoffrey described the problems he perceived in teaching the various major subjects. From these we identified certain activity dimensions that have implications for teacher training, for examination of the curriculum for meaningfulness, and for renewed effort in investigating development of skills, especially in varied school environments.

In examining the daily lesson as an activity, we noted the special problems the teacher faces in finding common experiences to utilize in introducing topics or units, in using textbooks that have great differences in approach, reading level, organization, and in making instruction relevant to pupil backgrounds and achievement. Additional problems were found in the matter of assigning work, especially homework. We also note that traditional textbook teaching, that is, highly structured, despite the problems suggested above, may be more effective than other methods of organizing instruction for the children with whom Mr. Geoffrey was dealing.

As we looked at the flow of teaching the *3 R*'s as activity dimensions, we identified few procedures as innovative. We also examined activities relative to the importance established by the teacher. We found what we called "selective emphasis"—Geoffrey's emphasizing the *3 R*'s is an example. Other elements identified were appropriateness, drama in teaching, difficulty level, the fractured quality of activities in the classroom, and the frequency of interrupted activities.

As we changed our focus and looked beyond the *3 R*'s we were struck by the indications that for most of Geoffrey's students, learning came slowly and hard. The teaching of intellectual skills was frustrating and often fruitless, and the reasons seemed again to be bound up in the curriculum. The emphasis was clearly on cognitive skills; affective goals were not highly visible. Although humor and banter played a major role in the classroom, the child's "joy of knowing" seemed to be a rare experience. The Halloween party was a special episode in the activities of the classroom. The observer used it as a vehicle for speaking about a number of notions regarding the education of the culturally deprived.

CHAPTER   SEVEN

THE CULTURALLY
DEPRIVED CHILD
IN THE CLASSROOM
AND THE SCHOOL

Recently the concept "cultural deprivation" has come into vogue. A major part of our interest centered on developing a clear and concrete image of cultural deprivation as this was exhibited by the children in the classroom and the school. As we observed the children, listened to other teachers, and took part in the day-to-day life of the school, we began to phrase our position around two central ideas—the ability problem and the mental health problem. These ideas soon differentiated themselves further into aspects of sensationalism, limited physical resources, defenselessness, and unrealized talents. The parade of the sensational refers to the newsworthy or "gossip-worthy" kinds of episodes that occur infrequently in middle-class elementary schools. The limited physical resources specifically mean the limits in physical health and well-being possessed by the children. Defenselessness is the pupils' impotence or powerlessness, created by a lack of family concern and support. By the expression "unrealized talents," we refer to pupil abilities that seemed to have little stimulation for development.

THE PARADE OF THE SENSATIONAL

Too frequently, in our judgment, teaching in lower-class schools is defined and illustrated with reference to episodes in the behavior of individuals or groups of pupils that are sensational in the context of a conservative middle-class community. By sensational we mean an occurrence that shows a discrepancy between a belief regarding what might happen and what actually does happen and that possesses content relevant to emotional or moral events. Usually the group that holds the expectation, notes the episode, and judges the discrepancy is the broad band of people described as middle class. The generalization we wish to make is this: lower-class schools, in contrast to middle-class schools, have a continuous series of sensational episodes. This variation in frequency we hypothesize is significant and important. The reservation we expressed in our introductory sentence refers to the fact that the sensational is only one thread, and although more visible and publicized, to the teacher it is a lesser thread in the fabric of "the culturally deprived child in the classroom."

If we content analyzed the coffee klatch conversations of the teachers and our own notes of observed incidents, we could present a sensational kind of narrative of the semester. Briefly, we would illustrate our point with reference to a series of these episodes.

Early in September, Miss Holt brought to Mr. Geoffrey a copy of a magazine of pornography and violence, which allegedly was not transportable through the public mails. One of her former students, now twenty-one or twenty-two, had published a story, needed a job, and hoped to become a writer. He was in trouble at home because of shooting at his stepfather—for the third time. Miss Holt wondered if there was anything we knew that might be helpful to him. She saw him as an able boy, "a real brain," and as "someone deserving a break."

In the middle of October an incident reflecting the children's environment more than the children themselves occurred.

> Another interesting event that occurred this morning as I sat finishing my dictating near Italo's restaurant involved a Negro man in his thirties or early forties, I presume, walking by with a kind of halting gait, carrying a six-pack of beer. In his hip pocket he had a bottle of whiskey. Even after this long in the neighborhood, it struck me that at 7:00 on a Monday morning that one should be getting started for the week in this fashion was a little bit early and depressing. The few people who were about gave him no mind.   (10/14)

As we have indicated, Italo's restaurant is only a block away from the school. A number of the children walk regularly by the restaurant and the parking lot where the observer was sitting and dictating his notes.

Closing this same week is another episode from the notes.

> Another brief incident that should be recorded occurred as we were walking out of the building. We met Mr. Inman who told us that one of the boys who had been suspended last year and who, it was thought, had a court record, but upon further inquiry had not had a court record according to the police, today was out in front of the school drinking a can of beer and generally behaving in a mildly obnoxious and hostile manner. Neither Mr. Inman nor Geoffrey, and especially the latter, had any sympathy at all for the boy. They would just as soon see him arrested and shipped off to a reformatory. The point of the illustration, however, is again the nature of the environment of the school and the fact that there would be a kid hanging around on the other side of the fence drinking a can of beer.

Joe K. about whom we speak at many points in the monograph adds another item to the sensational.

> Several observations of Joseph K. are warranted at this time. The first day, last week, when he came back to sit at my table, I noticed two tattoos, one on each arm. Both of these are crosses. At first I thought they were pen and ink affairs, but when I asked him about them it turned out that they were genuine tattoos, even though homemade. His brother had put them on using a needle and some ink or dye. They were not removable with soap and water. He commented that one was kind of messy and really hadn't been done very well while the other one was much better. He talked about getting rid of the one through the use of "white bleach," whatever that is. I asked him if it burned when he put it on; he said no, he didn't think so. Apparently he has not tried it. (10/21)

On the last day of October racial tempers exploded and the school was deluged by parents and relatives coming in for their children. The confusion, the excitement, and the emotion continue our illustrations of the sensational that constitutes life in a contemporary, urban slum school.

> Another aspect of the situation occurred in the halls shortly after lunch while Geoffrey's pupils were down at gym. This was the combined look of intense fear—really terror—that was dominating, and the hatred and anger that also seemed to be there. The cues on this are very, very difficult to pin down. Part of it was the quickness with which it was most vividly seen in the parents and the relatives of the children in the school. There was one mother who came to an eighth-grade girl inquiring about her children who were in the lower grades. This eighth-grade girl, a responsible and reliable kid, apparently walks the younger children to school and looks after them to and from the school. The mother was wondering where they were, how they were, and what had happened. She talked rapidly in short sentences; she obviously was quite emotional over the whole issue. Then there was the sister-in-law who was coming for one of the eighth-grade girls and the girl refused to go for she "wanted to stay with her friends." (That one is in the

field notes.)[1] The sister-in-law, who is probably in her twenties, wore blue jeans, scuffed shoes, a bandana over her head, and a jacket. She had a firm, determined look on her face in contrast to straight-out fear or hate. Then there was another sister and her boyfriend who had come. The boyfriend was a tough-looking character and walked around as if he were looking for a fight. Geoffrey turned some of these people away with a cool and almost abrupt "I can't tell you anything, you will have to see Mr. Inman in the office. He is the only one who can let the children out." These people were the poor, rural whites. One had a vision of the strong, more concealed type of southern prejudice typical of a community such as Big City or perhaps more typical of a suburban part of the city.   (10/31)

One incident, among the many, occurred on a day the observer was not in the building. The episode was relayed by the clerk and recorded in the notes.

On the way out I stopped by the office and talked to Miss Effingham for a few moments. I haven't seen her for several days and it was like talking to an old friend once again. She treats me as such also. She gave me the scoop on the incident of Tuesday afternoon with the caustic soda. Several children found a bucket or container of crystals that looked like rock candy sitting behind the store. Apparently one of the codiscoverers was Henry L. who is in Mr. Geoffrey's room. They took handfuls of the crystals, put them in their pockets and then offered them to the other children as candy. It must have involved about fifteen kids with the candy. There were some rumors that Henry L. had "made them try it" although these were never really corroborated. One or two of the kids were brought in by Miss Carr because they were complaining that they had been given some candy that burned their mouths. Mr. Inman had one of the children take him over to where they found it; they talked to Mrs. Maller[2] and found out what it was and took her suggestion that vinegar was the best remedy for it. Mr. Inman sent for all the kids and they were slushing out the kids' mouths with vinegar. One boy they were quite concerned about because he had reasonably deep burns on his lips and his tongue. He was hoarse and they thought that perhaps he had swallowed some of the soda also. That turned out not to be so, as the mother later called about the child and took him to the doctor. Apparently, Miss Effingham responded initially to this situation with a question to Mr. Inman, "Is Mr. Smith here today?" At least that's the way she reported it to me this morning.   (12/5)

In summary, the day-to-day existence of the school shows a narrative of sensational episodes. We have included some of these to clarify a part of the reality of teaching in an urban slum school. However, the larger truth, if one can use such an expression, lies more in the ability and mental health problems, the defenselessness of the children and other aspects of their behavior and outlook.

[1] See the appendix for the distinction between field notes written on the spot and the summary observations and interpretation dictated shortly afterward.

[2] The woman at the store where the "candy" had been found.

Table 7.1
Distribution of IQ scores based
on the most recent group test
recorded on permanent record
card.

110–114	l	
105–109	l l	
100–104		
95–99	l l l l l l l	Q_3
90–94	l l l l	
85–89	l l l l l l	
80–84	l l l	Q_1
75–79	l l	
70–74	l l	
65–69		
60–64	l	

THE ABILITY PROBLEM

The academic ability of children from a lower socioeconomic neighborhood is a greatly debated phenomenon. The data we have consists of our observations and some test scores. In regard to the latter, we have tabled the most recent test scores (Table 7.1) on those children for whom Geoffrey had cards on September 3. These were the children he was expecting to teach. On these standardized tests the children scored considerably below average. In many upper-middle-class suburban schools the distributions would overlap minimally, that is only a few pupils would score below 100.[3] On October 3 we tabled the scores on the new sixth graders and on the group of seventh graders who remained. Their scores are reported in Table 7.2.

Table 7.2
Distribution of IQ scores for
children enrolled in Geoffrey's
class on 10/3.

	Sixes	Sevens
105–109	l l	
100–104	l	
95–99	l l l	l l l
85–89	l	l l l
80–84	l l l l l l	l l
75–79	l l	l
70–74		l l
65–69		l

[3]At this point we do not wish to argue the point of "culture fair" tests nor the more general validity question.

The Map Incident

While there were many incidents that suggested the limited ability of the children, the map incident came to typify the problem. The episode developed this way as Geoffrey passed out blank maps of the United States and had the children fill in the names of the states:

11:22 "All for today. Put dictionaries away. I have a little test for you. When you come into seventh grade you are supposed to know something: $2 + 2 = 4$, C-a-t spells cat. Also should know states in your country." Explains. Some dallying questions. Urges them "Do your best. No excuses." (LMS—Sequence of influence attempts; comments before action rather than after.)

11:25 Everyone starts. (LMS—This turns out to be quite difficult for these kids.) Much hesitancy. Questions back and forth among pupils. These are met with shrugs and subvocal "I don't know."

11:29 Geoffrey begins moving around and about. Collects from lunch girls.[4]

11:34 "These maps of yours are miserable, stinking, terrible."[5] (LMS—Actually three or four states is about average. I was surprised at how poor the students were. Once again the limited knowledge.)

"Can't study history without knowing the states. . . ." Pulls down map and has them start writing and copying them in. Brings out map game for them to use at leisure. . . . "At some time in next two weeks we will have a test for real." Irma, with a horrified look, asks if it will go on their grade. As if there is something totally unfair about it.

11:38 Messenger. Cute little second grader. Geoffrey talks gently with her for a moment.

11:44 "How many have Mexico? TAKE IT OFF." (same as Canada).

11:45 Messenger back.
Sends Thelma for fifth- and sixth-grade geography books. Back and forth protesting (by Sandy, Irma, and others) about what they have or have not studied.

11:47 Thelma back.
"Here is fifth-grade geography book." With emphasis, *"You know the name of this,* young lady?" (To Sandy.)[6] Irma enters into discussion of how she thought Canada and Mexico were part of the states . . . This goes on for several minutes. Gets help from class. Sarah: "Cuba's on map." Dick: "Have 52 of them?" Pulls North American map: Canada, U.S., Mexico. Comes back on another tack "What makes a country?" "What makes a state?" "Which is bigger?" "What makes U.S.?" Raises question regarding representatives. Two senators? "Mexico send senators and representatives to Washington?" Dick: "Mexico has president." "Mexico has its own president and government." Other pupils about to give up on her.[7]

---

[4] Several of the girls work in the lunchroom and left class at 11:30.

[5] This is part of his "ferocious tiger" role about which we commented earlier.

[6] This is the year-before-last geography book on the United States; they had spent a year on this information.

[7] Irma argues for 2 days on the inclusion of Mexico and Canada. Geoffrey explained "til he was blue in the face" but she wouldn't give up. The observer even spent a half-hour with her. It was a striking performance on her part.

11:57 Messenger in (patrol boys needed)
11:58 Bell rings

"Sam, do you know what that desk costs? Neither do I. We'll both find out if it breaks. Not supposed to sit on it. Especially a boy like you."

After lunch the children have another 10 or 15 minutes to work on their maps.

When one extrapolates from the map exercise to the impending lessons in colonial history and distinctions among New England, Middle Atlantic, and Southern regions, much less the broader concepts of colonists' purposes in coming to the new continent and the beginnings of democratic government in such documents as the Mayflower Compact, one feels most uneasy.

Another aspect of the problem came into sharper focus in an offhand comment by one of the old hands who had been in the school for 10 years. He commented, "I used to feel angry with the lower grade teachers, then one year I had the kids two years in a row and they didn't know any of the language materials I had taught them the year before." He chuckled when the observer commented, "It made you wonder who the lousy teacher was?"

Soon we began to wonder at what seemed to be the assumptions of some educators and psychologists who haven't been in daily contact with these children. Many seem to believe that the deficits are mostly culturally imposed and are relatively easy to remedy, that research has shown the unreliability of intelligence tests, that most large school bureaucracies and their functionaries are not quite doing what they should be doing and that better teachers, more like themselves, could solve the problem.

In the course of the investigation, we began to look at the alternatives available to the teacher. This immediately raised the observer's most fundamental and characteristic response, "It's more complex than it looks at first." Typically, this complexity indicated a series of dilemmas. For instance, when a child falls behind in an activity or enterprise, generally he catches up by spending more time or working harder per unit of time. The whole "Weltanschauung" of the slum child is away from school activities. When extra pressure is needed, a teacher frequently turns to a parent for help. These parents often will volunteer permission for corporal punishment or they will "whip him good" if you desire. Neither parents nor children see the importance of regular school attendance—having the children proximal to learning experiences. Typically on Friday, and especially Friday afternoon, some five to ten of the thirty went "to the country." Usually this was a drive to outstate rural areas to visit "grandma" or an aunt and uncle. In reports from the children it seemed that the parents tacitly assumed the children were needed or would enjoy the trip. The pupils uniformly reported, in casual conversation, that they liked the country and would like to move back. When placed in the context of a conflict between main-

```
Dear Teacher

Harry went Fri. to Contry
with me because his Grandpa
is very sick & we did not
come home to Mon. nite?

        Please excaus him

             Joan
```

Figure 7.1   Parental note regarding Harry's absence.

taining and strengthening family ties versus developing competence and achievement, many of us would see some legitimacy also. We have included verbatim a note from a parent excusing the child's absence.

Often to increase learning, the prescription is to go back to the level of the children. In a sixth- and seventh-grade class such as this one, it means an average of fourth- and fifth-grade level. If you seriously conduct class activities at this level then you have the problem of the few children who are at grade level. While this is the ubiquitous problem of individual differences, it has overtones here that seem more onerous. This concerns the inability of the kids to function easily in small groups in independent work. For instance, differentiating assignments, especially those significant in meaning and interest, carry some unspoken requisites. In another context, we have had occasion to observe a seventh-grade child struggling with independent study and report-making. She was a strong and avid reader, was highly motivated, had skills with dictionaries and encyclopedias, had such resources available, and had verbal problem-solving skills. An omission in any one of these would have materially altered her success. As one lists these necessary skills, one describes what a culturally deprived child lacks.

To catch up, to reverse the tide of influence suggests you must start earlier. Although we did not observe primary classes, conversations with teachers at that level suggest that the difficulties are already appearing there. A strong public preschool program seems a very good idea. Our only hesitancy here is perhaps practicing the error about which we are preaching—the other man's job looks simpler when you have not lived it and you do not know anything about it. In short, the low ability and achievement of the slum child did not look in our semester sojourn like the simple-to-solve problem some commentators have indicated it was.

THE MENTAL HEALTH PROBLEM

Mental health, as an area of concern to educators and psychologists, frequently has been a pivotal point of attack against the public schools as well as a measure used by the middle-class schools to indicate their breadth of outlook. We wish to use the concept for further exploration of a series of issues. The field notes dictated after recess duty in mid-October suggest the general nature of the problem.

> I have just come in from recess and am leaving the school early for University business. Once again at recess I was struck by the drain of energy that results from just keeping on top of the scuffling and fighting and clowning of the pupils. Basically, you have to ignore it except when difficulty really arises or, as Geoffrey says, when there is a crowd or someone is getting hurt. Accumulating fatigue, however, is almost unendurable. This is the real problem of the aggression of the children. It is not that there is any fear of getting involved yourself, or of being afraid to teach in such a situation; it is just that coping and putting up with it wears you out.
>
> Another phenomenon, which struck me again today at recess, is the variety of individual differences in not only aggression, but in mental health more generally conceived. At one extreme, you have a kid like Billy, who is happy, who gets along as well as one might expect in terms of his intelligence, who is pretty responsible, can hold a job (he has one in the summer) and can make enough money to buy some of the things that he wants. The average pupil, however, is far to the left of Billy. . . . There is the listlessness and apathy of a girl such as Leona, who is so overweight; there is the confusion within a boy like Leonard. As I watch him, now that he sits very close to my desk, I keep feeling I am seeing someone who is tormented. For instance, he wrings his hands, he stammers, he has a facial tic, he looks totally pent-up. And, apparently, he does explode on occasion, as when he was caught beating up a girl. The social-class bias in mental-health scores reflects extreme differences in frustration, conflict, anxiety, and a host of adjustive mechanisms. Just where the school is to grab hold of this is not clear at the moment. Perhaps an ungraded school would be effective, if it could be

integrated with some type of a grade level program. The use of books and materials to make the lessons more systematic and to give continuity might be one way around this. The articulation with the high school could be planned in terms of a band of age levels that permitted a floating, but reasonably stable, achievement-test criterion. It should be noted that this would be a very complex administrative arrangement, and would take a good bit of trial and error to operate. This is predicated on the belief that, not only is the problem serious today, (a fact that I can support in terms of a general criterion of learning) but that it *is* possible to do something different that will alter this problem. At this point in my own experience, the possibility is a very real but untested assumption.   (10/17)

Aspects of Mental Health

Spliced into the notes were numerous illustrations and tentative hypotheses concerning the subproblems making up the general syndrome of mental ill health. For instance, Allison's volatility in her reaction toward her brother Edwin:

> Allison finally around to trading a desk. Geoffrey finally off to Gennep's room. About one-quarter of the class are working.
>
> Edwin snaps Allison on her bottom when she bends over. She turns on him with a snarl "You do that again and I'll kick you where it hurts." (LMS—The volatility; the awareness again fit the construct of the lower-socioeconomic-status child.)
>
> Lonny back to see me. Sandy also. Allison sings out about a crush.

The pupils showed considerable variability in behavior. Oliver, who played a clowning role in much of the early interaction, had his good and bad days as indicated in the notes:

> (LMS—On lower socioeconomic status personality: (1) Variability in reaction versus consistency. Suggested by Oliver who has been engaged in "gentle jesting", for example, he said he stayed out all week because of a dental exam. Very different from hostility showed toward Sam and other kids on another day. (2) The need for precision in directions. Witness the care given to filling out dental cards. Some kids don't know year of birth, spelling of street, and so forth.   (9/12)

A further interpretive hypothesis relating to the implications of the variability in the children's behavior was recorded in the notes:

> (LMS—Part of variability of behavior, for example, Sam, Sandy as Lolita, and so forth, raises issues of trusting an adult or authority-figure. Adult who gets too close has no leeway to absorb variability. Gets hurt, personally. Relate to Fromm's aloneness.)

Finally, we would sketch further the involved aspects of the mental health problem by a long quotation from the notes of December 17:

> Yesterday morning I saw the complications of the alternative of parent involvement. While it may not be a general principle, it does reflect

the difficulties involved. Walt G's mother came with him to school yesterday morning at 8:45. She was hostile and aggressive and ready to "get Geoffrey" (these are my terms). He had been lying in readiness for her literally since the time the first report cards came back a number of weeks ago. Walt's mother had made some remark then about returning Walt to the other teacher. This had made Geoffrey quite angry. He armed himself with his several books and notebooks of records and went out in the hall to discuss the problem with her. This lasted for only a moment and then she and he went down to the office to involve Mr. Inman. The situation turned out much as it had with Agnes. The parent was carefully informed about how much work had been assigned that the boy had not turned in and how little of his classwork he had been doing. Geoffrey's records are so immaculate that it is impossible to argue in terms of the data. This aspect of record-keeping probably should be explored more fully, particularly as it contrasts with the habits of an individual like Mr. Alton who in the past kept practically no records for an occasion such as this. Another issue that arose concerned the father's treatment of the boy, apparently just the night before last. Geoffrey had originally thought that the father's punishment was a result of the kid's skipping school, but apparently this was not so. As Geoffrey informed me yesterday afternoon as we were going out, the father had told the boy that he could sell his sled so the boy sold the sled, gave one of the two dollars he obtained to his mother and spent the other dollar. The father, apparently for this reason, whipped him severely. The whipping is the point of the whole paragraph. Geoffrey commented to me that the boy had welts and bruises all over his back. He later demonstrated this to me when Walt came up to class shortly before recess to stay in the room because "my back is sore." Geoffrey told him he wanted to see his back again and very artfully turned the boy toward the wall, away from me, where I was sitting across the room, and took another look. In that way I got a clear view of the boy's back. I saw approximately one-half of the back from the waist, half-way up to the shoulder. Half of this area looked like a combination of broad, inch-and-a-half-wide welts on a background of black-and-blue bruised areas. These welts and bruises were on the lower half of his back; presumably the top half was worse than this lower half. While my experience with bruises has not been wide, it was clearly the worst case I have ever seen. I don't have more details on what precipitated it, nor on the circumstances at the time the beating occurred. For instance, was the father drunk?

The basic point I would make concerns the issue of involving the parent in the problems of the child. With a number of the children, and how large this number is is not clear, there may be physical repercussions if you pressure the parents to take a more active and involved role with the kids. When you pressure them, you in fact frustrate them, and this can instigate aggressive behavior. When the instigation results in such overt behavior as this beating, it casts considerable doubt on the efficacy of this alternative for the teacher. As I have talked with a few of the kids, they have commented that when they do things wrong or bring home a poor report card, they are due for a whipping from their fathers. Just what the frequency of this behavior is, I don't know. Yet, I can remember kids like Irma, Esther, and Walt G. who have told me this explicitly.

It is important to remember that all of these kids are at least twelve years old and some of them range on up to fifteen. Just when this whipping stage, if it might be called that, passes is an interesting question, also. It may well be that it goes on until the child is old enough to leave the home, either by running away or going elsewhere to live, or until the child is big enough to retaliate in kind and curbs it through the fear the parent has. (12/17)

Broader Issues

Two boys we discussed earlier, Pete and Leonard, were similar in the seriousness of their problems; that is, the problems were chronic, they extended over many aspects of their lives, and they created new difficulties each day. They illustrate what we have called the "negative spiral," a vortex or whirlpool which leads away from such minimal goals of adulthood as economic self-support, stable parental and marital ties, and freedom from legal difficulties.

We might debate the public schools' responsibility for these as aspects of the children's development. Should the public schools remedy the situation? Are the public schools, by making academically strong demands furthering the difficulties? These are partly questions of values and goals of public education. They are also partly questions of fact—which alternatives lead to which consequences, and how are these judged as favorable and unfavorable?

Another side of this issue remains unsettled. During an informal conversation, one of the teachers commented about having been urged to "understand" a difficult child. The teacher's reaction was "Understand him? Hell, I wish someone would understand *me*." Lest we be misunderstood, the teacher who made this comment is one of the most patient, gentle, and dedicated individuals on the staff. Mental health, social work, psychology, understanding, were all dirty words. Each was a red flag when used by outsiders and a stimulus for humor when used with each other

To the observer, it seemed that the teachers referred to outsiders as those who offered advice but did not have to live in the teachers' day-to-day environment. This, we believe, is a very important point; the day-to-day existence as currently structured is exceedingly difficult and frustrating. Besides Leonard and Pete, Mr. Geoffrey's classroom contained a number of troublesome children and a number of marginal ones. Two boys were on probation from juvenile court. Several of the boys just sat in class; they would do no classwork, and if they did not disturb anyone, the teacher left them alone. This truce, rapprochement, or whatever, as we have indicated, is a most interesting problem in its own right. One of the girls, Leona, twelve years old, was very overweight, 170 pounds, and each day would present a run of psychosomatic problems: she couldn't see, she felt dizzy, her nose was bleeding and so forth. Several times a day she had to go to the restroom. She was absent a good deal also. Another girl,

Irma, was exceedingly dependent: she was up to the desk for instructions several times a day. Besides these children who wear you down, and the normal, fun-loving boys and boy-crazy girls, there were a half dozen boys who were extremely difficult and hard to work with. At best they would do an occasional assignment; generally they were engaged in all kinds of nonsense: they were inattentive, they were in trouble on the playground, they missed a lot of school, often would come in tardy, and so forth. Their major characteristic was what we called "neurotic stupidity." They just could not learn by simple experience. The teacher would make a suggestion, would ask them to do something or not to do something else, or would warn or threaten them—the verbal behavior of the teacher was quite varied as he sought techniques to cope with the kids—but five minutes later they were back into inattentiveness, nonsense, or difficulty. Although it is difficult to speak abstractly about their behavior, qualitatively it did not have a healthy, fun-loving adolescent dimension to it. There was a tenseness, a driven quality, and a purposeless, stupid quality about their behavior.

However, it was not just the analysis of the children's behavior itself which concerned us. For the teacher it meant long, hard, frustrating days. The conscientious teachers were faced with a large minority of kids who were highly resistive to academic work; they were individually troublesome and collectively fatiguing. The teachers faced their own demands to do a "good job." The school curriculum set certain demands which seemed to them to be unattainable. The school staff norms demanded that they work at their jobs in certain ways. The conflicts here increased the frustration. The psychometrists, social workers, or other specialized personnel who came by with brief truisms for advice were not looked upon with favor nor was their wisdom influential. To those in positions of consulting, supervising, or teacher training, we would urge some careful reexploration of what and how our knowledge can make a contribution to the mental health of pupils and teachers. Specifically, the analysis of teacher frustrations, the kinds and the quantity, seems very important. Which ones can be alleviated and to what degree? Also, what kinds of internal conflicts are provoked by demands from one's conscience, by special service personnel, by supervisors, and so forth?

LIMITED PHYSICAL RESOURCES

Personality theorists vary in the manner with which they treat physical and physiological variables. For some, these variables influence personality and for others they become taxonomic factors in their own right. In our scheme they are dimensions with bodily referents within the individual which are significant for classroom functioning. An analogy suggests the frame of reference: in a variety of sport contests, maximum performance is attained through careful attention to diet, exercise, training, rest, and so forth. The organism engaged in serious competitive interaction is tuned to machine-like readiness and proficiency in order to attain his highest level of performance. If school activities require physical stamina, and for the moment we can assume they do, and if the culturally deprived needs to move in a more accelerated fashion to catch up, or even to hold his own, then we realize that limited physical resources can further handicap the culturally deprived child.

Our data are extremely limited concerning the *diet* of the children. On several occasions, usually in conjunction with a health movie, Mr. Geoffrey informally asked the children about their breakfasts and lunches. A number of children ate little or no breakfast. A few would have a bottle of coke or soda and potato chips on the way to school. Only a few of the pupils took part in the school lunch program. Those who did not go home would have a hamburger at the Sandwich Diner on the corner, or candy, coke, and a pinball game at Rhody's Confectionary across the street. Our notes are replete with accounts of children of all ages eating candy apples, popcorn, penny candy, and so forth at all hours of the day—before school, at recess, noon and after school. Our several trips into the confectionary required elbowing through crowds of young people eating, smoking, talking, and playing the pinball machines.

While we don't wish to moralize, our records show also that a number of thirteen-, fourteen-, and fifteen-year-old boys were habitual smokers with well-stained fingers. One conversation with Alan indicated that he was aware of the cancer research summarized in the newspapers and on T.V. from the Surgeon General's report. He commented that he had been smoking since he was ten and he could outrun most of the boys he knew who did not smoke. He did not believe the reports of the medical consequences. Only one incident of serious drinking came to our attention. Edwin had gone "to the country" one weekend and had gone out on the town with an eighteen- or twenty-year-old cousin. He described with great relish the beer drinking and carousing that he had enjoyed. We did not probe for this kind of information; our guess is that considerably more occurred.

The physical illnesses and uncorrected chronic disabilities of the children also were not checked closely by the investigators. However, to the casual eye a variety of difficulties were apparent. Of the fifty children who were in the room at one time or another, only Thelma and Esther wore glasses. Thelma went without hers for several weeks when they were broken and she couldn't afford to get them repaired. Esther often refused to wear hers. Pete, from the time he had lye thrown in his eyes, had visual problems that never were corrected. Timmy had a hearing loss, which was evident if Mr. Geoffrey called on him when he was facing away. Others would have to poke him to make him respond. During one three-week period when he had a terrible cold and cough he seemed almost totally deaf. To extend the illustration and make the general point, Timmy also had low-average or dull-normal intelligence, minimal reading and arithmetic skills, serious restlessness, and a reputation among the children for being an odd boy. For him to run an academic race was impossible.

Many of these limited physical resources contributed to the absenteeism problem which we have documented. The children frequently stayed home.

General fatigue seemed in some instances, such as with Henry L., to be more a symptom of other problems than a cause. He often slept with his head on his desk for several hours during the day. Other pupils, Peggy, for instance, would sleep during days following late dates with a boyfriend from City High School.

To return to our analogy, the athletic coach needs to attend to the physical fitness of his team members with a rigorous general health regimen before he can begin to teach them the skills necessary for playing the game. The teacher who has little control over these variables often is forced to lower his expectations of performance and accomplishment.

UNREALIZED TALENTS

A number of facets of cultural deprivation come into focus as we discuss artistic abilities. By way of context we have argued that the "frills," art, music, and science, received little emphasis in Mr. Geoffrey's class and elsewhere in Washington School. This was argued within the faculty norms in the following manner: the special areas are time consuming and not enough time is available since the children are already behind in the basic subjects. Another drawback, perhaps, was the teacher's ability. For example, Mr. Gennep on more than one occasion commented on his musical and artistic ineptitudes. He had had a course or two in music education but he felt totally inadequate to present a music program. His efforts consisted in playing popular records and singing some familiar songs. In Mr. Geoffrey's class, a number of pupils went to choir with Miss Binder and several, for instance Kent, went to instrumental music. This trading—some of Miss Binder's students came in to his class for study period—was a mechanism helpful in resolving areas of deficiency.

Several of the original seventh-grade pupils, Henry L., Billy, and Dick, displayed considerable skill in tracing and copying. From time to time they were observed "mimicking" as it were, a picture in a book or magazine. The likenesses were quite close. The observer had no difficulty recognizing what they had copied. On one occasion, Dick sketched a profile as the observer watched. When quizzed, "Where did you learn to do that?" they replied that they had taught themselves. (This was not checked out carefully for truth and accuracy.) The point we would make concerns the limited instruction they received and the possibilities for some respite from the heavy wall of failure and inadequacy in their performance. One should recall that Billy was a cheerful, pleasant, cooperative boy—even though exceedingly dull. Henry L. slept or rested his head more than he sat up and attended (while this wasn't logged quantitatively, it is close to being literally true). He did almost no school work. Dick, however, in contrast did most of his work. He was among the better group of the seventh graders who were moved in the shift when a room was closed at the end of September.

An important experiment that should be made concerns the impact of intensive instruction in drawing upon the skills already possessed and upon the attitudes and attendance of the children. The necessary ingenuity this would require goes without saying.

While we did little observing during physical education classes, the limited game skills of a number of the boys were quite striking. In one of the softball games in which we participated, batting and catching skills of the majority seemed minimal for boys of twelve to fifteen.[8] Two individual illustrations will suffice: Joe K., one of the most troublesome of the sixth graders, seemed almost untutored in game skills, yet to watch him scale the 10 foot fence around the playyard was to observe a boy with catlike grace. The matching of special talents with particular games and sports remains almost trial and error in the research literature. The point we would make is that limited opportunities existed for extended trials with tuition. Leonard, a boy who appears throughout our records, would delight a high school football coach in size and strength. His interpersonal difficulties, academic limitations, and lack of athletic training suggest that he will not be in school for the ninth grade. While we don't wish to laud the contemporary emphasis on high school competitive sports and some of the problems this poses for adolescent societies, the assumptions we are making seem to be (1) untapped talent exists; (2) success in some socially acceptable area of endeavor can be an important condition for building self-esteem and tolerance for frustration in other areas; and (3) success and self-esteem are prerequisites for being a full-fledged participant member in an immediate peer group or in larger societies.

THE CHILD'S EDUCATIONAL FUTURE

A variety of events led us one day to visit City High School. As we think back on our brief observation of the high school, our interpretations seem to make most sense in the context of our discussion of the culturally

---

[8] This seemed particularly true when contrasted in the exclusively coached and equipped middle-class suburban children observed informally by the authors.

deprived child in the classroom and the school. A fundamental truth in all teaching is that the child has an educational future as well as an educational past. Educators frequently talk about these issues as the "articulation" of one institution with another. Our notes and discussion elaborate this at many points within Washington School as we discuss the faculty social system, sequences of learning, and problems of promotion and retention. The dilemma of the teacher and her academic efforts is seen no more vividly perhaps than in the world that will face the child in high school, a scant year or two from the time they leave Mr. Geoffrey. We reproduce verbatim several long passages of summary notes, observations and interpretations, to indicate our concerns.

> Mr. Geoffrey and I went to the high school this afternoon. At this time, as I am driving home, the myriad of impressions have not formed into any pattern. I will report them in free association fashion. As we walked up to the door, I was struck by the fact that there were monitors, students standing guard at all of the entrances and exits. I was reminded of my old high school. The monitors inquired if we were there to see Mr. Sullivan.[9] We said we were. The monitor said that he would be here in just a moment, and we should wait for him in the hallway. Mr. Sullivan had cleared the way very neatly with the skill he possesses to a high degree. He took us immediately to lunch. Immediately was a well-chosen word for the lunch periods are 27 minutes long and individuals have to get in and get out in this brief time, so that any lost motion will make someone late for class. Tokens are used instead of money. We had a hamburger, french fries, and a glass of milk; coffee, salad, and dessert were also available. Many renovation projects are going on at the present time. The girls' gym and part of the cafeteria have been finished while the biology and chemistry rooms are now being redone. In one corner of the cafeteria they are making a partitioned teachers' room. Mr. Sullivan said that there had been a close vote on this. They went ahead even after they found that the majority on a second vote would have voted no because of the lack of ventilation in that corner. It was about this time that I was in the middle of the experience that reminded me of Buz Marrow in *The War Lover*. The undifferentiated blob that might be called adolescence or might be called high school, and which in one sense is a kind of fearful picture, began to get structured as I had images of teachers and pupils in lunchrooms and hallways and images of the commonality of the children sitting in these classes and the children sitting in other classes and other places. We met the principal and received a warm welcome. She told us an extended anecdote of her experience as Washington School principal with a student who defended a parcel against overwhelming odds one day in the office. Meanwhile Mr. Sullivan was trying to get down the hall to his study hall to relieve a teacher who was sitting in for him. By the time we got there, she gave him an interesting look implying "where have you been?" He introduced us to a girl named Jean who is one of the "queens" of the school. A real Jill.[10] She gave us

---

[9] A high school teacher the authors had known from earlier professional contacts.
[10] This was in reference to a *Life* magazine article on Jill, "golden girl" of a high school in California.

a tour of the building. Along the way we met a music teacher who was disturbed because of the physical arrangement of his class, for he could not keep an eye on everyone at once. He thought that music, though an elective, should also be a privilege. He wanted to get rid of two or three who were making trouble for him and who were making it sometimes difficult to reach the musical standards that he, and his supervisor, thought appropriate and necessary. He had to speak to the class for a moment to quiet them down. One of the girls had the giggles and just could not stop. I thought I was in the sixth grade at Washington School. We met a home economics teacher who showed us the kitchen arrangements that they have—six new alcoves. She also had one room with a special kitchen in it, but said she does not use it very much because— she arched her eyebrows—"I can't keep my eye on them here."

Several interesting comments were made along the way. First, Mr. Sullivan commented about the problem of keeping order in studyhall, saying that fourth-hour studyhall, right before lunchtime, was the most difficult one because the kids are restless and hungry. He had found a very satisfactory "club" that he wields whenever necessary. This involves the time in which they line up to go to lunch. If they line up before the bell rings, they can beat about fifty or seventy-five kids into the lunch line. If they line up just as the bell rings, they lose some ground, and if they have been giving him trouble they have to stay a minute or maybe two minutes, which literally destroys their goof-off time at the lunch period. Mr. Sullivan has a very easy, informal way with the kids. As we walked about the hall he commented to this one or that one about something he had seen in the school paper or something that they had been doing. He individualized his approach very neatly. This is quite similar to some of the tactics that Geoffrey uses with his elementary school group. It takes time, and it takes an interest in the kids. It means also that you go to basketball games or the football games or you take part in some of the school activities. He, also, apparently has affiliated very well with the ruling clique of the school. The girl he chose to lead our tour was quite friendly with him even to reporting a question we had asked her, "How many kids do you know in the school?" Both Geoffrey and I had asked independently of each other. It was at that time that Mr. Sullivan told us about her career in the high school. I should write to him and get him to comment on the "Jill" article in *Life* magazine. We had been gathering the same impression of her as she talked about the yearbook activities that she was involved in and we began to quiz her about the kinds of things she did in the school. She made a comment or two about the football and the basketball team. The former is most unsuccessful, but the latter are slated to be city champions. Jean commented that most of the kids on the basketball team were all bigger than 6 foot 1 inch and that most of them were colored kids. I asked her where they lived and she commented "over that way" pointing to the east. Actually, they are kids from a housing project and its school. She did make a very interesting remark that "they live over there—most of us live over here," pointing to the other side. I believe the "they" and "us" distinctions are very important particularly as they relate to the Washington kids because most of the Washington kids come over from the "they" area which is the other side of the park. Most of the "us" kids come from the area immediately adjacent to the high school. As Mr. Geoffrey and I drove back, the differences in the neighborhood were very apparent. Around the high school the homes are in at least an upper-lower-class category and many of them look like "good, solid middle-class homes." (10/4)

The observer picked up remaining impressions on his tape recorder the next morning:

Several points remain from the trip to the high school. In the course of making conversation, Jean began talking about the high school and about the nature of the kids that go there. One of her comments was that there were no "snobs" in the high school, or, as she said, maybe only one or two. She contrasted this with some other high schools in town where there were sororities and very strong cliques in the school. She said none of this existed at City High School. In my mind there is no question that there is variability in such a phenomenon, but I would question whether she accurately perceived the existence or nonexistence of her own clique in the school.

Another point of importance concerned the general appearance of the kids in the school. There certainly is not a great deal of wealth among the students, and as Mr. Sullivan mentioned, the kids work in the cafeteria for not only their lunch but for the little spending or cigarette money that they can make by selling some of the tokens that they earn. But in one way or another, either by working for lunch, or by earning the money themselves, or possibly by the fact that some of the poorer students drop out, the kids at the high school manage to give a better appearance than the children in the current sixth-grade and some of the younger children of our school. City High School just does not look as poor as Washington Elementary School. It is interesting in this light of the general improvement of the social-class conditions at the high school (contrasted to the Washington School) that Mr. Sullivan commented that the faculty feels quite proud of what they do with "the material they have" in the way of students. While the number of pupils that go on to college is low compared to some of the other high schools in town or the typical suburban high schools, City High does have its share of scholarship winners, and occasionally it has pupils who rank high in the City in academic achievement and aptitude. The critical comment here is what they have to work with, which seems to be the perennial plea of the teacher in any circumstances or situation that is less than ideal. In response to my question concerning faculty pride, he commented that the staff at City High School uniformly has training at the Master's degree level and three or four of the teachers have Doctorates. Most of them seem to like to be where they are.

It might be worthwhile to comment a bit about the physical facilities of City High School. They are as close to intolerable as one can imagine. As indicated above, just this last year they have built additions onto the school. One of these is a gym for both the boys and the girls. Prior to this time, the boys' gym was a small, elementary-school-type playroom with pillars scattered through the room to support the auditorium upstairs or the floor of the upstairs classroom wing. It was ludicrous. It was impossible for anyone to play basketball and move about. Currently in the renovations there are two academic classes that meet at opposite ends of the old girls' gym. They happen to be quite small classes but you can hear the discussion at the other end as well as at this end. Some of the classrooms, Sullivan's class for instance, can only be reached by walking along the back end of someone else's classroom. As Geoffrey and I went in to see him before we left, we observed the teacher and some of the pupils. The door that led into Mr. Sullivan's classroom squeaked horribly and disturbed a few more. On the way out the same thing happened. The faculty lounge, while homey, was small, and the overstuffed furniture was popping out of its covers. Similarly, the main office was a jumble of staff, students, desks, papers, benches, and so forth. Nevertheless, there was a real hum to the place. The library was small but seemed to be pretty busy also.

One might comment about the problems that would be imposed on a college-bound child as he went to the Washington School or the City High School. The major reaction I have is that the home would have to supplement the school fare in the elementary school to a very high degree. At the high school, I would see the tracking program (ability grouping) as a major innovation in culling out the able students and giving them a different curriculum—considerably more stimulating than would be provided to the run-of-the-mill students. This in itself holds some very interesting possible implications for the future in terms of living in the downtown area.

The extended quotations from the summary observations and interpretations need little further comment. The reader might well want to imagine who of Mr. Geoffrey's class will reach City High and which of those will complete the four-year trek.

DEFENSELESSNESS

In our discussion of the nature of cultural deprivation as it appears in the classroom, an additional phase centers on the defenselessness of the children. We see this as a corollary of the "child as a decision-maker" focus and of the noninvolvement of the parent. More specifically, the point we would raise concerns the powerlessness of the child and the consequences which flow from this.[11] Several illustrations will suffice. In the shift of students during the "October change" both Rose and Patty remained with Mr. Geoffrey. One of the pupils coming from Mr. Gennep's room was their younger sister, Evelyn. Rose protested. She didn't want to be in class with her two younger sisters. The essential reason for her staying behind was her low achievement and her inability to meet the criteria for promotion into the eighth grade at the end of the year. But the consequence was a negative relationship, a reversal in age and achievement status, where

[11] The image we are trying to evoke is similar to the "total power" conception which the guards possess in a maximum security prison such as Sykes describes in *The Society of Captives*. (Princeton University Press, 1962)

the youngest sister was the best student and the oldest was the poorest. The high reading group included the youngest sibling and the low reading group had the oldest. They had to live daily with this direct and vivid reality. The point we wish to make is not to second-guess the staff decision nor to trace the rising absence rate of the older girl, but to indicate that the battle was fought and lost by the child without a parent to intervene in her behalf. Although we do not have cross-cultural data, our guess would be that such an incident occurs infrequently in middle-class society. Pairs of siblings in the same room and grade (Allison and Edwin) and in the same room (Billy and Harry) were quite common at the Washington School.

A second illustration of the defenselessness centered on the demotion of Norman. Again, the reasons were detailed and real: he was one of the "impossible aggregate," although not a great deal worse than some of the others. He was demoted and traded for another boy, Henry L. The child had been warned repeatedly. He had been in continuous trouble. He had made his "choices." No one stood by him to aid, comfort, or defend him against losing a full year's progress in school.

During one of the incidents of racial conflict, Harry got caught up in the issue in a way that makes concrete, again, our concept of defenselessness. The summary in the notebook states it this way:

> Several things might be mentioned about the incidents of this week. First, they have precipitated a visit by Mr. Willower, the supervisor. He should come today.
>
> Second, the incidents have resulted in one boy's being suspended. This was the boy who threw rocks. Also, there was a second boy suspended, Harry, for swearing at the principal. As the story was told to me by Mr. Geoffrey and by Harry's brother, Billy, it went something like this: Harry had been over at the confectionary across the street, and had come out with the rest of the boys on Tuesday, when the first of the racial incidents began. There had been considerable excitement and Mr. Inman was trying to calm everyone down. Harry had left his pen in the confectionary and wanted to go back across the street to get it. Mr. Inman told him to wait for a few minutes. A little while later, he asked the question again and was told to wait. Then, or the third time he asked and was turned down and told not to bother Mr. Inman, Harry walked off and made a muttered comment of the order of "Fuck you." This was the end of it for him. There is a real tragedy in his being suspended for of all of the kids in Mr. Geoffrey's class, this fellow is one of the lowest on the test scores, and yet he comes through with the correct answers a fair number of times. Also he was crystallizing in the social structure as one of the boys who help make the class move academically. In the low reading group he was one of the most able of the kids, and I think the notes will show in the last few days that Geoffrey was able to work with him to pull the group along in the direction he wanted to go. Similarly, in geography it often was Harry who could make the sensible guess, the common-sense interpre-

tation, or provide the necessary interest or enthusiasm. While he carried some very strong overtones of hostility in his makeup, he did not have the "kookie" qualities of many of the boys in the sixth grade.

Such illustrations suggest points in the "negative spiral" which might be broken if the schools had the necessary resources available. Note, however, the elements: (1) special classes or teachers for these children, for they could not be handled with thirty others; (2) the honestly held reasons—the school must teach the children basic knowledge in reading, arithmetic, and so forth, and these children cannot (Rose) or will not (Norman) carry out the assignments and activities that lead to these cognitive goals; (3) the promotion policies—if not actually in the directives—at least as perceived by the staff;[12] (4) the parents who did not come to school, who often wrote notes indicating that the child (Rose) needed to stay home to help with the laundry and the babysitting, and so on; (5) the "inevitability" of these children becoming at best dropouts and at worst serious individual and community problems.

PUPIL SCHEMA: A FINAL GLIMPSE

Schema, or cognitive map, is the psychologist's attempt to say something about the broad class of variables related to images, concepts, or ideas of people. Gradually as the semester wore on we came to have greater contacts with the children and clearer perceptions of their views. In the summary observations and interpretations early in January, a lengthy report on a conversation occurs. We include the verbatim notes to indicate the pupil schemata and the beginning interpretations of the authors.

> The next episode I wish to report concerns the conversation I had with four of the children: Leona, Agnes, Esther, and Peggy. They jabbered so incessantly for approximately twenty-five to thirty minutes that it is hard to recapture the total flavor of their conversation. Let me try listing a number of observations and interpretations. First, a good part of the time they were talking among themselves and only occasionally to me as I would interrupt with a question about who was this or what exactly happened. This gives a more interesting perspective on their more generalized conversations when they are alone and when they are not with an adult. Once, again, I tended to evaporate out of the situation and they went on about their business regardless of whether I was there or not. Second, this point in contrast to the first, wove in very interestingly with the other. At times the children seemed to want to have my attending ear, and they would talk incessantly at me and run through their whole verbal repertoire to gain my attention as they would be competing with the other three children. I am reminded

---

[12] Before one (such as a college professor, an outsider) judges too harshly, let him consider his own admissions, grading, and failure policies in his classes and in his institution as he "maintains standards" and "strives for excellence and quality."

particularly of Leona, who would tell me something as if to say "listen to me, too, I've got something important." (These are my quotes and my interpretations.) Substantively I was overwhelmed by the variety of references to family, boys, life, death, and generally the world of persons. Let me illustrate with several examples. Much of the discussion centered around Peggy's boyfriend of the moment and her past boyfriends. While I do not have a totally clear picture, I think at the present time she is dating an eighteen-year-old boy who is Agnes' uncle. Previously she had been dating another boy, who I believe was Esther's older brother or perhaps her cousin. There was considerable speculation on how nice it would be if Peggy became Agnes' aunt. The kinship relationships here are quite intriguing, or as the kids say in reference to their "kin." Or, as Mr. Geoffrey sometimes comments "Is he your kin?" Thirdly, the kids talk a good bit about half-brothers, their father's first wife, somebody's divorce, and so forth. My guess is that they take part in and listen to a good bit of this kind of relative talk with their parents and their "kin." Leona kept breaking in with discussions about how she could hardly wait and how her family could hardly wait until she becomes an aunt this March. It sounded to me as if the pregnant one of the family becomes the focus of attention and everyone is excited about whether it will be a boy or a girl, and this too becomes part of family lore. As they talk about nieces and nephews and younger brothers or sisters (and Esther is about to have a younger brother or sister this spring and she is excited about it too), the inference I draw is that the kids get considerable enjoyment out of playing with, fondling, spoiling, and generally making a fuss over infants. Apparently this is a high point in their lives. It suggests the interesting problems of the immediate satisfactions derivable from a young child and the anticipation of the next one, and the gradual abandonment of the kids as they get older and go out on the street and begin to get on their own to a considerable extent. They talk with considerable freedom about this aspect of their lives. Agnes mentioned, for instance, "that her mother was married at seventeen and had her at eighteen." Peggy talked about "living a little" and not getting married right away. Several of them commented about the contrast between this "living a little" and being married in that when you are married you are always "arguing and fighting and stuff." The image I have (but with no real strong evidence upon which to base it) is that the kids, as they grow up and move into their middle and older teens, find a good deal of pleasure and excitement in the attention of boys, the dating and the partying, and that this should go on for a few years. Then they get married and life becomes one of feuding and fighting with husbands, and the sociable pleasures arise in the contact among other women, young mothers, and their variety of kinfolk. It is almost as if the women didn't expect much help from the husbands nor much companionship with them. Doing things as a couple, which pervades the middle-class mores, seems to be not a part of the way in which these girls think and talk about their current lives and their future lives.

Another item or two that entered into the conversation: Early in the discussion, Leona told me about their pet dog who had distemper and "had to be put away." She seems to have some kind of morbid fascination with death for she commented on an earlier occasion about a younger brother or sister who had died and how upset she had been. These items keep coming up in the conversation from time to time. The only references they made to school were comments about how they hoped they wouldn't "flunk." Agnes was the strongest in talking about not wishing to fail. Leona said that she was going to flunk, and I asked her why, and she said because she didn't do her work. I asked her why she didn't do her work and she said "she wasn't interested." In the same way that life and death is an easy part of their conversation, so is passing and failing. The tenor of the difference in which they talk about this as compared to the way a suburban youth and her friends might talk about this is very striking indeed. By tenor of the difference, I mean "the naturalness" of the discussion. It is as though it's an item that comes up regularly in life from time to time and that one knows about, understands, lives with, and isn't really concerned about. Failing is not fun but it is something that happens and is not something that you worry about a good deal. You don't like it when it comes, but you live with it and it passes on. The girls talked about going to the show and Peggy and Agnes talked about going downtown on Saturday to buy some belated Christmas presents that didn't get bought beforehand. Peggy is going to buy one for Agnes and also for Agnes' uncle, Peggy's boyfriend. Agnes has gotten a radio for Christmas; Peggy got a nail file set which she was using profusely while she was talking with us in the back of the room.

The point I am trying to grope for here is the nature of existence for these kids. At this point in time, with the economic system as it is, most of the children have enough to eat, enough to wear, and presumably a reasonably good shelter. There are an array of satisfactions based upon interpersonal relationships, small and inexpensive material items, the earrings and necklaces and pins of the girls and the whistles and mechanical items that the boys possess from time to time, and the day-to-day events around the house and the neighborhood. On occasion the kids will talk about other places to live and other kinds of things, as Agnes did once when asking me about Oakdale and the suburbs generally. If I recall correctly, she made some comment of "it's pretty out there." There is a kind of stoicism about their outlook. The range of goals, the desire to get ahead, the future orientation, are all practically nonexistent. Life is much more of a "here and now." Things happen to you and you accept them and live with them and try to select the better parts as well as you can, although you don't plan very far ahead for them.

I am struck by how different the whole framework is. It raises the question of whether this, then, demands day-by-day assignments, which Mr. Geoffrey utilizes, and whether it prevents the utilization of long-term project activities. Interestingly enough, it raises also the question of the directive-autocratic environment, which, in effect, impinges upon the children and pushes and shoves and moves them about and which they stoically react to. What I am trying to say is that there is a curious kind of fit to the kid's outlook, as I'm trying to phrase it and describe it here. Their world is not one that they shape and alter toward long-range goals and developments. Their world is a world that happens to them. In this sense, the directive-autocratic teacher is a "natural" part of this world. In this sense, the directiveness doesn't carry the emotional overtones that it carries in other groups and societies. In this sense you might say "It's the way it's supposed to be. And while you don't like it, there really isn't any effective way to resist it, so you have to bear with it, but do as little as possible to work with it."

In one sense the above might be a first-class rationalization, and yet in another sense it seems to me to fit very well this part of the "real world" that I'm observing. The implications for the "ideal world" are also far-reaching. What are the pluses and the minuses of the one alternative or the other? What would be the sequencing if you are to move toward a different kind of world?

Unless I am misreading some of this, there is one kind of inner freedom in that your battles are with the outside environment, the necessities, and the day-to-day issues. The intra-psychic conflict, at least for these girls, in contrast to some of the boys, seems much less evident. The presence of anxiety and guilt, as they arise from the superego-versus-ego conflict, is not apparent with these children. While there may be an anomic reaction to the overwhelming outside environment, there is no intervening, self-imposed neurotic anxiety. If I were to try to explain the behavior of the children along these lines, it would suggest that Agnes and Esther were reasonably healthy kids in this context, although Esther has some religious problems that come up from time to time which don't fit too well. Peggy has an overwhelmed look much of the time, but that may be situational because of her schoolwork that is much too difficult for her very limited intelligence. Leona, on the other hand, with her terrible weight problem and the variety of psychosomatic symptoms that go along with her obesity, may well have learned these techniques of appearing ill as simple reactions to frustration. Her behavior has become generalized and unconscious, or partly so, in that she still uses her obesity occasionally in a malingering fashion to escape things that she doesn't like. Yet her actions do not seem to carry the usual, whatever usual means here, reaction to anxiety.

The children make comments about several of the others that should be mentioned also. They refer to Timmy as if they don't like him, and they talk about how he is always "acting crazy" and making noises and sounds like a barking dog, and so on. They also cite an occasion when he and Leonard, the tall boy who left our class a month or two ago, (and they did not like him either) apparently took Peggy's purse. She got it back and hit Timmy on the head and then ran off. The boys were trying to trade the purse for a kiss. She didn't like this at all. As far as I could gather this was mostly because she didn't like either one of the boys. They were creepy. (I think that last word is mine, not theirs.)

In the same boy-girl area, Agnes talked about playing some kind of game, a variation of hide-and-seek, and the teasing she would do when she would run and tell her mother that the "boys" were grabbing her. This wasn't running as a little girl would run but running to tease and provoke the other kids. As she talked I had the feeling that she well understood the implications of what she was doing and the way in which she was doing it. There were also several comments about hitting boys or whacking them with purses, and so on. The point I would make is that aggression is also a major part of their lives.   (1/4)

SUMMARY

If one teaches in this slum school, one finds the sensational, the difficult, the exciting, and the satisfying. We would hypothesize that most schools in lower socioeconomic areas will have similar children. Behind the slogans of wars-on-poverty and the sensational accounts that creep into the newspapers are the day-to-day struggles-in-conflict that face the classroom teacher. Two ideas seemed central as we looked at the children—the ability problem and the mental health problem. As far as ability is concerned, our semester's work suggested that the problem is not so simple to solve as some commentators have indicated. When we add to this the mental health problem, then the task confronting the teacher in such a school as Washington becomes demanding indeed.

Limited physical resources beyond the control of the teacher, that is, the children's diet, further complicated the teaching situation. Within the teacher's control, however, if he himself is talented enough, is the task of tapping the skills the children already have. Unfortunately, these skills may not be in the mainstream of instruction, the *3 R*'s, but may instead reside in areas, such as art, that were not emphasized at Washington School. As we looked at the culturally deprived child in the classroom and the school, his defenselessness struck us. He is caught in a negative spiral whose grip is hard to break in the present organization and operation of the school. Our trip to the high school showed us how others think about the children who go on through Washington School and other elementary schools. Indeed, we wonder how many students in Geoffrey's class or in Washington School will reach City High and how many of these will last four years there. The negative spiral has already weeded out many and no doubt will weed out more before the senior year of high school. A final glimpse of pupil schema reviews for us that life with these children is pretty much a "here and now" matter. A range of goals, a desire to get ahead, and a future orientation are not a part of their make-up. They do not control their environment. Their environment controls them. The nature of the culturally deprived child minimizes the degree to which the teacher can bring changes in pupil behavior in the classroom.

How much of the children's behavior and personality, are shaped by the school and the teacher who have bureaucratic and short-term demands, and how much of the children's behavior and personality are shaped by broader social conditions of poverty and by the more intimate interactions of family life, we do not know. Nonetheless, this is how we found the culturally deprived child in school and classroom.

CHAPTER EIGHT

REFLECTIONS ON CLASSROOM ANALYSIS

INTRODUCTION

In an earlier investigation of the "correlates of classroom functioning," the investigators had concluded:

> The mosaic in the lower socioeconomic groups seems less satisfying than the mosaic in the middle socioeconomic groups. The authors have barely begun to satisfy themselves as to an 'educational psychology of the classroom of the culturally deprived.' [Smith and Hudgins, 1966, p. 253]

From this dissatisfaction grew the problem of the present monograph, the manner in which a middle-class teacher copes with a group of lower-class youngsters.

Other antecedents existed as well. We found dictums of advice such as Goodwin Watson's (1962) comment on teacher-pupil relationships: "The starting point is respect. Nothing else that we have to give will help very

much if it is offered with a resentful, contemptuous, or patronizing attitude."
(p. xi) Later, in the book to which Watson had written his comment as
part of a foreward, Riessman (1962) wrote dramatically about a number of
issues in the educational psychology of the culturally deprived. He tended
to have little to say about the processes of teaching, although one comment
remained with us as an irritant and goad for further efforts. In a few words
Riessman suggested several alternative strategies for teaching lower-class
youngsters.

> She can concentrate on those values which she holds in common with the
> pupils and ignore the differences . . . She can ignore value questions entirely
> and focus on teaching basic skills and knowledge. . . . There is one more
> option, . . . The teacher may, in a designated area, explicitly and openly
> disagree with a value bias like anti-intellectualism. If she does this directly
> and honestly, not snobbishly or manipulatively, she may be able to sway
> students, and may also be more at ease in her relationship to them.   [p. 82]

And then he states, almost as a second thought:

> Of course, disagreement, to be fruitful, has to take place within a frame-
> work of general acceptance, and so the teacher, in order to be effective in
> opposing certain beliefs, has to be able to share, or at least respect other
> sentiments.   [p. 82]

We were concerned with that "framework" and had some feelings
that it was probably more complicated than the strand of "general acceptance." Homans' (1950) discussions of other human groups, in an industrial
setting, on street corners, and in a south seas island community clearly
argued for a more complex view—a social system of interdependent elements.
General acceptance is a sentiment. Disagreement is a kind of interaction.
We asked ourselves: What of activities and norms? What of situations, times
and places? And what of environments—physical, technical, and social?
These questions became the foreshadowed problems about which Malinowski
(1922) spoke and which could be, we thought, distinguished from "pre-
conceived ideas" treated as conclusions. In short, the problem developed an
initial focus. But problems attain part of their definition and focus from
the procedural style used to attack them. Once again we found ourselves
listening to Homans as he chided his fellow sociologists that methodology
was a matter of strategy, not a matter of morals.

Not only did Homans provide the caveat, but also he presented a
simple set of "rules of scientific procedure" which could provide a focus for
observers who wanted to behave in an analytical style as they quested for
a theory of classroom teaching. Explicitly, he stated his position:

> All these ideas can be summed up in a set of rules that, as experience
> seems to show, are wisely followed in setting up a theory of the kind we pro

pose. A theory, we will remember, is a form in which the results of observation may be expressed. The rules are:

1. Look first at the obvious, the familiar, the common. In a science that has not established its foundations, these are the things that best repay study.

2. State the obvious in its full generality. Science is an economy of thought only if its hypotheses sum up in a simple form a large number of facts.

3. Talk about one thing at a time. That is, in choosing your words (or, more pedantically, concepts) see that they refer not to several classes of fact at the same time but to one and one only. Corollary: Once you have chosen your words, always use the same words when referring to the same things.

4. Cut down as far as you dare the number of things you are talking about. 'As few as you may; as many as you must,' is the rule governing the number of classes of fact you take into account.

5. Once you have started to talk, do not stop until you have finished. That is, describe systematically the relationships between the facts designated by your words.

6. Recognize that your analysis must be abstract, because it deals with only a few elements of the concrete situation. Admit the dangers of abstraction, especially when action is required, but do not be afraid of abstraction. [1950, pp. 16–17]

In effect, we had a problem, an approach for gathering data, and some tentative guidelines for analyzing and interpreting the results.

In a monograph as long as this and as full of illustrative detail, difficulties arise in choosing final summary statements, in explicating particular implications and focusing on the various readers to whom the volume has been directed. As we noted in the introduction, an interested citizen developing images of issues in urban education may not be reading the same book that a prospective teacher reads as he is about to face thirty or forty children in his next semester's practice-teaching in a slum classroom. Also, the reflective practitioner, with many years of experience, who examines his own perspective vis-à-vis ours, looks for a different set of summary implications than the graduate student expects to find when he seeks a thesis or dissertation hypothesis and a few hints for operational procedures and design tactics. Rather than dealing explicitly with such dilemmas, we selected another alternative, the specification of several items that struck us as intriguing, that have wide generality, and that have led us into further investigation. In this manner, we hope to remain "all things to all readers."

We felt also that a partial criterion of research lies in the new problems to which one is alerted. In our view, new issues remain implicitly in the three major conceptions of the book's title—complexities, urban, and classroom. When we first addressed ourselves to the problem, we accented the classroom as a closed or self-contained system. We were interested in the teacher's behavior in coping with the children. Hardly had the study begun when the realities of the organization, formally and especially informally, struck us as major issues needing analysis. Our contract, the agreements we had made to stay within Geoffrey's classroom, and our limited resources precluded following those problems at the time.

Not only do school buildings as organizations have a history and structure, but so do the individual teachers. They are socialized into teaching and into the cultures of particular schools. This we saw in Mr. Miller, an apprentice from City Teachers College. This process struck us as intriguing and as exceedingly important for a clear understanding of the complexities of teaching in urban as well as other classrooms. Also, we have hinted, Big City School's attempts at integration were focused, in our semester at the Washington School, on the "bussing" solution, moving intact classrooms from overcrowded Negro areas into less crowded predominantly white schools. A host of problems arose in this area, and though they fell outside the scope of this analysis, they need careful consideration in a study of urban education. In our judgment, a number of things need to be changed in the urban classroom and school. Our contract and our unwillingness to "second guess" ourselves and our colleagues in the Washington School prevented the research from moving in such new directions. The dimensions and problems of change in schools and classrooms need careful analysis as well as creative suggestions. To us, the most significant contribution of the study lay in the dynamics of classroom events. Considerably more needs to be done here also before we have a powerful theory of teaching.

Finally, our methodology, so new to us, which we found stimulating and captivating, needs more intensive consideration. While anthropologists and sociologists might find "microethnography" or participant-observation standard procedures for the study of human behavior, the educational psychologist does not. The latter must see it in the context of the multiple classical approaches more usually utilized in educational and psychological research.

A TEACHER AND HIS CLASS

An Initial Problem

As we have indicated, we started in part with a Homans (1950) perspective. We wanted a classroom case study to supplement his more general studies. Such a study would aid the teacher and educator to translate and utilize a more general social science perspective. However, as we began to talk about Geoffrey's relationship to the pupils, and especially his attempt to influence them, we could not move easily with *The Human Group's* thrust; it seemed to deal less adequately with the individual's relationship to a group with well-catalogued dimensions than it had with the analysis of the group itself.[1] Consequently we struggled with a set of diagrams, the final result of which appeared in Figures 3.1 and 3.3 of Chapter Three. In these figures the abscissa is a time line, our attempt to capture the ephemeral dimension of process. However, it is the ordinate which is of critical importance in this discussion. After "stating the obvious in its full generality" we found that we needed to categorize Geoffrey, the teacher, into elements of personality[2] and behavior. For instance, Geoffrey had conceptions of recitation, feelings of concern for humor to enliven the classroom, and a remarkable ability to quip. These internal personality processes received expression in his classroom behavior. Similarly, as we have indicated, our diagram needed a category for an individual pupil and his personality and behavior. In the instance of Sam, his ability to quip and his responsiveness to termination cues were important elements of his personality.[3] As we talked further, we found not only were concepts of interaction, sentiment, and activity necessary, but that our discussion moved more easily and more carefully by introducing such additional concepts as beliefs and roles. Each of these we defined conceptually and they became part of our glossary and cumulating theory.

In other diagrams, our mode of representing conceptual analyses, we found it more convenient to assume the time line along the abscissa and to weave the relevant concepts into hypothetical relationships and miniature theories without forcing them into the more exhaustive scheme. For instance, in Figure 4.5 the analysis of the "provisional try" uses such general rubrics as teacher personality and group structure and more specific concepts of anxiety, freedom, and alterability of teacher plans.

Teacher Decision-making

The heart of our model of the processes of teaching lies in the decision-making of teachers. Rationality, so it seems to us, means that one's goals and their accompanying highly probable means are in control of one's behavior. While the broad and more ultimate goals of public education have been formalized by committees and commissions, we have been impressed by the degree to which means have become ends in the urban classroom. To phrase the situation more positively, proximate goals have replaced distal

[1]Once again we make a distinction between Homans' insightful clinical analysis of leader behavior (Chap. 16) and his inability to integrate these materials into the conceptual structure he had been developing earlier. Also, we did not want to engage in a reductionism to a different level of analysis, which we felt occurred in the *Social Behavior: Its Elementary Forms* (1961).

[2]In other places we have followed McClelland's split of personality into the domains of schemas, motives, and traits.

[3]Recall our contrast with Elma who had the ability to make "wise" remarks but did not have the ability to terminate the developing interaction.

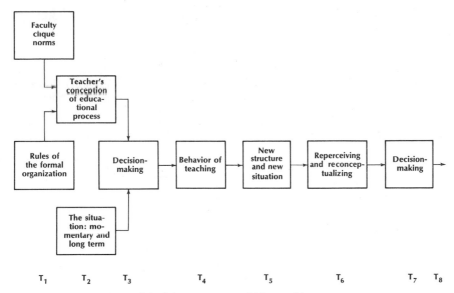

Figure 8.1 Summary model of the processes within teaching.

goals. Concretely, "appreciation of one's heritage in western civilization" has become a number of pages in a social studies textbook. As the latter is accomplished, the former is assumed. Although educational psychology has produced a number of documented generalizations connecting particular learning experiences with particular outcomes, for example, advance organizers in meaningful reception learning, number and kind of examples in concept attainment, and communicator prestige in attitude learning, the awareness of such generalizations in the teacher's thought processes has not been carefully ascertained. In effect, no careful assessment of the subjective probabilities of teachers has been made. Also, as we have argued, extra classroom events, the school organization, and the teacher's reference groups were important in Geoffrey's thinking. Consequences occurred in those domains. Within the classroom, the situation included the time of the year, fixed parts of the schedule and the particular pupils constituting his group of pupils. These events and thinking led to behavioral alternatives which he invoked.

As we have looked at teaching in this monograph, we have been impressed with the several meanings of "process" as they apply to the analysis. Conceptually, our references to process are changes occurring over time. Operationally, this has been handled as a time line in our models, most of which read sequentially as Time 1 (T_1), Time 2 (T_2), Time 3 (T_3), and so forth. In a sense, these are simple ideas, which are responded to intuitively by practitioners, but which are much more difficult to handle theoretically and even more difficult empirically. As we saw the classroom processes, two references to time were critical. First, and the simpler, was time in the context of the year. The beginning of the year had a number of qualities, essentially establishing a social structure, which the remainder of the year did not have. The second use of process involved a consideration of the flow of events during an hour, a lesson, or a similar brief episode. It is this usage that contains our major concerns. In Figure 8.1 we try to focus on several critical elements.

The Behavior of Teaching

A most significant concern in the decision-making model has a twin or dual characteristic. Cognitively, the concepts teachers use to describe what they do have been extremely limited. We have argued that a theory of teaching needs considerable differentiation into more complex structures. It is these concepts that need to be built into prediction systems, and a teacher needs to assess their probabilities in relationship with his goals. At the same time, the educational psychologist interested in a psychology of teaching must get on with the difficult theoretical and empirical job of clarifying the concepts and establishing the propositions, that is, ascertaining the objective probabilities.

In an earlier paper (Smith and Hudgins, 1966), we commented specifically regarding teacher behavior:

> What the teacher 'really does' is a most important and complex problem in its own right. For instance, if educational psychology is to have something to say to the classroom teacher, it must be able to specify behavior on her part, under her control, that will lead to altered pupil perceptions and then to altered pupil behavior. But what she 'really does' can be assessed at varying levels of specificity and generality—the long standing molecular-molar controversy. . . . The authors' comments, at this point, are not to suggest a resolution of just what the teacher does, but to suggest that the problem is important, complex, and theoretical.   [p. 256]

An initial map of this domain in the art of teaching contains a number of elements.

As Geoffrey taught and as he talked about what he was doing and as the observer watched and listened, the elusiveness of the art of teaching seemed to lose some of its undefinable quality. For instance, teachers face a situation that is far more complex than educational psychologists and other educators have seemed to appreciate and which we have called *a distinction between "here and out there."* No simple choice seems appropriate for accenting what one is teaching. Possibilities exist that (1) the learning applies only to pupils' behavior in the classroom, (2) the learning should change the pupils' behavior in the community outside of school, and (3) the application of the learning is more subtle, "it depends on the situation." Each course of action has its potential positive outcomes—conflict avoidance, transfer, and flexibility, and a number of unknown and uninvestigated consequences.

Geoffrey tended to initiate a number of mundane interactional episodes that the naïve outsider might see as petty or insignificant. In time we came to call these *preparations for contingencies*. They foresaw events and provided resources to deal with them. The uninitiated might be unprepared for these events and would not only stub a toe but might fall as well. The monitors, the safety pins, the keeping of records all meshed nicely. He was prepared; he was ready. We have not pursued the phenomenon far enough to have a taxonomy of problems and issues that one can utilize to provide observable indicators by which the researcher can specify the degree to which a teacher is high or low on the dimension. We are confident that this can be done, that variation in teachers exists, and that demonstrable relationships, such as those hypothesized in Figure 4.3, will be found.

We think that teachers vary in another way, the degree to which they do things tentatively or provisionally. The *provisional try*, as we called the idea, is reflected best in an offhand statement such as "we'll try it this way for a while." Such behavior should promote a tentativeness about class-room organization and learning activities and should prevent recriminations from pupils when the teacher elects to change activities for the short term. Setting the context of a high degree of such provisional trials and a high degree of actual changes seem to be different variables. The freedom you guarantee with the former kind of behavior may be disastrous if practiced greatly in actuality. Useful discriminations might be made also between the teacher's behavior so typified and the pupil's behavior as he engages in problematic learning tasks.

As teachers work and live in the classroom, the *awareness* they have of their pupils and the social structure of the classroom probably vary to a marked degree. Such alertness to the nuances of the daily lives and the give-and-take of pupils should facilitate a number of additional processes of teaching. The degree to which teachers maintain *continuity* in commenting upon past events and building into future situations seems quite significant. The multiple contemporaneous strands of events demand behavior such as we have called *ringmastership*. The teacher who can keep the proverbial three balls in the air is a very different kind of person from the individual who becomes rattled or disorganized in the face of multiple stimuli. While we have not commented upon the genesis of such skill, a provocative question lies in the degree to which this is readily trainable in a sophisticated teacher-training program and the degree to which it relates to more stable personality traits. Casual observations of children suggest that such variability occurs at least as early as middle childhood or preadolescence. Perhaps a special case of this is *sequential smoothness,* the degree to which the teacher blends activities and makes one part follow smoothly upon another. The rate of flow of activities over time, we have called *pacing.* The teacher can manip ulate or adjust this depending on his goals and his perception of the situation. Physically, elementary school teachers vary in the degree to which they *teach-in-motion.* We hypothesize that this is another element in the artistry and process of teaching, and that it should relate to *personalized interaction, preparation for contingencies, awareness,* and other such variables.

In many classrooms the potentiality for teacher-pupil conflict seems quite high. As children move toward adulthood they progressively move toward the give-and-take of peerage. They come to have an identity, to speak their minds, and to expect to shape, in part, their destiny. Also, as individuals come from varying social backgrounds their interests and goals vary; a middle-class teacher with a group of lower-class youngsters typifies this. Similarly, individuals and organizations often pursue different ends. In a slum school the teacher mediates such potential conflict situations. We found ourselves talking about *aloofness and autonomy* as qualities of teacher behavior when "illegitimate" demands were being made and pupils refused through disinterest or "fun." The teacher did not plead, haggle, or force the issue. He withdrew, went about his business, and assumed the problem would be solved and that he was in control of the situation. *Skirmishing,* verbal exchanges in the lesser battles of the game of teaching, occurred as Geoffrey probed and directed in more legitimate areas and as he indicated that the class was to keep moving toward its goals, and he was not only willing and able to handle any problem which might arise, but that he would do so. *Banter,* the use of humor in interaction, and usually with only a few who played appropriate roles, provided a highly acceptable mode of dealing with problems and gave a liveliness and a fun quality to the classroom. The basic quipping skills of the teacher, the subtleties in pupil-role development, and the correlated skills of the pupil indicate the context of this dimension of teaching process. Geoffrey's mock anger in the *ferocious tiger role* occurred mostly in total group situations after hard-teaching, strong-pupil efforts, and limited accomplishment. The fierceness of his display seemed only a minimal sample of his own anguish and torment. It served as a prelude to the return to a task difficult for both teacher and pupils. With individuals who were having difficulties with learning problems, who were apt to be embarrassed, and who were willing to make an effort, the *lamblike gentleness* appeared.

Finally, we thought that a portion of the confusion surrounding individualized instruction could be solved with a more restricted conception of *personalized interaction,* the degree to which a teacher attends to an individual child. We hypothesized that arguments about textbook teaching, recitational teaching, and independent study can be clarified, in part, by such analysis.

The Situation

In our analysis, two of the critical elements constituting the situation were the time of the year and the particular collection of children who were pupils in the classroom. At the Washington School these proved important. The beginning of the year shaped Geoffrey's goals and his actions to implement the goals. He was preoccupied with developing a livable, workable social structure. The presumption was that such a structure, once established, would lead economically to the variety of more distal learning goals. The role of pupil was clarified and accented. The children were in class to work and to learn. They were to do better, to improve. They were responsible for their behavior and responsible to him. A series of small but clear rules on assignments, talking, classroom behavior, and so forth rounded out this general picture. Significantly a series of more individualized roles as monitors for classroom duties and as specialized persons in interaction with him and with each other were established. The court jester with Sam as incumbent brought fun and vitality; the nonworker role with Pete as incumbent illustrated tragedy.

The initial aspects of the teacher's role involved establishing control and getting the program of activities underway. Control involved the development of pupil readiness to comply with teacher requests and directives. This process seemed to have elements of clarity, what we called *grooving the children;* elements of forcefulness, an "I mean it" quality; elements of potential and actual consequences, a following through; and elements of softness and gentleness as beliefs were shifted to norms and commitment of the children was sought. In great detail also we saw Geoffrey's efforts to establish the activity structure, the daily pattern of study of the eight curricular areas. The scheduling of these, passing out the relevant texts, building in meaningful and recurrent weekly schedules, as in spelling, took a major portion of his time and efforts in the initial days of the year. Later the program "ran itself" and Geoffrey turned to the individual learning problems in what we called personalized interaction. He had settled a whole series of problems. Presumably they would have stayed settled, but this year the closing of a room brought in a new group of students and the process had to be initiated again.

Parenthetically, we would comment that if our hypotheses on the establishment of a social structure are tenable in classes other than Geoffrey's, much of the correlational analysis of teacher behavior and pupil reactions must be carefully reconsidered. For instance, the correlations of classroom climate indices and teacher behavior may really be epiphenomena or residual byproducts. The cause-effect interpretations that one is prone to read into correlations may be very serious errors. The teacher behavior critical to the formation of pupil roles, beliefs, and sentiments may have been expressed long ago and the system may be maintained mostly through reputations and a rare overt comment or act by the teacher. Such hypotheses pose a number of interesting researchable questions on distinctions between the genesis and maintenance of social systems such as classrooms.

As teachers plan and make decisions, their thinking often distinguishes between the fixed and the flexible items in the totality. In Geoffrey's case, such items as opening and closing time of school, recess, and lunch times were fixed by system directive; they were hard parts of the schedule. Geoffrey noted them early for all of the remaining decisions were contingent upon them. Similarly, the physical education classes, taught by a specialist who worked throughout the building, were in a master schedule over which the individual teacher had minimal control. The remedial reading teacher had a bit more negotiable flexibility, although not much. If one had special or idiosyncratic personal biases or needs, as in Geoffrey's preference for "straight line" scheduling, the meeting of major subjects at regular times each day, the weighing of pros and cons among alternative consequences becomes a smaller and less difficult intellectual problem. The hard or fixed quality of the schedule is an important part of the situation which must be incorporated into one's thinking and deciding.

As a particular group of thirty or thirty-five pupils walk into a classroom shortly after Labor Day, a further part of the situation becomes defined. Early in the year we were struck by the *ability problem,* the limited knowledge and intellectual skills possessed by the children. Every decision made by the teacher seemed conditioned by the pupils' lack of information, the pupils' inability to meaningfully read related materials, and the pupils' problems in working independently on academic problems that were broad in scope and lengthy in time allotments. We have sketched a number of thoughts on shaping such pupil behavior through successive approximations. The incoming group of sixth graders caused us to see more clearly an issue we came to call the *mental health problem.* Particularly among those twenty children, but also among the other pupils, their mental health was an important fact of life for the urban teacher to understand. Perhaps we have not been analytical enough here in not going beyond the broad categories of active mastery of the environment, clear and positively evaluated self-conceptions, need-free perception of the world, and lack of conformity to broader cultural values. These characteristics are part of the urban pupils and considerable sophistication and behavioral skill are required of the teacher who must cope with the children on a day-to-day basis and build a continuing and workable relationship for the days, weeks, and months of the school year. The dimensions of Geoffrey's behavior we have indicated as awareness, continuity, ringmastership, sequential smoothness and so forth. They integrate neatly as one thinks about the salient characteristics of the pupils who constitute a classroom in a slum neighborhood.

Further specification of pupil personality and behavior in the slum school occurred to us and seemed important as elements in the teacher's thinking and action. We have commented upon the everpresent sensational episodes which occur constantly and which make good gossip but which are not as critical as the ability and mental health variables. The children's deficits in physical resources seemed most important. The special abilities and talents which went unnurtured also were a part of the fabric of the child's life. The defenselessness and impotency of the child from a lower social-class neighborhood has not been emphasized and analyzed to the degree to which it seems important.

Activity-structures as Functional Equivalents

Somewhere between the overt behavior of the teacher and the growth of pupils, one needs a set of intermediary variables. We have chosen to speak of activity-structures. Operationally, the dominant themes were recitational lessons centered around the textbook. While one might have conceptualized these as teacher variables, they seemed to belong more to the authors of the text materials who created the content, its scope and sequence, and the questions utilized to guide the pupils' independent study in class and as homework. In an instructional sense we would argue that a functional equivalency exists between teacher statements of facts and generalizations and text statements of facts and generalizations, between teacher questions and text questions, and between textual prompts and teacher prompts. A theory of teaching more sophisticated than ours will one day synthesize the discussion in Chapters Four and Six into an integrated sets of concepts and propositions. At the Washington School they seemed, phenotypically, a different class of events, and we have treated them as such. Dimensions such as difficulty level of materials, the interrupted quality of lessons, the appropriateness of the content, the openness and creative potential in the materials, seem to be variables necessary for further thought about teaching.

Verificational Research

As one project draws to a close, it is appropriate to speculate on the next project, the new directions for future work. While this process, the flow of research, has not been studied systematically, several positions in educational psychology (defined broadly) have impressed us with images clear enough to function as ideal types. Some years ago we discovered Redl and Wineman's (1957) beautiful study of a residential treatment center for young aggressive boys. The second half of their volume, *Controls from Within*, described a social system geared for total rehabilitation: the structure and strategy of a treatment center, programs geared for ego-support, "techniques for the antiseptic manipulation of surface behavior," and interview techniques for particular therapeutic objectives. Redl and Wineman's colleagues at Wayne State University, Kounin, Gump, Sutton-Smith, and Ryan, worked independently, concurrently, and collaboratively on similar problems and concepts. They moved toward more quantitative verificational research in the laboratory and in the field. A classic summary of several studies of antiseptic manipulation of surface behavior, influence techniques, interference and desist techniques appeared as "Explorations in classroom management," by Kounin, Gump, and Ryan (1961). Desist techniques were studied in relation to their effects on pupil perceptions and attitudes, in relation to "prevailing variables", for example, high and low motivation, and in relation to such other group structural variables as teacher reputation and pupil power. Verificational attempts were made though correlational analyses, interviews, research regarding ongoing classrooms, and field experiments in a specially constructed summer school for "studying different methods of teaching." More recently Kounin and several of his colleagues (1966) have reported an intensive study, "Managing emotionally disturbed children in regular classrooms," in which they tested many of their desist technique hypotheses using video tapes of a half-day's teaching from thirty classrooms. When many of their hypotheses were not supported, they moved inventively to such new ideas as "with-it-ness" and "overlappingness." In short, the Wayne State group had made a most creative and intensive attack on the age-old problem of classroom discipline. If their research approach and strategy are viable, they suggest several further steps.

In adapting the model to our situation, we have a number of concepts and propositions now ready for verificational analysis. In Chapter One we illustrated the axiomatic model utilizing the miniature theory of "personalized interaction." As we look back at this discussion several further remarks seem in order. First, the variables on the left-hand side of Figure 1.2 seem to fall neatly into the broader rubrics of formal organization, informal organization, and teacher personality. Incorporating them in this fashion suggests additional variables that might be linked into the analysis for fuller appreciation of the complexities of this or any other classroom. For instance, in considering changes in urban schools one immediately thinks of class size as an important organizational variable. A move toward smaller loads and toward influence attempts, through appropriately designed teacher training as sketched in our ideal school notions, could bring about a shift in personalized interaction.

At this point we would need further analysis of personalized interaction into dimensions of affective tone, supportive to nonsupportive, and into content relevant to specific subject matter and academic goals. Similarly, such a concept as "individuality of self-conceptions" would need clarity in terms of the variety of positive self-images our society supports. For instance, does a boy like Sam or a girl like Sandy, two of the most prominent of the seventh graders in our data, come away from the year's experience with more self-esteem and respect from classmates? Our hypotheses go beyond the classroom to link these peer and personal estimates with broader social variables such as decisions concerning remaining in school, mental health, and vocational choices.

Perhaps even more intriguing are the potential interrelations among concepts of personalized interaction (Fig. 1.2), continuity (Fig. 4.7), awareness (Fig. 4.4), and "getting off the hook" (Fig. 4.14). In Figure 4.4 we argue that teacher awareness should lead to increased informal teacher-pupil interaction. One form of the latter might well be personalized inter-action. In Figure 1.2 we argue that personalized interaction leads to differ-entiated classroom roles. In Figure 4.14 we argue that such roles lead to "getting off the hook" and that the latter leads to continuity, which in turn, as hypothesized in Figure 4.7, leads to meaningful verbal learning. Briefly, and illustratively, this kind of interdependence is the essence of viewing the classroom as a social system. These concepts and hypotheses are ready to be operationalized and tested more systematically in verifica-tional studies in the field and in the laboratory. As these several miniature theories are codified, they tighten the analysis of classrooms as closed sys-tems. Correlational analyses and projected experiments would put further concrete meaning into the paradigm suggested by the example of the Wayne State University group.

Classroom Microethnography

The next microethnographic classroom study we hope to pursue may be a simple extension of the present study. In our discussion of decision-making we talked of the lesson plan as a vehicle for operationalizing our model, because objectives, alternatives, barriers, and subjective probabilities could be obtained quite readily. With the cooperation of a secondary school teacher we hope to gather data on each lesson as the teaching moves from the first day to the end of the semester. Also, we hope to describe the class activity in great detail. While field notes will remain a major source of data, particularly for the interpretive asides and for informal conversa-tions with students, the primary source of the events will be audio and video recordings of the process. The nuances in the rapid verbal exchanges will be recorded as closely as possible. Finally, a careful post-lesson inter-view or questionnaire will elicit teacher comments on her departures from the plan, the stimuli that she perceived to be critical, and the flow of inter-action afterwards. Such an intensive case study is unique in its emphasis on the context or situation, the accent on teaching process (for example, the careful integration over time of the teacher's planning and thinking with the acting and interacting in the classroom), and theoretical under-pinning in decision-making. Some of the literature which seems relevant at this point and which we would hope to speak about includes the work of Aschner, Bellack, Bruner, Piaget, B. O. Smith, and Taba. To our knowl-edge a processual study such as this has not been completed before.

THE ENVIRONMENT OF THE CLASSROOM

We had another conceptual problem with *The Human Group.* Although Homans stressed the environment as an important part of his theory, for example, the external system as the group's responsiveness to this environment, we felt that our classroom data were analyzed more profitably if we interpreted the environment as mediated through the teacher's personality, especially his cognitive or decision-making processes. As we distinguished between an ideal world of education and the real world of teaching in the Washington School, we found Geoffrey's decisions, and consequently his teaching behavior, influenced, both as constraints and as opportunities, by a number of organization variables. We did not find total isolation and automony in the self-contained classroom. While a number of variables need analysis and careful accounting in this regard, two of the most important will illustrate our intent. A theory of teaching, if it is to handle our case, needs a way of incorporating the broader organizational rules, directives, and activities. For example, Geoffrey was furnished a set of textbooks in each of the curricular areas, and in some instances, for example, language arts, he was also given evaluation devices, simple tests of grammar and usage. The results of his efforts at teaching, the pupil test scores, were then recorded on cumulative record cards. Supervisors from the central office checked these from time to time, particularly the record cards of teachers who were on probation, a more tentative position in the total organization structure. As we have indicated, the supervisors were around from time to time, and they did their job. Several teachers at the Washington School heard from them. Our point is simple: the teacher's lesson plan, the operational measure of his decision-making, does not usually contain a category such as "integration into school policy." In our judgment it should. Part of the complexity of an urban classroom is that it is part of a larger totality, a school system that may contain several hundreds of schools and several thousands of classrooms. The people in control of the total enterprise, the downtown office, do have mechanisms to reach into the life of the individual teacher.

To follow, for the moment, an overly simplified formal-informal distinction within organization theory, we have noted that Geoffrey was part of a clique of teachers within the building. Presumably teachers have a number of reference groups, although this has not been explored carefully by research. At the Washington School we found the staff cliques to be of major importance as the teachers decided on a number of courses of action. Once again, lesson plans do not have categories of "integration into staff norms" as a part of their outline, and once again in our judgment the plans should. "The way things are done around here" is an important dimension of the teacher's life. We are not arguing here for conformity or for individuality. We are arguing that the choices a teacher makes will have implications for his collegial relationships as well as for pupil learning and for his own professional identity. A person who knows this presumably can control to a better degree the kinds and amounts of rewards and punishments he will receive. From our system of values this is a highly desirable professional position.

A further outcome for Geoffrey involved the trading of pupils with Norton. Because they "got along" and had good working relations with the remedial reading teacher, they were able to constitute ability groups in which the most able children went to the specialist—an enrichment course in this context—the least able pupils came to Geoffrey, and the largest group went to Norton. On the surface this may seem simple, but it involved role specialization, solution of the "equity" problem (varying numbers of pupils per teacher), and individual teacher decisions in scheduling around another fixed point in the day. Our theory of teaching processes indicates the importance of such phenomena.

The School as an Organization

During the spring following the semester in the Washington School, we had occasion to phrase formally a new study that grew from our concern for the environment outside of the classroom. The research proposal stated the purpose this way:

> The problem to be studied in this investigation has several components. We are trying to capitalize on an unusual event, the building of a new and uniquely designed elementary school.
> In a general sense, what happens in such a situation is the focus of the research. The specific problems to be analyzed will include: (1) the development of the faculty social system; (2) the principal's role vis-à-vis the faculty social system; (3) the teachers' innovations in instruction; (4) the development of the schoolwide pupil social system.
> In a prior investigation (Smith and Geoffrey, *Toward a Model of Teacher Decision-making in an Urban Classroom*, 1965)[4] we were impressed with the importance of a faculty peer group as an element in the classroom teacher's decision-making. The influence it exerted was not widely recognized in the building. This clique had been in operation for a number of years. In this study we will have an opportunity to observe the formation of an entire faculty system (eighteen of the twenty-three teachers are new to the school district), to see in what ways it is a totality, what and how cliques are formed, the influence processes, and the resulting impact, consonant or dissonant, on the teacher.

As the study grew, it became an investigation in the theory of organizations.[5] We immersed ourselves in sociology. The Merton, Selznick, Gouldner, and Blau tradition opened vistas seldom considered by educational administrators and even less considered by educational psychologists. To us, the complexities of a classroom require such a consideration.

---

[4]This was the phrasing of *The Complexities of an Urban Classroom* in 1964.
[5] The results of this investigation are in a final report to the U.S. Office of Education:
L. M. Smith and P. M. Keith, *Social Psychological Aspects of School Building Design.*

The Integration Issues

The larger community is demanding that the public schools rectify several centuries of injustice created by and exhibited in slavery, segregation, and "separate but equal," facilities. As yet these new demands are not being accompanied by new resources, financial and otherwise. The demands are made in the crosscurrents of multiple and conflicting public viewpoints. The magnitude of the problem, the limits in resources, and the conflicting pressures are wreaking havoc on even the best intentioned of public school personnel. This is an educational tragedy of the gravest proportion. Every urban classroom lives with that shadow over its shoulder, if not directly with the reality in its lap. One story of such havoc we hope to describe and interpret as an aid to further understanding. We would argue that the multitude of resolutions of this problem in individual schools need study. In our judgment, the participant-observer methodology seems especially appropriate, for we do not anticipate overwhelming and clear-cut resolutions but rather long and difficult struggles. The processes underlying these struggles need to be made known in great detail.

The complexity of these issues poses problems large enough to challenge the best of social science research, theory, and practice. One proposed study[6] of extended magnitude was initiated through the feasibility stage by a group of social scientists. The preliminary report phrased the study in this manner:

> The kind of investigation the Institute staff regards as fruitful for a full understanding of the Project is reflected in the nature of the pilot studies conducted during the spring. An extended investigation should be multi-faceted, involving the contributions of behavioral scientists, educators, and historians of diverse talents and research approaches. The investigation must focus on the school system *in process*—on what people are doing and saying, how they are thinking and feeling, what their intentions are and how they are attempting to implement them. The school system should be conceived as an ongoing social institution, set in a larger historical and social context and one in which social relations are as significant to explore as educational plans. The staff agrees that a traditional evaluation, which assesses certain inputs (operational programs) against certain closely measured outputs (such as academic achievement of students), would not be productive of significant generalizable knowledge regarding the Project, even were rigorous, dependable data concerning inputs and outputs available for the time period covered by the Project. In as complex and poorly understood a situation as the urban school district, significant knowledge can come only by investigating the social system itself, by tracing the processes by which inputs are linked to outputs.   [Charters, and others, 1965, pp. 2-3]

[6]We were unable to obtain funding for the full three year study.

The Socialization of Teachers

Teachers come and go, but organizations seem to go on forever—unchanged. While such an assertion overstates the case, it does suggest that the socialization of teachers into the organization is an additional important and much neglected part of the complexity of an urban classroom. In a new research proposal we have phrased part of the issues this way:

> The objective of this study is to gain a preliminary understanding of some of the different kinds of consequences that occur in the education of teachers as a result of different patterns in the organization of the student teaching experience.
>
> City Teachers College has an apprentice teaching program which involves elementary teacher trainees in a series of two week programs. Each student participates for two weeks in each grade level (Kindergarten through 8th) during the course of the semester. City University provides its student teachers with a sixteen week program in which each student spends the entire semester with one teacher at one grade level.[7] Both programs have been in operation for a number of years. We propose to describe carefully these ongoing institutions and develop models of their functioning.
>
> Theoretically, the study may be viewed as a problem in functional analysis. Our attempt will be to take Merton's general position and utilize it in the study of this important educational problem. (Connor and Smith, 1967)

Classrooms have a variety of contexts. The educational psychologist needs to look at the environments—both present and past—that bear upon the teachers and pupils who currently are the focus of his analysis. Teacher careers, the apprenticeships from which they come and the promotions to which they aspire, have an influence on what the teacher thinks and does today in the classroom. The faculty social systems and the community problems seem critical also.

THE RENOVATION OF THE URBAN SCHOOL

While our major purpose lay in describing and conceptualizing the real world of teaching in a lower socioeconomic neighborhood, we also kept one eye open for developing a conception of an "ideal" situation. Concretely, we talked of setting up an experimental school in a slum community with Mr. Geoffrey as the principal, directly responsible to the school administration, and Mr. Smith as research director, directly responsible for the accumulation of data relevant to innovations and experimental pro-

---

[7]Other patterns exist; for instance, the Chicago Teachers College has two eight-week experiences for each teacher.

grams. Jointly they would select staff. The staff, in conjunction with the principal and research director, would settle on specific ideas and alterations of program. The plans would entail perhaps a five-year commitment. At this point in our present analysis we would like to mention several insights that we had along the way in our data collection and analysis, and several concrete and specific ideas generated by considering each individual pupil to imagine what might be done to facilitate his development. While these ideas will be most relevant to these specific children, they indicate aspects we would argue for with our teachers in our experimental school.[8]

Professional education has a long history and a not-so-proud reputation in lay and academic circles as being uninteresting and possibly insignificant. Among teachers and professional educators the same beliefs and sentiments often exist. One aspect of our ideal school would center upon generating an excitement in the analysis of teaching.[9] The summary notes in November indicate one instance of this in our experience.

> This morning was very productive for Geoffrey's class. The pace in reading, in arithmetic, and in language arts was quite intense. For just a moment we began to talk about the differences between teaching arithmetic and language arts. The problem arose out of a very brief discussion of the difficulty that the kids were having with regular and irregular verbs. They had missed the concept initially and Geoffrey was surprised, for their slowness was in contrast to the way they had handled the arithmetic. In my notes I have comments about the breadth of development that Geoffrey gave to the arithmetic that he did not give to the language arts. He expressed some surprise at the differences in his behavior. (1) This suggests a whole host of other problems in the ability to perceive what one is doing while actually in the process of doing it. Geoffrey then began in a very exciting way to lay out some of the differences he saw between language arts teaching and the teaching of arithmetic. The crux seems to lie in the interdependency of all the elements in the language arts program in contrast to the more independence of the elements in arithmetic. For example, in Geoffrey's words, "it is difficult to get a good example in language" for you are always coming up with an infinitive or a gerund or some such thing. In arithmetic, in contrast, you can deal with addition as addition while not having to do anything with multiplication or division, and so on. Also, the language systems are very different for the children in contrast to the adults. For instance, at this point you can't talk about past participles even though this is what you are dealing with. In arithmetic adding is adding to a child or to an adult.

[8] At a later time we must return to the analysis of this kind of general framework, which contains several important social psychological principles: experience, participation in decisions, role *expertise,* clinical research, administrative freedom, and staff rapport.

[9] Our general indebtedness for this position lies in our long association with Dean Robert J. Schaefer of Teachers College, Columbia University. Our illustration is one concrete instance of his more general argument, which is now elaborated in book form, *The School as a Center for Inquiry* (1967).

Beyond beginning to lay out some of these similarities and differences, Geoffrey made a comment or two indicating that "until this year I never thought about most of these things." He really seemed to have caught the bug of the analysis of the instructional process. With his experience and observations as the teacher in the ongoing situation and with my somewhat naïve but more objective outside view, we have the possibility of making a very exciting statement in this area. There is an interesting contrast between his reactions now and what they were when we were talking earlier about concrete experiences and the dates in the geography lessons. Then he could not see any point in the issues I was trying to raise. Now he is obviously intrigued and excited about speculating on the whole conceptual structure of teaching and learning in the various subject matter areas. An interesting sidelight occurred as Geoffrey and I were talking during lunch. Mr. Inman happened upon us at the time that Geoffrey was "lecturing" about the differences in language arts teaching and arithmetic teaching. We extended the analysis a step or two further and then quit. The very naturalness of our conversation and the fact that we were dealing with educational incidents should further specify in concrete detail what we are doing at the school. I personally feel very good about this.   (11/9)

Whether large numbers of teachers can be intrigued in such a manner as this is, of course, an hypothesis. In our judgment, the elements in the design of an experimental school (see footnote 8 in this chapter) are exceedingly important. For instance, teacher participation in decisions, rather than university or administrative domination, is a rare phenomenon in our perception of the educational scene. Similarly, the degree of *expertise*—in teaching or research skills—brought by the outside agency leaves much to be desired.

An additional illustration of the excitement, the kind of problems one would raise, and the interesting byways one might traverse we labeled "meaningfulness: Pandora's box in social studies." The reader will recall that earlier in our discussion of dimensions of activities, the things done by a group, we raised the issue of meaningfulness, the degree to which one's day-to-day experience is integral to what the group does. Mr. Geoffrey's lament, "History and geography, however, seem to have no relevance at all," suggests a point of departure. The gamble we would take, cautiously, in the "ideal education" would involve factors such as these:

1. If "Backgrounds of American Freedom" is a social studies topic, then explore with each child in the group his national origins in Europe, Africa, or Asia.

2. If religious freedom was a source of emigration, then explore its manifestations in the current group. Some of the class members, such as Esther, who had commented at length on Christian aspects of Thanksgiving, and Sydney, who did not dance at the Halloween Party because of religious reasons, hold strong and diverse beliefs. The scope and grandeur of this kind of variation, the enhancement that it can make for one's identity, and the problems that have occurred historically seem most significant.

3. If the slavery issue was significant in the colonies and in the post-Colonial period, as well as in the Civil War and Reconstruction Period, then the residual issues and problems in the South, in Big City, and in the Washington School where Negroes and Appalachian whites are in residence seem most meaningful.

In January after listening to a half-hour of the children's free chatter, some of which concerned racial problems, the observer speculated in this fashion:

> Perhaps the most interesting commentary I can make on this is first, Mr. Geoffrey exhibits in class absolutely no racial prejudice as far as I can tell. He would just as soon chew out Joe G. or Joe K. or one of the others without any regard for the fact that one is Negro and one is not. Similarly, he will tease Susan and Elma about as readily and with about as much effectiveness and sympathy as he will any other child in class. The second comment I would make is that there has been, as far as I can tell, a *lack* of discussion of any of the issues surrounding the racial situation either locally or in terms of the school building itself. The difficulties they had in the building are secondary to those in the broader metropolitan community. The problems associated with this area are certainly possible in the discussion of history or current events, particularly surrounding Africa and the connected problems. One of the major issues that I would be concerned about trying experimentally in a group like this would be a very strong Taba-type program in intergroup relations.[10] Can you tackle the problem directly, with objectivity, and with the intent of building some conception of democratic ideals, showing how the conception ripples over into the day-to-day lives of individuals and how it produces some kinds of conflict with other groups that one is associated with? Without question, you are apt to get into difficulties with the families and the communities and so on. Is this the point where you want to do this kind of battle and where you want to spend some of your credits? This would be one of the unsolved problems that we might try on another occasion.   (1/14)

The several kinds of existing interdependencies suggest the following problems: First, additional dimensions of the teacher-pupil interaction are brought out. For instance, at one point Elma accused Mr. Geoffrey of prejudice and unfairness because she was black and he was white. His immediate reaction was anger because of an unjust accusation. Secondly, he attempted to suppress further incidents by making her repeat the accusation in front of the principal and then apologize when no evidence could be brought to support her position. The exploration of those problems about which they did in fact conflict and her use of the racial issue as a rationalization, the conflict among other children and the teachers, and the development of a viable general building policy (district policy?) all would become salient and significant. Second, in the observer's view the whole administration is "touchy" over the racial issue, or, as some would

[10]The reference here is to Hilda Taba's several publications (1948, 1952).

say, is "running scared." The teacher who opens issues such as these might be confronted with official reprimand or stony silence if he needed outside resources. Third, the norms of the staff are essentially "hear no evil, see no evil, and speak no evil" regarding religious and racial matters. Fourth, the general total authority pattern, both in interaction and as upheld in norms, does not permit children's questions. To allow such questioning, and in sensitive areas, would throw open the possibility of questioning all aspects of authority which, while potentially a very desirable end, would provoke immediate shortrun anxiety for the teachers and result in lack of clarity around central modes of interaction. Fifth, the parents, who normally stay at arm's length from the school and are kept powerless, as poor rural Southern whites, have extremely strong feelings regarding integration and the school's role in this social problem. In short, making social studies meaningful—beyond the perhaps trite aspect of going to the museum—may entangle the teacher and the school in a very exciting experience, but one not to be entered into lightly.

CONCLUSION: THEORY, RESEARCH, AND PRACTICE

Early in our account, on page 1, we stated our purposes, the description and the conceptualization of a single classroom. We hope that in these pages the silent language of a middle-class teacher coping with a group of lower-class youngsters has become manifest and audible. The special problems of beginning school, the building of a viable social structure through establishing control and getting the instructional program underway, have been described and analyzed. The more general issues in instructional processes and teacher behavior were spelled out in the continuous coping in

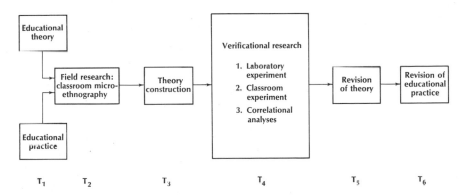

Figure 8.1 A process model integrating educational research styles, educational practice, and educational theory.

which the teacher is engaged. The subtitle of this book is "An analysis toward a general theory of teaching." Ultimately a theory of teaching is our goal. The methodology, which has excited and charmed us, seems open to considerable debate, and we have tried to entertain the first rounds of that discussion. If the methodology is placed in the context of a broader scheme of theory, research, and practice, as we have tried to do generally throughout the discussion and specifically in the appendix, it seems to offer important potential. Figure 8.2 presents a sketch of these relationships.

The accent we make is upon the primacy of theory as the strand or theme that must integrate the usual dichotomies of research and practice, classroom versus laboratory research, and clinical or case-study research and verificational research. As the theorizing improves, the gaps will narrow, the dichotomies will dissolve, and issues of individual classrooms will yield to more abstract and powerful conceptualizations. At that time we will have a theory of teaching worthy of its name and worthy of the complexities of an urban classroom.

A P P E N D I X

FURTHER REFLECTIONS
ON THE METHODOLOGY

The research methodology utilized in this investigation was new to us and is relatively rare in educational psychology. In other disciplines it is more common and goes by such labels as ethnography, field work, and participant-observation. As is obvious, we became enamoured of the technique and the possibilities it provided for exploring significant issues in the psychology of teaching. A self-consciousness about our procedures has led us toward these further reflections on the methodology of "classroom microethnography."

When we began this methodological discussion we had envisioned a larger and more final essay. Specifically we had wanted to present, and we have, an account of the "microethnography of classroom research," plus an integration of several other lines of work. First, we wanted to assess, vis-à-vis our approach, the strengths and weaknesses of the more popular "quantitative observation" which has received considerable recent emphasis in educational research. Second, we wished to synthesize the literature on concept formation and attainment, which seems intuitively to have much to say to the observer who builds and verifies models and theorics. The rapid expansion of this literature and our waning energies prevented carrying out this option. Third, the "commonalities in the related disciplines" of natural history, clinical method in psychology, and historical method strike us as very significant. The scholars working in such areas often see themselves apart from the endeavors of the scientists in the laboratory. This separation seems to us reconcilable in both possibility and desirability. Fourth, our pleasure in the novel as a form of literature and the insights of acute observers of the passing scene suggests that the social scientist must attend to the methodologies of this dimension of observation and reporting.[1] An illustration from O'Hara has remained with us:

> If you are an author, and not just a writer, you keep learning all the time. Today for instance, I was thinking about dialogue, listening to dialogue of some characters in my mind's ear, and I learned for the first time in my life that almost no woman who has gone beyond the eighth grade ever calls a fifty cent piece a half-a-dollar. A male author, writing dialogue carelessly, might easily have a female character say 'half-a-dollar' because it sounded right to him. But it would be wrong, it would harm his characterization, and he would never know why.   [O'Hara, 1961, p. *ix*]

Finally, we had wanted to read, summarize, and integrate the large literature on the nature of legal evidence which seems so close to the kind of reasoning engaged in by the participant observer. This, then, was the methodology discussion to which we aspired; hopefully a more industrious scholar will tread that path.[2]

MODEL-BUILDING

The behavior of the participant- and nonparticipant-observers has been described sufficiently in Chapter One to give the reader a clear indication of the conduct of the research. Our intent here is to raise an additional general issue or two relevant to "microethnography as science." As we have commented, we came to the method from skeptical positions. One, trained in a "dustbowl empiricism" at Minnesota where anthropology and nonquantitative notes harken back to a prescientific era and the other, experienced over several years in difficult and trying situations were "scientific" results seldom seem to have applicability, have considerable doubts as to whether our investigation qualifies as legitimate or as scientific. One phase of this doubt concerns the investigator's bias; that is, "Does he see what he wants to see?" The questions can be handled best, we think, by an extended discussion of the problems of description and "model-building." To enter this discussion, we present several more classical positions which we hope ultimately to synthesize.

In his study of Melanesia, Malinowski, who argues for scientific anthropology, makes a major distinction between "perconceived ideas" and "foreshadowed problems." These have been presented in Chapter One.

Becker, in his classical analysis of inference and proof in participant observation comments:

[1] Truman Capote's use of the term "a nonfiction novel" for his book, *In Cold Blood*, suggests a new midpoint on the dimension.

[2] We have included in the bibliography some of the relevant references upon which we had begun.

The final stage of analysis in the field consists of incorporating individual findings into a generalized model of the social system or organization under study or some part of that organization. The concept of social system is a basic intellectual tool of modern sociology. The kind of participant observation discussed here is related directly to this concept, explaining particular social facts by explicit reference to their involvement in a complex of interconnected variables that the observer constructs as a theoretical model of the organization. In this final stage, the observer designs a descriptive model which best explains the data he has assembled.   [Becker, 1958]

Our own experience has been this. In talking about the problems of teaching a group of slum children, there was little literature which we knew that made much sense for helping a teacher carry out his day-to-day activities. These discussions led to a preliminary statement in a research proposal under the general heading of teacher strategies.[3] We report that statement verbatim from the initial proposal.

The Preliminary Model: Teacher Strategies

As it is used here, the term "teacher strategies" is broadly conceived and includes the construing, hypothesizing, decision-making of the teacher. It includes also the action she takes upon such thinking, the perception of the consequences of this action, and the reconstruing, hypothesizing, and decision-making she then undertakes. The concept "classroom social system" refers to the educational setting, the pupils, and the interdependency of the aspects of the classroom, that is, the activities, interaction, sentiment, and norms. The uniqueness of the combination of the elements is a function of environment and the personality systems of the teacher and children. Over a period of time, new elaborations appear and become standardized.

In recent years the concept of group norms has become central in the theories of many social psychologists and sociologists (Sherif, and others, 1956, 1961; Schachter, 1951; Homans, 1950; Thibaut and Kelley, 1959). In his extensive analysis of the structure of group norms, Jackson (1960, 1962) has presented a return potential model that incorporates a number of phenomena related to norms. One aspect of this is norm correspondence or noncorrespondence. Essentially this is the degree of similarity in the values or schemata of an individual group member and the more general norm of the group. Jackson's analysis has had obvious consequences in general social psychology. It seems to offer a point of departure for a number of important educational and classroom issues relating the teacher's behavior with the classroom group.

To this investigator's knowledge there has been no significant breakthrough in conceptualizing a middle-class teacher's coping with a class of children from a lower social class. Recently, strategies for dealing with lower-class children have been suggested in a number of sources. They are impressive in their vividness, their variety, and, to the present, their lack of synthesis. Becker (1951, 1952) suggests that the teacher must be showy, dramatic, and acceptant of minimal effort. Watson (1962)

[3] For which we were unable to obtain funds.

suggests "The starting point is respect. Nothing else that we have to give will help very much if it is offered with a resentful, contemptuous, or patronizing attitude (p. *xi*)."

It is precisely at this point that the understanding of the context surrounding this problem area would be assessed carefully through interviews; the teacher's behavior would be observed carefully; and the responses of the individual pupils and the class group would be observed carefully and tested objectively. This is the theoretical and practical clarification of the social system concepts dealing with the interdependency of the teacher and the group. A more intimate and vivid concrete view of this sort should, in the broad programmatic context of the whole proposal, then permit abstraction to a wider and more general point of view.

It is our hunch that this problem may yield conceptually because it seems to be an instance of the more general case of noncorresponding normative structure. If we can extend Jackson's theorizing, if we can collate the findings of such relevant literature as Merei's (1949) work with child leaders and "institutionalization," Lippitt's (1958) modification of Lewin in the *Dynamics of Planned Change* and Coch and French's (1953) field experimentation in "Overcoming resistance to change," then case study observations of a teacher working with such a problem should be a fruitful addition to educational literature.

Development of the Model

At this point we began systematic observation. As we have indicated, the strategy model came to be seen as a portion of the larger decision-making conception. Once this conception was suggested, we began to pursue ideas from Simon, Bross, Brim and so forth.

Briefly, we might indicate that seminar discussions, faculty reactions, and general discussions in classes raised points which had not been seen before. The senior author recalls vividly giving a talk to a group of student teachers and the development of the "best of a bad situation" conception in trying to handle a question regarding some of the ideas from the project.

It is not parenthetical to include two additional pieces of evidence about the development of the model in field work, or as an English teacher might say, finding a thesis or theme for one's paper. William F. Whyte comments in the foreward of his book (1955):

"John Howard spent two years of field work in Cornerville. In this book, I have found it wise to concentrate upon my own material, which I know best, but discussions of our separate observations were exceedingly valuable in clarifying my ideas. *Mr. Howard was the first to suggest that an analysis of leadership would provide means of integrating the study.*" (our italics) [Whyte, 1955 rev. ed., p. *vii*]

If we read that last sentence correctly, the unifying theme, the major ordering construct of the monograph, developed quite fortuitously out of a casual conversation or an intense discussion. For our purposes, it illustrates well the interplay between data, active concept formation behavior on the part of the investigator, prior theory, outside stimulation and "chance" combinations of these factors:

Later Whyte comments:

> "The ideas that we have in research are only in part a logical product growing out of a careful weighing of evidence. We do not generally think problems through in a straight line. Often we have the experience of being immersed in a mass of confusing data. We study the data carefully, bringing all of our powers of logical analysis to bear upon them. We come up with an idea or two. But still the data do not fall in any coherent pattern. Then we go on living with the data—and the people—until perhaps some chance occurrence casts a totally different light upon the data, and we begin to see a pattern that we have not seen before. This pattern is not purely an artistic creation. Once we think we see it, we must reexamine our notes and perhaps set out to gather new data in order to determine whether the pattern adequately represents the life we are observing or is simply a product of our imagination. [Whyte, 1955 rev. ed., pp. 279–280]

RAW DATA: THE TWO-REALITIES PROBLEM

Methodologically, one of the most critical problems with which we have struggled we named "the two-realities problem." When the observer goes into the field, he perceives a reality—the flux. Such a process continues day by day. Eventually, as we have begun to indicate, the observer leaves the field and has his notes typed into multiple copies so that analysis might proceed easily. These notes become now a second reality. For most field workers they are the basis for analysis.

Several implications occur. The more recent attempts (Becker, and others, 1961) to quantify participant observer data rest on twin assumptions: first, that everything in the notes, the second reality, represents events in the first reality, the real flux; and second, that the proportion of events to one another in the notes is a total sample or contains proportionality with the events in the real world. We would contend that these are separate assumptions and important for the kind of analysis possible. For illustrative purposes, we would select a simple example, interruptions from outside the room. In regard to the two assumptions, we would argue that every interruption, whether a pupil or teacher who entered the room and obtained Mr. Geoffrey's attention at least momentarily, that is stated in the notes, actually occurred. However, to argue that we have information on the proportion of staff-to-student interruptions is another issue. Similarly, to argue that interruptions occur more or less frequently in mornings or afternoons raises the second assumption.

To content analyze the notes and quantify such percentages seems open to serious question. To continue the illustration, on several days we specifically attended to the problem of interruptions and made formal counts of how many occurred. On other days we were more interested in other problems and only incidentally noted who was coming in and out of the room. To go back to the notes now and to test hypotheses of the order—interruptions occur more frequently on Monday and Friday—seems inappropriate. However, to have a tentative belief, an hypothesis that this is so and to use the belief in reasoning through problems of teacher strategy in organizing lessons for Mondays and Fridays seems most feasible.[4]

In this sense we are arguing our basic thesis, the methodology is much more appropriate for model-building rather then verificational research. We would urge one final related caution. Living in another institution for so many hours per day for such a long period of time, and with the single clear purpose of understanding the institution, leaves one with a vivid view of a reality. Later, as persons raise hypotheses, of many orders, one feels compelled to validate, supplement or criticize on the basis of this experience. This seems to be moving implicitly toward the second assumption. For instance, at the time of this writing, we have been stimulated by Professor Lortie of the University of Chicago.[5] His conception of the autonomy-equality pattern and the authority pattern of the school is a fascinating analysis, but it only partially fits the Washington School as we saw the school. As we criticized the conception, primarily for underestimating the informal teacher-teacher and teacher-principal interactions and reciprocities, we are presenting what latently are quantifiable relationships. While informally the arguments are posed in terms such as "you haven't quite caught the tenor of the system" or "more frequently it goes like this," a more careful analysis requires further documentation. Because the participant-observer was not specifically testing this pattern of hypotheses, he cannot present quantified results on this point. The notes will not contain the data that meet the second assumption. Also the conception by its very originality may cue images and verbal memories of events that did *not* get into the notes but that are within the memory of the investigator. This suggests, really, a third reality—the unwritten recollections of the investigator—which may or may not be adequately represented in the notes. We raise this because of the important value such critiques might possess and because of the frequency with which it seems to occur without awareness among participant-observers.[6]

ADEQUACY OF THE MODEL

We have used the term "model" as a schematic complex of interconnected variables explaining a phenomenon. When one asks the question, "Is the model adequate?," one raises the classical issues of explanation in science. Briefly our reasoning proceeds in this way:

1. Explanation is the deduction of hypotheses from other propositions.
2. Deduction is a logical process governed by rules.
3. An hypothesis is an unverified proposition.
4. A proposition[7] is the relationship between two concepts.
5. A concept is a unitary-abstraction used to order experience.
6. Verification is the process of obtaining concrete observations on the relationship between concepts.

[4] Most assuredly other hypotheses concerning absences, rhythms of work, pupil norms, and so on, need to be entered into concerning Friday lesson planning.

[5] Personal communication and also through his chapter in Shaplin and Olds *Team Teaching* (1964).

[6] If this really be true then this kind of experience for practitioners in the use of theory is very significant in their training.

[7] Principles and generalizations are synonyms for proposition.

Zetterberg's Analysis

The organization of these definitions is illustrated best, in our experience, by Zetterberg (1965) in his discussion of "the confirmation of a proposition." He relates two concepts, conformity and promotion, into an hypothesis: the more a member conforms to the norms of a formal organization, the greater the likelihood that he will be promoted." While he does not formally deduce this from more general propositions, one might do so from concepts such as those presented by Homans in his discussion of *Social Behavior: Its Elementary Forms*. Zetterberg then reports indicators, concrete observations or operational definitions of his concepts; these are items from an attitude scale and records of promotion in an organization —in this instance, the Army. He argues for the validity[8] of the indicators, their relationship to the concepts, and their reliability. Finally, a test of the proposition is made through determining its likelihood of arising by chance. Zetterberg raises questions of items such as controls, representativeness of the sample, and control of alternative propositions.

The classical solution of the control of alternative hypotheses in scientific research is through the experimental method and its corollary, randomization. In descriptive or correlative research, one cannot carry out such procedures. Consequently, the major alternative hypotheses in Zetterberg's illustrations of such ideas as seniority relating to promotion or education relating to promotion are investigated and tested. Unfortunately, alternatives are limited only by ingenuity of the critic—physical attractiveness, physical size, ascendancy, and so on, might also be suggested.

These issues become exceedingly crucial for the microethnographer in that he is trying not to test a single proposition but to construct a network of interdependent propositions. At the operational or concrete level, his observations suggest interrelations but are susceptible to alternative interpretations. At the conceptual level his explanation is vulnerable to others' explanations. To handle these problems we have resorted to two lines of thinking. First, we argue that this methodology is most appropriate for model-building, and experimental methodology is most appropriate for hypothesis-testing. Second, we have sought to handle the alternative hypothesis through what Polya (1954) calls "plausible reasoning."

Polya's Analysis

Part of our effort methodologically centered on integrating our approach with the more usual traditions in education and psychology. Specifically we were intrigued with the possibilities of axiomatic and deductive theories as a means for defining "proof" of hypotheses. Also we were concerned with the power of the experimental method in controlling alternative hypotheses through randomization and in permitting one to make explicit probability statements about obtained differences in results. Our efforts have been aided materially by the analysis suggested by the mathematician George Polya in his book, *Patterns of Plausible Reasoning*.

[8]Validity is a complex operation itself involving both logical and empirical aspects, for example, the recent psychological attempts to formulate construct and content validity as well as predictive and concurrent validity. In a sense one never can escape into a neat category of "this is theoretical" or "this is empirical." One shifts levels of abstraction and employs "evidence" of various sorts.

Essentially he raises distinctions between "proof" and "plausible reasoning" and illustrates his ideas by reference to a wide variety of mathematical and common-sense illustrations. Proof he defines as the deduction of a proposition from more general theory. Many mathematical propositions have been discovered and accepted as plausible long before they have been proved. As an illustration he presents an hypothesis or conjecture discovered by Euler, "Any integer of the form 8n + 3 is the sum of a square and of the double of a prime." When n = 1, the integer is 11 which equals 1 + 2 × 5. When n = 2, the integer is 19 which equals 9 + 2 × 5. When n = 3, the integer is 27 which equals 1 + 2 × 13. Polya comments that empirical verification has occurred in numbers through 1000 but the theoretical proof does not yet exist. He argues that each succeeding demonstration does make the proposition more credible. The generalization he makes concerning this pattern of plausible reasoning he calls *verification of a consequence* and he argues such verification renders conjectures (hypotheses) more credible.

He extends this idea of verification of a consequence to *successive verification of several consequences*. The illustration he uses here concerns the theorem for the area of the lateral surface of the frustum of a cone, $\pi(R + r)\sqrt{(R - r)^2 + h^2}$, where R is the radius of the base, r is the radius of the top, and h is the altitude. He then proceeds to several consequences: if R = r, the frustum of the cone becomes a cylinder and the equation reduces to $2\pi rh$ which is the area of the lateral surface of a cylinder. Similarly, he sets h equal to zero and obtains the area of annulus between two concentric circles. A final consequence, r = h = 0, provides the formula for the area of a circle. As several such consequences are verified, the original proposition takes on greater credibility.

Polya presents both a mathematical and a common-sense illustration of a third case: the *verification of an improbable consequence*. His illustration[9] clarifies the point:

> A defendant is accused of having blown up the yacht of his girlfriend's father, and the prosecution produces a receipt signed by the defendant acknowledging the purchase of such and such amount of dynamite. Such evidence strengthens the prosecution's case immensely. Why? Because the purchase of dynamite by an ordinary citizen is a very unusual event in itself, but such a purchase is completely understandable if the purchaser intends to blow up something or somebody.   [p. 8]

We cite one further pattern, *"our confidence in a conjecture can only increase when an incompatible rival conjecture is exploded."* (p. 20) If proposition *A* is incompatible with *B* and *B* is false, than *A* becomes more credible.

> We consider a situation which is not too usual in mathematical research but frequently occurs in the natural sciences. We examine two conflicting, incompatible conjectures *A* and *B*. When we say that *A* conflicts with *B* or *A* is incompatible with *B* we mean that the truth of one of the two propositions *A* and *B* necessarily implies the falsity of the other. Thus, *A* may be true or not and *B* may be true or not; we do not know which is the case except that we know that both cannot be true. They could both be false, however. A naturalist proposed the conjecture *A* to explain some phenomenon, another naturalist proposed the conjecture *B* to explain the same

[9] This kind of illustration is leading us into a consideration of legal proof as well. The analogy seems quite relevant.

phenomenon differently. The explanations are incompatible; both naturalists cannot be right, but both could be wrong.

If one of the conjectures, say B, has been proved to be right, then the fate of the other is also definitely decided: A must be wrong. If, however, B has been disproved, the fate of A is not yet definitely settled: also A could be wrong. Yet, undeniably, by the disproof of a rival conjecture incompatible with it, A can only gain.   [p. 20]

Briefly, as we state such a proposition as the clerk in the elementary school is an important part of the informal organization of the school, we can illustrate the tenor of Polya's analysis. In the very first occasion of the observer's being in the school, he had the impression that his conversation with the principal was monitored casually by the clerk. On a much later occasion she expressed a frank and diverging opinion in a discussion with the principal. She regularly ate lunch with a group of the teachers, one of whom was acting principal when the principal was out of the building. She was invited to informal staff parties and social functions. Information from outside the system, for instance, which families had moved, was conveyed by her to other members of the staff in the casual and informal chatting and "passing the time of day." In short, our confidence increases with the developing web of consequences, individual, successive, and improbable that surrounds the clerk and her interrelationships.

"When Prophecy Fails": An Exception

Perhaps the classical exception to our general point that participant-observer methodology is utilizable more for model-building than for verificational research occurred in *When Prophecy Fails,* a study by Festinger and his colleagues. (Festinger, and others, 1956) The research team were full participants[10] and were unknown as researchers to the members of the group under study. The observers

> . . . were informed that we needed to know about each individual in the movement, the degree to which he was sincerely convinced of the truth of the various components of the belief system; the kind of actions he had taken (or failed to take) in committing himself to participation in the movement; and, finally, the extent to which he had engaged in proselyting or propagandizing for the belief system.   [Festinger, and others, 1956, p. 244]

While they could not write notes as they participated, trips to the restroom, pleas that one "needed to think alone," and accessible tape recorders facilitated careful recording.

The critical element, however, in a verificational study concerns carefully drawn hypotheses available before entering the field situation. The researchers had developed their theoretical position from many social data and had given it limited test in historical analyses of "unfulfilled prophecies and disappointed messiahs." Their position led them to state five interrelated propositions:

1. A belief must be held with deep conviction and it must have some

---

[10] This adds another shade to the multiple meanings of "participant observer." See their discussion, pp. 234–249.

relevance to action, that is, to what the believer does or how he behaves.

2. The person holding the belief must have committed himself to it; that is, for the sake of his belief, he must have taken some important action that is difficult to undo.

In general, the more important such actions are, and the more difficult they are to undo, the greater is the individual's commitment to the belief.

3. The belief must be sufficiently specific and sufficiently concerned with the real world so that events may unequivocally refute the belief.

4. Such undeniable disconfirmatory evidence must occur and must be recognized by the individual holding the belief . . .

5. The individual believer must have social support. It is unlikely that one isolated believer could withstand the kind of disconfirming evidence we have specified. If, however, the believer in a member of a group of convinced persons who can support one another, we would expect the belief to be maintained and the believers to attempt to proselyte or to persuade non-members that the belief is correct. [Festinger, and others, 1956, p. 4]

In effect, the observers had specific instructions relevant to concepts and propositions central in the theory. They, in contrast to most participant-observers, were not to wander intellectually nor to free associate on mental health implications of messianic movements, the role of public news media in formations of cults, adolescent hostility to holders of deviant belief systems, and so forth. Such questions, and many others that a reader might find of interest, were not posed and built into a more general conceptual structure.

CONCLUSION

As we look back at our procedures, the methodology seems an appropriate way to begin attacking important and significant problems in the psychology of teaching and in broader issues of public education. In considering participant-observation we have placed our emphasis on concept formation and model-building in contrast to verificational research. The interplay between first ideas, the raw data, outside stimulation from colleagues and from reading, and the developing interpretations seems very significant though largely unanalyzed. We have alluded to several sources as investigators found the thesis in their data. Underlying the interpretations is the quality of the raw data. The degree to which the field notes represent the "flux" which has passed by is very important when the observer moves out of the situation and seeks to reconstruct events in the lay language and then seeks to build more abstract interpretations and formulations. Issues of quantification shade into this. The impressions one receives from knowing a case so well often loom up as a test for criticizing new theoretical developments presented by other investigators; for example, is his new idea congruent with the way life was at the Washington School? On occasion, such considerations evoke further images that were not in the field notes and one has the problem of a third reality. Careful exploration of such phenomena seems mandatory. We have appealed to a synthesis from Zetterberg's conception of verificational research and Polya's plausible reasoning as a means for judging the adequacy of the interpretive models we develop.

In summary, the argument we are making is that our observations make us privy to an immense number of sequences of events. As we try to shape these into empirical and conceptual order, hypotheses arise. In checking back to the written record we keep looking for exceptions to our generalizations that would make the model less credible. As we find consequences congruent with the model, we move toward greater credibleness. In all of this it is not possible to attach clear .05 or .01 probability statements. Nonetheless, the strategy seems significant and important.

GLOSSARY

THE BEGINNINGS OF A GENERAL THEORY OF TEACHING

As we have reiterated continually, our interests lie in description, model and theory building, and interpretation. As description moves beyond the rough categories and concepts of the layman, the issue of a language system appropriate to the classroom arises. We have started essentially with the concepts of George Homans and quickly moved well beyond.[1] Our early hopes of developing an axiomatic theory of classroom processes have given way to the wisdom that we do not have the time, the resources, and probably the talent for such an accomplishment. Instead we present a glossary, a partial dictionary. Even though it is much less than our original aspirations, we are pleased with it in several ways: First, it is comprehensive in its scope—our classroom. Second, it possesses an internal con-

---

[1]Parenthetically we might add that Professor Homans, also, even in his early book *The Human Group* seemed to be thinking well beyond his formal theory. For instance, his excellent Chapter 16, "The job of the leader," clinically outstrips his theory.

sistency in that it has a few undefined terms and builds all the others upon the original. This, we think, will greatly reduce the "slippage" in classroom argument and discussion wherein a party introduces concepts new to the discussion, as he explains predictions that go awry or situations outside his usual generalizations. Third, the concepts seem to be of real importance for the teacher who wishes to control, alter, or guide his classroom. Finally, for the educational researcher, the concepts seem readily transformable into operations pertinent to laboratory experiments and operations relevant to observational schedules or questionnaires useful in verificational research in field settings.

CONCEPTS IN THE PSYCHOLOGY OF TEACHING

ability: 1) a dimension of personality; 2) personal resources available for carrying out activities.

academic achievement: 1) pupil learning; 2) degree to which classroom goals have been reached.

activity: 1) an undefined term; 2) events engaged in by a group; 3) comparable to "behavior" in reference to the individual or response as a unit of behavior; 4) task.

aggression: a kind of interaction in which one person hurts another.

alternative: 1) an element of a decision; 2) may be an activity, interaction, or response.

appropriateness: a dimension of activities indicating their ability to stimulate and reinforce pupil ideas and behavior.

assumption: a proposition held to be true for purposes of argument.

attending: 1) a kind of activity in which the children are engaged with the academic materials; 2) a kind of interaction in which the children listen and follow the content of the teacher's verbal statements.

autonomy: behavior indicating that its causes or determinants lie within the individual rather than in the physical or social structure or environment.

awareness: 1) dimension of teacher behavior in which teacher knows information important in the group members' lives and indicates his knowledge to the group; 2) may be applied to pupils as well.

banter: a kind of interaction involving humor and at least a three response sequence (t-p-t or p-t-p).

barrier (specific to learning): an unknown activity lying between the individual and his goal which prevents attainment of the goal.

behavior: 1) an undefined term; 2) things an individual does.

belief: 1) an undefined term; 2) a group variable referring to a common perception among members.

best-of-a-bad-situation: an alternative which is better than any of the available alternatives but which is quite discrepant from an absolute standard.

boredom: a negative sentiment arising because of slow pace and lack of variety in activity or interaction.

breaking the spiral: an individual response which alters the vicious circle interaction.

choice: selection of an alternative in a decision.

clarity: degree to which an element of individual personality or group is perceived correctly.

clique: subgroup.

clown: 1) a role in which a pupil provokes humor, usually at his own expense; 2) contrasts with court jester who provides humor at the teacher's expense; 3) in Geoffrey's class the incumbent was Oliver.

cognition: an element of schema.

compliance: behavior or activity in accord with the intent of a directive.

concept: an abstraction noting a commonality among discrete objects.

confidence: 1) a schema variable characterized by ability perceived to be adequate for the task or activity; 2) lack of anxiety.

conflict: an interaction in which two individuals have incompatible goals and which usually produces negative sentiment.

conformity: 1) activities in accord with norms; 2) one conforms when one acts in ways prescribed by group norms.

consideration: 1) a dimension of teacher-pupil interaction involving concern for individual needs; 2) dimension of leader behavior.

constraint: 1) a variable (or element) which inhibits activity; 2) may be temporary or permanent; 3) may be in any part of the system—personal, social or cultural; 4) often used to justify (rationalize) action or inaction and in this sense is reducible to lack of ability, high reward and costs, and other "undeniable" expectations.

contingency preparation: dimension of teacher behavior that averts situations that have a high probability of negative consequences.

continuity: a dimension of activity and interaction referring to connections with past and future.

control: a type of interaction in which teacher directives elicit pupil compliance.

cooperation: a kind of interaction in which each individual's goal attainment is facilitated by the other.

coping: a sequence of responses in which an individual tries to shape another individual or a group.

court jester: 1) a classroom role in which a pupil engages in humorous, taunting teasing of the teacher; 2) often but not necessarily the class clown; 3) in Geoffrey's class the incumbent was Sam.

cultural deprivation: 1) environmental experiences producing deficits in mental ability and mental health; 2) correlated with social class.

decision: 1) the cognitive process in which an individual (or group) takes one alternative among two or more; 2) usually connotes active and serious intellectual effort although on occasion it does not—as in a thoughtless decision; 3) choice, judgment.

decision tree: a graphic display of a sequence over time of choice, alternatives, and consequences.

defenselessness: a characteristic of culturally deprived children involving lack of support by parents during crisis period.

differentiation in classroom role-structure: degree of complexity in pupil roles.

difficulty level: a dimension of activity characterized by probability of adequate pupil response.

directive: 1) behavior indicating appropriate goals or activities for a group or individual; 2) an order.

discipline problems: pupil behavior, activity, or interaction not conforming to school norms or to teacher beliefs.

discriminal ability: an ability of the children to make subtle distinctions in parts of the environment, for example, in language.

dissonance: an internal response of incongruent or conflicting elements—perceptions, ideas, attitudes, or overt behavior.

drama: a dimension of teacher behavior characterized by the unexpected, the theatrical.

dyad: a two-person subgroup.

effectiveness: the degree to which a group accomplishes its goals.

element: 1) an undefined term; 2) a part or unit.

embarrassment: a sentiment in which an individual is uncomfortable due to discrepancy between behavior and ideal.

emotionality: a response characterized more by feeling and emotion than by rational problem-solving behavior.

emphasis: a dimension of assignments indicating degree of reward and punishment involved.

energy: 1) personality variable; 2) personal resources available to aid group in reaching its goals.

environment: "Everything that is not part of the social system is part of the environment in which the system exists." (Homans, 1950, p. 57.)

episode: a time unit of the belief system.

esteem: a sentiment of positive regard for another person.

expectation: 1) a group variable, 2) a synonym for norm.

experience: personality variable indicating past history with a social situation.

external system: 1) the group's solution to the demands of the environment. (In a school, the organization of the classroom which approximates system directives.) 2) technical organization, formal structure.

fatigue: a state of the individual reflecting a negative ratio of resources to tasks to be done.

fixed point of schedule: 1) the "hard" part of the schedule; 2) that part of the schedule that is usually set by outside forces, and that all other parts of the activity must be scheduled around.

fluidity of group structure: ease in change of structure.

friendship: 1) a sentiment; 2) mutual attraction between two or more individuals.

frustration: 1) failure to satisfy; 2) blocking of goal attainment; 3) a state of tension resulting from 1) or 2).

functional equivalent: 1) an item or dimension of social structure that, although different in form, accomplishes the same ends as another; 2) after Merton (1957).

getting-off-the-hook: a type of interaction enabling the teacher to leave a difficult situation.

goal: 1) group variable; 2) comparable to norm; 3) sentiment regarding desirable ends of activity.

goal displacement: shifting of sentiment from end products to activities or other elements believed to be closely related to end product.

grooving the children: a kind of interaction in which the teacher issues a series of minor directives and obtains a series of minor complying responses from the children.

group: two or more persons who interact together or who are believed to interact together.

group pressure: the increase of rewards and punishments of several individuals, usually legitimized by group norms.

here-and-out-there: a discrimination between behavior in class and outside of class.

humor: 1) interaction and beliefs focused on the unusual, unexpected, or whimsical; 2) fun.

hypothesis: 1) an untested proposition; 2) a conjecture.

individual: person.

individuality in self-conceptions: uniqueness of individual pupil schemas about self.

individualized instruction: a broad multiple meaning concept, for example, nontextbook, multiple activities, high teacher-pupil interaction rate.

influence process: interaction over time in which one person or group tries to change another person or group.

institutional goals: goals established by the school system.

institutional rhythm: the sequence of organizational processes wherein a cycle or series of episodes repeats itself.

isolate: a person who belongs to no subgroup.

interruption: an irrelevant activity or interaction within another episode.

involvement: 1) high interaction and positive sentiment between two individuals; 2) used especially regarding teachers and pupils.

knowledge: 1) a fact, concept, or proposition; 2) usually our usage applies to propositions, that is, a relationship between two concepts, x leads to y.

learning: 1) the change in the probability of occurrence of a response in a particular situation; 2) pupil change.

legitimized: behavior ordinarily arousing guilt but diminished by group norms.

lesson: a subpart of an activity which contains a specific teaching purpose.

liking children: 1) a dimension of teacher personality; 2) attitude.

meaningful verbal learning: 1) pupil change regarding relevant symbolically related materials; 2) after Ausubel (1963).

member: a person defined (by group or others) as within a group.

mental health: 1) a broad collection of individual attributes involving apathy, anomie, hostility, aggression, anxiety, frustration, and volatility; 2) personality evaluated.

model: 1) a schematic designation of a theory; 2) usually a tentative conceptualization.

multiple strands: 1) at any moment in time the classroom contains multiple dimensions of activity and interaction; 2) strands implies a past and future orientation as well as the momentary present.

negative behavior: responses which prevent attainment of group goals or generally accepted individual outcomes.

nonworkers: 1) a pupil role in which the pupil engages in few or none of the class activities; 2) in Geoffrey's class Pete, Henry H., and Henry L. are clearest examples.

norm: group variable, indicating common sentiment for activities or behavior to be carried out by individuals, roles, or groups.

norm change: instability or alteration in norms.

norm clarity: 1) relatively little disagreement among group members regarding a norm; 2) clarity of expectations.

norm integration: 1) ordering or priority in expectations; 2) role or norm conflict.

openness: the degree to which an activity specifies future behavior.

operationalizing: moving from a concept to its indicators.

organization: group with explicitly defined goals, activities, roles, and structure.

organizational pressure: comparable to individual and group pressure but with increased legitimation and usually with more extended ramifications.

pacing: a ratio of amount of activity to time.

path: 1) alternative; 2) usually used in relation to goal.

patience: a dimension of teacher behavior characterized by acceptance of pupil who moves more slowly or inappropriately than the teacher expected.

pay-off table: anticipated consequences (outcomes) of various alternatives in a decision.

peer: an individual of equal social rank.

person: 1) an undefined term—that glob of protoplasm within a skin commonly referred to as a human being; 2) individual.

personalized interaction: 1) a dyadic interaction between the teacher and one pupil; 2) operationally a teacher or pupil comment and a reaction of aware ness on the part of the other.

plan: a schema relating alternatives to goals.

planning: 1) the process of developing a plan; 2) in teaching usually done prior to interacting with the class.

position: 1) an element of social structure; 2) defined in terms of the group's belief system; 3) dynamically—viewed as a role; 4) status.

practice: the repetition of a response series as an aid in learning.

preciseness: a dimension of assignment-giving indicating clarity.

prediction system: the scheme of relationships among choices, alternatives, and consequences.

preparation for contingencies: behavior of a teacher or teacher-pupil interaction which anticipates a problem, alternatives, and consequences.

pressure: a threatened or actual increase or decrease in rewards and punishments.

principle: a proposition with some empirical support.

problem: a situation in which alternate paths to goals are not clear.

process: the change in elements over time.

proposition: relationship between two or more concepts.

provisional try: dimension of tentativeness in teacher behavior or teacher-pupil interaction.

rank: a sentiment indicating one's position in a group.

rational decision: 1) a decision based upon probabilities that a selected alternative will have the highest probability of reaching the goal; 2) subjectively rational—in judgment of actor; 3) organizationally rational—in terms of institutional goals; 4) objectively rational—in terms of expert's judgment.

recitation: 1) a unit of a lesson; 2) part of the body of the lesson.

reject: low social rank.

reputation: 1) a unit of a group belief system or an individual schema indicating probabilities concerning the behavior of others (child, or teacher); 2) in Washington School used especially regarding a pupil's trouble-making propensities, and his ability and willingness to do schoolwork.

resources: 1) an undefined term; 2) the funds of time, energy, and materials available to a group.

ringmastership: a dimension of teacher behavior reflecting an ability to handle multiple and simultaneous strands of activity and interaction.

role: 1) position; 2) a pattern of activities, interactions, and sentiments bound together by a group belief.

role conflict: 1) varying and conflicting expectations for a group member; 2) conflict from expectations from two different groups.

role incumbent: person occupying a position or role.

role structure: the interlocking pattern of roles in a group.

routine: activity or interaction which has reached a stable sequence and is perceived by the children as stable.

satisfaction: 1) a kind of sentiment; 2) an emotional reaction indicating pleasure.

schedule: the time sequence of activities.

schema: 1) an individual's view of the world; 2) a cognition.

sensational: activities or interactions showing a discrepancy between belief and actual events which carry moral overtones.

sentiment: 1) an undefined term; 2) a dimension of a group comparable to emotion in an individual.

sequential smoothness: the flow of activities and interactions toward goals with minimal interruptions.

shaping: individual behavior attempting to change an individual or a group toward a predetermined criterion.

situational thinking: 1) cognitive processes accenting the context in which propositions are considered; 2) after Selznick (1949).

skirmish: an interactional episode of a minor sort that is relevant to the larger game of teaching.

social class: 1) a unit of society; 2) composites of economic, educational and valuational dimensions.

social-class value conflict: a conflict in goals held by members of two or more social classes.

sociometry: an operational procedure for measuring classroom social structure—especially pupil sentiments.

social structure: the pattern or equilibrium of the elements of a group.

status: 1) an ambiguous concept; 2) see position; 3) see rank.

subgroup: 1) group members who interact more frequently with one another; 2) a clique.

successive approximation: a process of teacher-pupil interaction in which the teacher aids the shift in the pupil behavior towards a specified criterion.

superior: 1) an individual with higher social rank; 2) a superordinate.

system: an interrelated set of elements.

task-focused behavior: behavior relevant to the activity intended by the teacher.

teacher: a role in the school in which an individual tries to change the learning of another, the pupil.

teaching in motion: teacher behavior reflecting proportion of time spent at one's desk to time spent in other parts of the room.

teaching program: the formal statement of the activity structure.

teaching style: 1) a broad rubric summarizing several aspects or dimensions of teacher behavior, teacher-pupil interaction, 2) possibly the total classroom equilibrium which is alleged to be under the teacher's control.

teacher understanding: 1) intimate, specific, and organized knowledge about pupils; 2) the translation of this knowledge into teaching problems.

tension 1) negative sentiment; 2) group dissatisfaction.

time: 1) an undefined term; 2) our sense of things happening one after the other; 3) operationally—movement of clock hands.

troublesome: a role in which a pupil engages in behavior undesired by the teacher.

value system: 1) the conception of goals or ends; 2) objectives.

variety: a ratio of kinds of activity to time.

vicarious experience: perception of and participation in another's experience.

vicious circle: 1) a kind of interaction; 2) negative behavior by a pupil arouses negative teacher behavior which in turn arouses more negative pupil behavior; 3) usual consequence is an equilibrium in which teacher-pupil cooperation is minimal.

SELECTED REFERENCES

Ausubel, D. P., *The psychology of meaningful verbal learning*. New York: Grune and Stratton, Inc., 1963.

Becker, H. S., "Problems of inference and proof in participant observation." *American Sociological Review*, Vol. 28 (1958), pp. 652–660.

Becker, H. S., "Role and career problems of the Chicago public school teacher." Unpublished doctoral dissertation, University of Chicago, 1951.

Becker, H. S., "Social class variations in the teacher-pupil relationship." *Journal of Educational Sociology*, Vol. 25 (1952), pp. 451–461.

Becker, H. S., and others, *Boys in white*. Chicago: University of Chicago Press, 1961.

Bloom, B. S., and others, *Taxonomy of educational objectives, Handbook I: Cognitive domain*. New York: David McKay Company, Inc., 1956.

Bross, I. D., *Design for decision*. New York: Crowell-Collier and Macmillan, Inc., 1953.

Charters, W. W., Jr., and others, *The Ghetto Schools: A report on the feasibility of an extended investigation*. Proposal submitted to The Human Development Corporation, August 1965.

269

Coch, L., and J. R. P. French, Jr., "Overcoming resistance to change." In D. Cartwright and A. Zander (Eds.), *Group dynamics.* Second ed.; New York: Harper & Row, Publishers, 1960.

Connor, W. H., and L. M. Smith, *Analysis of patterns of student teaching.* Washington, D.C.: U.S. Office of Education, Co-op. Res. Report No. 5–8204, 1967.

Davis, J., "Impulsivity and situational structure in behavioral contagion." Unpublished doctoral dissertation, Washington University, 1965.

Festinger, L., and others, *When prophecy fails.* New York: Harper & Row, Publishers, 1964.

Festinger, L., and E. Aronson, "The arousal and reduction of dissonance in social contexts." In D. Cartwright and A. Zander (Eds.), *Group Dynamics.* Second ed.; New York: Harper & Row, Publishers, 1960.

Frankel, H., "The author (Truman Capote)." *Saturday Review,* Vol. 49 (1966), pp. 36–37.

Griffiths, D., and others, *Teacher mobility in New York City.* New York: New York University, 1963 (Mimeo.).

Hall, E. T., *The silent language.* New York: Doubleday & Company, Inc., 1959.

Halpin, A., *Manual: leader behavior description questionnaire (LBDQ).* Columbus, Ohio: Ohio State University, 1957.

Haring, N. G., and E. L. Phillips, *Educating emotionally disturbed children.* New York: McGraw-Hill, Inc., 1962.

Hilgard, E. R., *Theories of learning.* Rev. ed.; New York: Appleton-Century-Crofts, 1956.

Hollander, E., "Conformity, status, and idiosyncracy credit." *Psychological Review,* Vol. 65 (1958), pp. 117–127.

Homans, G. C., *The human group.* New York: Harcourt, Brace & World, Inc., 1950.

Homans, G. C., *Social behavior: its elementary forms.* New York: Harcourt, Brace & World, Inc., 1961.

Homans, G. C., *Sentiments and activities.* New York: Crowell-Collier and Macmillan, Inc., 1962.

Jackson, J. M., "Structural characteristics of norms." In National Society for the Study of Education Yearbook, *The dynamics of instructional groups.* Chicago: University of Chicago Press, 1960.

Jackson, J. M., "Normative structure in educational systems." Paper read at Washington University Conference, "The classroom as a social system." February 1962.

Kahn, R. L., and D. Katz, "Leadership practices in relationship to productivity and morale." In D. Cartwright and A. Zander (Eds.), *Group dynamics.* Second ed.; New York: Harper & Row, Publishers, 1960.

Kottmeyer, W., and K. Ware, *Basic spelling goals: 7.* St. Louis, Mo.: Webster Publishing Division, McGraw-Hill, Inc., 1960.

Kounin, J., and others, "Explorations in classroom management." *Journal of Teacher Education,* Vol. 12 (1961), pp. 235–246.

Kounin, J., and others, "Managing emotionally disturbed children in regular classrooms." *Journal of Educational Psychology,* Vol. 57 (1966), pp. 1–13.

Lippitt, R., and others, *Dynamics of planned change.* New York: Harcourt, Brace & World, Inc., 1958.

Lippitt, R., and others, "The dynamics of power." *Human Relations,* Vol. 5 (1952), pp. 37–64.

Lortie, D., "The teacher and team teaching: suggestions for long range research." In J. Shaplin and H. Olds (Eds.), *Team teaching.* New York: Harper & Row, Publishers, 1964.

Malinowski, B., *The argonauts of the Western Pacific.* London: Routledge & Kagan Paul, Ltd., 1922.

McClelland, D., *Personality.* New York: Holt, Rinehart and Winston, Inc., 1951.

McGuire, Edna, *Backgrounds of American freedom.* New York: Crowell-Collier and Macmillan, Inc., 1953.

Merei, F., "Group leadership and institutionalization." *Human Relations,* Vol. 2 (1949) pp. 23–39.

Merton, R. K., *Social theory and social structure.* Revised ed.; New York: Crowell-Collier and Macmillan, Inc., 1957.

Miller, G. A., and others, *Plans and the structure of behavior.* New York: Holt, Rinehart and Winston, Inc., 1960.

O'Hara, J., *Assembly.* New York: Random House Inc., 1961.

Ojemann, R. H., "The human relations program at S.U.I." *Personnel Guidance Journal,* Vol. 37 (1958), pp. 199–206.

Pollock, T. C., and R. W. Rounds, *Words and ideas.* New York: Crowell-Collier and Macmillan, Inc., 1960.

Polya, G., *Patterns of plausible inference.* Princeton, N.J.: Princeton University Press, 1954.

Redl, F., and D. Wineman, *The aggressive child.* New York: Crowell-Collier and Macmillan, Inc., 1957.

Riessman, F., *The culturally deprived child.* New York: Harper & Row, Publishers, 1962.

Schachter, S., "Deviation, rejection and communication." *Journal of Abnormal and Social Psychology,* Vol. 46 (1951), pp. 190–207.

Schaefer, R. J., *The school as a center of inquiry.* New York: Harper & Row, Publishers, 1967.

Selznick, P., *The organizational weapon: a study of bolshevik strategy and tactics.* New York: McGraw-Hill, Inc., 1952.

Shaplin, J., and H. Olds, *Team teaching.* New York: Harper & Row, Publishers, 1964.

Sherif, M., and others, *Intergroup conflict and cooperation.* Norman, Okla.: University of Oklahoma Press, 1961.

Simon, H., *Administrative behavior.* Second ed.; New York: Crowell-Collier and Macmillan, Inc., 1961.

Skinner, B. F., *Walden two.* New York: Crowell-Collier and Macmillan, Inc., 1948.

Skinner, B. F., *Science and human behavior.* New York: Crowell-Collier and Macmillan, Inc., 1953.

Smith, L. M., *Group processes in elementary and secondary schools.* Washington, D.C.: National Education Association, 1959.

Smith, L. M., "Classroom social systems and pupil personality." *Psychology in the Schools,* Vol. 1 (1964), pp. 118–129.

Smith, L. M., "The social psychological complexities of an urban classroom." In P. Knoblock (Ed.), *Educational programming for emotionally disturbed children: the decade ahead.* Syracuse, N. Y.: Syracuse University Press, 1965.

Smith, L. M., and W. Geoffrey, *Toward a model of teacher decision-making in an urban classroom.* Washington, D.C.: U.S. Office of Education, Co-op. Res. Report No. S-048, 1965.

Smith, L. M., and B. B. Hudgins, *Educational psychology.* New York: Alfred A. Knopf, Inc., 1964.

Smith, L. M., and B. B. Hudgins, "Correlates of classroom functioning." *Genetic Psychology Monographs* 1966.

Smith, L. M., and P. Keith, *Social psychological aspects of school building design.* Washington, D.C.: U.S. Office of Education, Co-op. Res. Report No. S-223, 1967.

Stephens, J. M., "Spontaneous schooling and success in teaching." *School Review*, Vol. 68 (1960), pp. 152–163.

Stogdill, R. M., and A. E. Coons (Eds.), *Leader behavior: its description and measurement.* Columbus, Ohio: Ohio State University Press, 1957.

Sykes, G. M., *The society of captives.* Princeton, N.J.: Princeton University Press, 1962.

Taba, H., (Ed.), *Literature for human understanding.* Washington, D.C.: American Council of Education, 1948.

Taba, H., and others, *Intergroup education in public schools.* Washington, D.C.: American Council of Education, 1952.

Thibaut, J., and H. Kelley, *The social psychology of groups.* New York: John Wiley & Sons, Inc., 1959.

Traylor, E., "Set, programmed instruction, and emotionally laden conclusions in teacher decision making." Unpublished doctoral dissertation, Washington University, 1966.

Warner, W. L., R. Havighurst, and M. Loeb, *Who shall be educated?* New York: Harper & Row, Publishers, 1944.

Watson, G., "Foreword" in F. Riessman, *The culturally deprived child.* New York: Harper & Row, Publishers, 1962.

Whyte, W. F., *Street corner society.* Revised ed.; Chicago: University of Chicago Press, 1955.

Wientge, K., "Teacher decision making: improvement in syllogistic reasoning." Unpublished doctoral dissertation, Washington University, 1965.

Williamson, E. G., *Counseling adolescents.* New York: McGraw-Hill, Inc., 1950.

Zetterberg, H. L., *On theory and verification in sociology.* Totowa, N.J.: Bedminster Press, 1965.

INDEX

273